Economics without Preferences

Economics without Preferences lays out a new microeconomics – a theory of choice behavior, markets, and welfare – for agents who lack the preferences and marginal judgments that economics normally relies on. Agents without preferences defy the rules of the traditional model of rational choice but they can still systematically pursue their interests. The theory that results resolves several puzzles in economics. Status quo bias and other anomalies of behavioral economics shield agents from harm; they are expressions rather than violations of rationality. Parts of economic orthodoxy go out the window. Agents will fail to make the fine-grained trade-offs ingrained in conventional economics, leading market prices to be volatile and cost-benefit analysis to break down. This book provides policy alternatives to fill this void. Governments can spur innovation, the main benefit markets can deliver, while sheltering agents from the upheavals that accompany economic change.

Michael Mandler is a Professor of Economics at Royal Holloway College, University of London. He is an economic theorist who has taught at the University of Pennsylvania and Harvard University and is the author of *Dilemmas in Economic Theory* (1999).

STUDIES IN NEW ECONOMIC THINKING

The 2008 financial crisis pointed to problems in economic theory that require more than just big data to solve. INET's series in New Economic Thinking exists to ensure that innovative work that advances economics and better integrates it with other social sciences and the study of history and institutions can reach a broad audience in a timely way.

Economics without Preferences

Microeconomics and Policymaking Beyond the Maximizing Individual

MICHAEL MANDLER

Royal Holloway College, University of London

CAMBRIDGE
UNIVERSITY PRESS

Shaftesbury Road, Cambridge CB2 8EA, United Kingdom

One Liberty Plaza, 20th Floor, New York, NY 10006, USA

477 Williamstown Road, Port Melbourne, VIC 3207, Australia

314–321, 3rd Floor, Plot 3, Splendor Forum, Jasola District Centre,
New Delhi – 110025, India

103 Penang Road, #05–06/07, Visioncrest Commercial, Singapore 238467

Cambridge University Press is part of Cambridge University Press & Assessment,
a department of the University of Cambridge.

We share the University's mission to contribute to society through the pursuit of
education, learning and research at the highest international levels of excellence.

www.cambridge.org
Information on this title: www.cambridge.org/9781009340700

DOI: 10.1017/9781009340731

First published 2025

A catalogue record for this publication is available from the British Library

Library of Congress Cataloging-in-Publication Data
Names: Mandler, Michael, author.
Title: Economics without preferences : microeconomics and policymaking
beyond the maximizing individual / Michael Mandler, Royal Holloway,
University of London.
Description: Cambridge, United Kingdom ; New York, NY, USA : Cambridge
University Press, [2025] | Series: Studies in new economic thinking |
Includes bibliographical references and index.
Identifiers: LCCN 2023050858 | ISBN 9781009340700 |
ISBN 9781009340731 (ebook)
Subjects: LCSH: Microeconomics. | Capital productivity. | Economics.
Classification: LCC HB172 .M3447 2025 | DDC 338.5–dc23/eng/20240224
LC record available at https://lccn.loc.gov/2023050858

ISBN 978-1-009-34070-0 Hardback

Contents

Figures

Preface

Economics without Preferences explores the theory of markets and economic behavior when individuals cannot form the preference judgments and marginal trade-offs taken for granted in economics. Books on economic theory have fallen out of fashion, particularly when they consider competitive markets and prices. With the exception of textbooks, the few still published tend to be technical monographs. This book addresses the entire community of economists – from behavioral economists to decision theorists to welfare economists to general equilibrium theorists – and shows how the absence of preferences recasts each of these areas.

Once upon a time, each generation of economic theorists told the story of how they had superseded the past – from Marshall in the *Principles of Economics* to Samuelson in his triumphant excursions into the history of economic thought. Everything they could say we can say better. This pattern came to a halt as the study of markets turned from theoretical fundamentals to extensions and applications, often in outlying fields such as public finance or macroeconomics. More recently, an avalanche of behavioral evidence has buried the neoclassical theory of the rational consumer and has launched new fields – behavioral and experimental economics – but it has not led to a new chapter in the 200-year history of the economic theory of value. I will therefore retell the story of how equilibrium and decision theory have developed through the last century; the tale explains why the present difficulties of microeconomic theory arose and how to overcome them.

In the clash between the classical theory of rationality and the evidence of behavioral economics, this book aims for reconciliation. The first article of the proposed settlement argues that the classical theory's claims of

rationality are unjustified; much of the dispute between orthodox preference theory and behavioral economics then dissipates. The second article
will show that many putative violations of rationality not only do agents
no harm but are in fact evidence of a deliberate pursuit of self-interest.

The agents in this book will always be able to form some preference
judgments. Orderings come readily when agents are offered a good deal –
if for example the terms of trade are tilted in their favor – or when they
can reduce a complex decision to simple elements that they do know how
to weigh. But agents often do not come to judgment nor do they have a
reason to do so. Agents still of course have to make choices. The book's
title skips over these nuances. But the more precise alternatives – *Economics without some of the preference judgments normally assumed* or
Economic theory with incomplete and nonsmooth preferences (the latter an actual suggestion) – were worse. A title closer to the mark would
underscore the absence of marginal preference judgments, the cornerstone
on which prices and social decision-making are ordinarily built.

Theorists who have read the manuscript conclude that it targets a
general readership, nontheorists consider it a book of mathematical
economics. Although the issues I discuss are not inherently of great mathematical complexity, their treatment in economics has been thoroughly
mathematicized and I must engage those analyses. The problems of how
to speak to theorists and nontheorists and how to combine text and formal modeling have no obvious solution. I have aimed for a Switzerland
that both parties can enter peacefully rather than a demilitarized zone
where no one will tread comfortably.

The lion's share of comments on the ideas herein came while I
presented and published the 15 or so interrelated papers I wrote in antic-
ipation of this book. It would be difficult to exaggerate how much I
learned in the process and I will not try to summarize those debts. I
am delighted however to thank Sophie Bade, Duncan Foley, Daniel Kahneman, M. Ali Khan, Mark Steitz, Chris Udry, Peter Wakker, and a
clear-sighted anonymous reader for detailed comments on several chapters. My initial discussions with Andreu Mas-Colell were indispensable.
Finally, I thank Patricia Craig for her patient sifting between plausible and
misguided ideas for a book cover and the British Academy for financial
support.

1

Introduction: Marginal Utility Matters

1.1 THREE VIEWS OF DECISION-MAKING

In a textbook that capped a generation of work on axiomatic preference theory, David Kreps introduced Totrep or "trade-off talking rational economic person" to ease students into the mathematical models they would need to master.[1] Totrep became a celebrity, by the standards of fictional economics personalities, and served as an exemplar of the economic agent who must choose among alternative actions. Curiously the reader never learns if Totrep can pin down the marginal trade-offs that economics is famous for. Totrep's preferences must satisfy the classical axioms of rationality that hold that all pairs of alternatives can both be judged and judged consistently, but it remains open whether Totrep can determine the marginal value of one good in terms of another.

The classical axioms of rationality do not require agents to make judgments of the form "I am willing to accept x units of good 2 for a small amount of good 1 and to give up x units of good 2 to receive the same small amount of good 1." These are the judgments that underlie the first graph drawn on the blackboards of Econ 101, the smooth indifference curve that pictures an agent's marginal trade-offs of one good for another. One of the hallmarks of economics is therefore missing from the mathematical model of Totrep's preferences.

The divide between Totrep and the intro economics classroom mirrors the grand development of neoclassical economics, where two views

---

[1] The textbook, Kreps (1988), explains that Michael Harrison has parental rights over Totrep.

1

of economic decision-making have dominated the intellectual landscape and divide it into two eras of roughly equal length. In the origin story of the indifference curve in the late 19th century, marginal utility played the lead: economic agents use the pleasure delivered by increments of various goods to figure out which combinations of goods will keep them at the same level of satisfaction. For the next 75 years or so, in the marginalist period of neoclassical economics, agents were accordingly modeled by utility functions with derivatives that represent the agents' marginal utilities. The smooth indifference curve is the perennial survivor of this epoch and, to this day, the smooth indifference curve makes the most sense when it is built from the ground up by agents who weigh the increments of some primordial benefit that different options can deliver.

For the last 75 years, beginning shortly after World War II, a more spare model of rationality has ruled the seminar rooms of economic theory: it requires an agent's preferences to satisfy two axioms, completeness and transitivity, and further assumptions in more specific choice contexts. The smooth indifference curve appeared difficult to defend to the best and the brightest of postwar economic theory; it was also unnecessary for the Arrow-Debreu agenda that dominated economic theory in the initial decades of this era. The existence and optimality of competitive equilibria were the crown jewels of economic theory and, for these results, marginal utilities and marginal rates of substitution are irrelevant. Since it seemed to serve no purpose, the smooth indifference curve was abandoned by those theoretically in the know.

Much of the economics profession paid little attention to the changing of the guard. The everyday models of economics continue to rest on smooth indifference curves and differentiable utility functions, and consumer optimization is still explained to undergraduates with the story that agents equate the marginal utilities of their expenditure on different goods. The transition in economic theory also passed unnoticed in the outside world. In the public imagination, economics comes down to the maxim that "everything has its price": agents will trade away anything of value if offered enough in exchange. While this saying is something of a caricature, an agent with smooth indifference curves is remarkably malleable: if after buying positive amounts of two goods, the relative price of good 1 in terms of good 2 were to rise even slightly then the agent would happily trade away some quantity of good 1. A readiness to substitute and trade goods remains a benchmark of economic orthodoxy. But this flexibility does not follow from the axioms that describe Totrep's decisions.

There is a third position to consider. When goods do not deliver different quantities of a common homogeneous benefit, agents may be of several minds about the trade-offs they confront. Individuals can then conclude that their options are incomparable and that they are unable to come to a preference judgment: their preferences are incomplete. Incompleteness does not imply that an agent has somehow fallen prey to irrationality; the incomparability view challenges the claim that the rational pursuit of one's interests requires an agent to form preferences. Agents must still choose, of course, even when they cannot figure out which options are best. Whether facing simple or complex choices, between apples and oranges or between detailed state-contingent plans, agents may conclude that all of their conflicting attitudes must be in agreement to approve a change over the status quo or a customary decision. Or they may resort to the safest course of action, say, the plan that makes the worst-case outcome as desirable as possible. These and other choice strategies that agents turn to when they cannot form preference judgments overshadow the pleasure calculations that economists in the 19th century, eager to apply calculus, imagined to be dominant.

When agents cannot form preferences, the options they do not know how to compare cannot be grouped into conventional indifference curves: if an agent cannot compare alternatives a and b then an improvement to a need not make it superior to b. When agents resort to safe options, it may be possible for their choices to be modeled by ordered families of indifference curves, but those curves will not display the smooth trade-offs we expect of Homo Economicus. For example, the marginal value of a good might fall discontinuously as it crosses the threshold of consumption that an agent regards as safe. In both scenarios, the smooth indifference curve disappears.

Agents who lack preference judgments cannot make arbitrary choices without jeopardizing the goals such as greater material wealth that they can identify. Sticking to the status quo is the most obvious way for agents to eliminate those dangers. Seen in this light, some of the characteristic findings of behavioral economics no longer appear as inexplicable outbreaks of irrationality. Status quo bias and kindred patterns of choice lay out exactly the decisions that individuals without preferences should take to safeguard their interests. The verdict of the economics profession is that the behavioral evidence has toppled classical rationality as a positive theory of decision-making – despite its persistence in economic theory. But if the incompleteness of preferences lies behind the manifold violations of standard choice theory, then a unified explanation of economic decision-making must go beyond the empirics of behavioral economics; a reformulation of rationality is needed.

This book will ask and answer basic questions. Which of the three views of economic decision-making is correct? Can agents always smoothly trade off disparate benefits? Why is there a discrepancy between contemporary economic theory, which has dropped the smooth indifference curve and the differentiable utility function, and the routine work of economics? Do agents obey the narrower axioms of rationality that economic theory currently backs and, if not, are they acting irrationally? How do markets perform when agents cannot make smooth trade-offs? And can government policymaking be decisive when the individuals in society are not?

It is common for economists to view the differentiable utility function as a technical convenience, not a statement of principle. In combination with the convexity of preferences, a differentiable utility allows an agent to be modeled by a system of first-order conditions, the solution of which will normally identify unique utility-maximizing demands. If instead an agent cannot form a complete set of preference judgments and thus cannot be represented by a utility function, demands are not as easy to characterize and there are multiple ways to define optimization, a morass that economists would prefer to avoid. When preference judgments are complete but utility functions fail to be differentiable, even less seems to be at stake; with some tweaks to the standard toolkit, nondifferentiable utilities can be maximized almost as easily as differentiable utilities. After going through the ritual undergraduate exercise of discovering that the demand functions for Leontief utilities appear to be well-behaved, economists mostly leave the nondifferentiable utility function behind.

The capacity of agents to trade off benefits smoothly in fact lies at the heart of conventional economics: although the Totrep axioms may omit any mention of trade-offs, the character is aptly named. But to see what trade-offs accomplish in economics, we cannot simply accept the criteria of successful model-building that the present era of economic theory has set for itself. The main results of decision and general equilibrium theory, not surprisingly, meet the tests of theoretical consistency that those traditions have laid out. In the theory of individual behavior, we instead need to examine whether rational self-interest in fact requires agents to make choices that obey the classical axioms of rationality. And we must look beyond individual optimization to the system-wide features of economic models that depend on smooth trade-offs but that general equilibrium theory has glossed over.

I will argue that the absence of smooth trade-offs leads to challenges that cannot be resolved by existing theoretical means. Before previewing this claim, let me underscore that I am not advocating a revival of the old-time religion. The smooth trade-offs and indifference curves of early neoclassical economics provided an internal theoretical coherence that the second era of economic theory has not been able to match. In terms of empirical validity, however, those assumptions and the marginal utility mechanics that lay behind them were failures and later economists have been understandably embarrassed by them. Smooth trade-offs lie at the heart of economic analysis but not of economic reality. I therefore back the third horse.

An agent that cannot pin down a marginal trade-off between goods can usually be described by a set or band of margins or supporting prices: an incremental increase in the consumption of a good will have a strictly smaller value (in terms of a comparison good) than an incremental decrease. This multiplicity of margins or valuations can be systematic, occurring not just at isolated points but at many or all consumption bundles. I will not however assume at any point in this book that agents are incapable of judging all trade-offs between goods. Agents will for example agree to part with a unit of a good when offered enough of another good in exchange. What will be missing are the marginal trade-offs and valuations that economic analysis relies on to rule over market prices and single out which government policies are optimal.

Neoclassical economics has from the outset exaggerated the importance of substitution in consumption. Economic agents do make trade-offs in consumption based in part on their preference judgments. But the magnitude of substitution may not be great enough to buffer an economy from shocks and the gains from trade that exploit differences among agents' valuations can be small. If you are seeking an explanation of the wealth of capitalist economies or of its fluctuations, substitution in consumption is not the right place to look.

The well-defined marginal rates of substitution that stem from smooth indifference curves once provided the go-to explanation of why relative prices do not move erratically through time. If instead agents are resistant to substitution and stick to particular patterns of consumption then demand will be relatively inelastic and small changes in endowments can lead relative prices to spike or plunge – a small contraction in the supply of power from the electrical grid will cause its price to jump. The neoclassical invention of smooth trade-offs assuaged these worries: the willingness of consumers to make marginal substitutions will dampen the volatility scenarios.

Once the differentiable utility function lost its standing, economists had to find an alternative argument for the stability of relative prices over time. The answer that descended from high theory was that the endowments that generate volatility are highly unlikely to occur. This account requires an economy to begin de novo at every date with a new stock of goods and therefore does not apply to societies where goods are produced. When production is present – and enough time passes for production to affect output levels – the absence of smooth trade-offs will again lead to erratic relative prices. Production can also deliver a better explanation of what curbs price volatility: firms can transfer resources across time to tamp down the price swings that unstable individual valuations can generate.

In normative economics, determinate marginal rates of substitution play an equally pivotal role: they underlie the decisiveness of the dominant concepts of economic efficiency, both social welfare maximization and Pareto efficiency. When in contrast agents' marginal valuations are ill-defined, a wide range of policy decisions will qualify as efficient. In public goods decisions, about environmental quality for example, agents consistently declare the harm done by an incremental fouling of the environment to dwarf the value gained by an incremental clean-up. A cost-benefit test will then fail to discriminate effectively: substantial intervals of environmental quality levels will pass the test. Applied welfare economics has avoided reckoning with this paralysis by ignoring, when possible, the ample evidence that agents wield bands of marginal valuations. For the practically minded economist, the way forward has been instead to employ the smallest valuations that agents report. This footwork lets the throughput of policy recommendations flow unimpeded, but that advice will be biased against public goods.

In the welfare parables of general equilibrium theory, efficiency in an exchange economy requires there to be price lines with a common slope that *support* (are tangent to) the sets of bundles that agents prefer to their own consumption. But if the smooth indifference curve is absent and is replaced by a set of margins, the discriminatory power of this requirement collapses. Economics then loses its role of showing how to fine-tune government policies. As in the case of public goods, many and sometimes every allocation will qualify as optimal and the pursuit of efficiency will therefore lead to few nonvacuous policy recommendations. If, say, an externality appears no policy response may be called for and any policy change that has even a minute impact on relative prices will usually fail to qualify as an efficiency improvement. When no policy can be dismissed as inefficient – even policies that every economist would judge to be distorting – economics becomes useless as a policy guide.

As with volatility, production rather than exchange paves the way forward. Increases in productivity, not the alignment of hypothetical indifference curves, drive the growth of social wealth. Technological change at the same time leads to sharp changes in the relative prices of factors and consumption goods and thus swings in the distribution of income. Economists tend to gloss over this conflict. The harm done by opening industries to productivity-enhancing competition either disappears into the black hole of distributional value judgments or is met with reassurances that injured parties can be made whole by carefully engineered compensation payments. Compensations accordingly became a centerpiece of how economic theory has dealt with the diverse repercussions of economic change. Under the best of circumstances, compensationism requires formidably detailed information about agents' preferences and trades. But with incomplete preferences, agents' decisions need not reveal their preferences; when agents are unable to judge and go for the safe option or the status quo, they may not view their selections as superior to their other alternatives. Discovering the information needed for compensation payments then becomes much harder.

The solution I propose provides an alternative design and rationale for policymaking that omits any mention of preferences. Compensations should give agents the opportunity to undertake the same trades they made previously; the policies that emerge then will not face any credible objections. When compensations based on ex ante trades are infeasible, policymakers can instead modulate the relative price changes that can undermine the fortunes of agents. A government moreover can constrain the relative prices facing households while still incentivizing efficient production via the prices that firms face; policies can thus both harness the efficiency gains of competition and avoid the price changes that inflict harm. This alternative approach can free welfare analysis from the apparent logjams where every policy option qualifies as efficient. Policymakers do need not acquiesce to the arbitrary programs and practices they inherit. A government need not stand by, for example, when technological change and international trade wreak harm on those caught on the losing side of dynamic comparative advantage; and the government's policy responses do not have to slow economic growth.

These economy-wide repercussions of missing preference judgments form Part II of this book.

Part I addresses individual decision-making. I begin by setting the 19th century dogma of marginal utility against the more parsimonious model of rationality that succeeded it in the mid-20th century, Robinson Crusoe comparing the gains of an extra minute gathering bananas or spearing fish against the completeness and transitivity axioms that model Totrep's preferences. Economic theory did not emerge unscathed from this transition. Utility and marginal utility not only allowed agents to pin down marginal trade-offs and thus find optimal decisions; they also showed that individuals can determine which of any pair of options is the better choice.

Once doubt was cast on marginal utility and pleasure-seeking, the larger principle that agents can order their options lost its justification. Without an explanatory psychology to fall back on, contemporary decision theory has remained silent on why an individual should satisfy the most basic axiom of rationality, the completeness assumption that individuals can form a preference judgment between any pair of options. In the face of this lacuna, the standing of completeness as a benchmark of rationality begins to wobble.

Agents find many decisions easy to judge. Everyone has favored clothes, foods, pastimes, and so forth. Agents will also readily come to preference judgments when choosing the best means to a known end – as when a worker opts for the highest-paying job. And difficult choices can sometimes be reduced to simpler alternatives that are easier to weigh. If say you compare two job options with disparate features – one offers higher salary and a longer commute – you may find the decision straightforward once you realize that the high-salary option will implicitly pay a trivial wage for your drive to work. But even in the simplest cases, you may not be able to pin down the marginal trade-offs essential to economics: you may reject a small return to a long commute but not be able to form sharper judgments.

Making matters worse, the comparisons that the agents of modern economics need to make are herculean. Jevons posited agents who faced small self-contained comparisons – how to allocate food on an ocean voyage for example – and he did not suggest that agents could compare disparate types of pleasure. The agents that live in current-day economic models, in contrast, must compare detailed state-contingent plans over a lifetime of consumption. But incomplete preferences do not have to stem from the complexity of decisions or a shortage of information. A well-informed agent facing clear alternatives might not have a best choice: there may be no bedrock of true preference that lies below.

Economists have a well-rehearsed answer to claims that agents cannot form a preference between options: make agents choose and declare that their choices reveal their preferences. I will show, however, that the "revealed preferences" that emerge from such exercises will not satisfy the classical axioms of rationality, even when agents follow decision rules that never lead to dominated outcomes. An agent in short can be rational without satisfying the axioms that supposedly characterize rationality. As a body of empirical predictions, classical rationality was therefore bound to fail, though it has taken decades of documentation for that failure to be recognized.

Our era of economics has responded to the empirical defeat of rational choice theory with a shrug: "who cares what is labeled rational, what matters is behavior." This book lays out two replies, given in embryo in this chapter, first that only the rational pursuit of self-interest can explain the apparent anomalies of real-world decision-making, and second that the appraisal of social institutions depends on a valid classification of actions as rational and irrational.

There is moreover an alternative to a divorce between rationality and behavior: characterize rationality with greater precision. When individuals face static one-shot decisions, the amendments needed are relatively minor. Instead of choosing options superior to all alternatives, agents must select undominated options. Since incomplete preferences reduce the opportunities for one decision to dominate another, decision-making then becomes easier, and indeed agents may confront an embarrassment of optima. While not a wholly new phenomenon – an agent with weakly convex indifference curves can occasionally face a budget set with more than one optimum – the multiplicity that comes with incompleteness is far-reaching. Despite this difference, the mischief that incomplete preferences can cause for the static demand for goods is limited. After all, preference theory has never been able to deliver on its promise of foundations for the downward-sloping demand function; as Becker (1962) pointed out long ago, it is easier to generate well-behaved demands from irrational behavior – specifically choices uniformly distributed on budget lines – than it is from utility maximization.

The terrain is different when agents face dynamic sequences of decisions. Individuals with incomplete preferences must then take care to avoid manipulation. The simplest way for an agent to steer clear of risks is to refuse any offer to switch to an option that the agent cannot judge

relative to the pre-existing status quo, a rigidity that stands in contrast
to the agents with smooth indifference curves who adapt their consumption to every relative price change. Status quo bias, the endowment effect,
loss aversion – the iconic choice strategies of behavioral economics – thus
emerge as validations rather than breaches of rationality. If we define
agents' interests by the outcomes their decisions yield, rather than the
axioms popular in economic theory, we can predict more accurately
which economic behaviors will persist and which self-interest will chip
away.

Incomplete preferences also resolve the puzzle of why agents so frequently fail to find a dominant option from a set of alternatives. With
classical preferences, indifference is a fluke event but with incomplete
preferences, an inability to judge alternatives arises systematically. In fact,
once the door is open to incomplete preferences, it becomes even harder
to attribute waffling to indifference: in models where agents can both
be indifferent between some options and unable to form preferences for
other options, indifference comes near to disappearing altogether.

The three views of decision-making adopt conflicting positions:
smooth trade-offs determined by marginal utilities versus rationality
axioms on preferences versus agents that cannot always come to preference judgments. The history of the contest between the first two views
was written by the victors. The psychology of pleasure-seeking peddled
by the early neoclassical economists appeared pointless to their mid-20th
century successors and stood in the way of their scientific aspirations.
Not only did the new orthodoxy hold that individual decision-making
could be based on axioms of rationality rather than utility, but the smooth
indifference curve appeared to be unnecessary. As I have mentioned, the
features of competitive markets identified by the Arrow-Debreu model,
the unifier of postwar economic theory, did not turn on marginal utilities or any of the other derivatives in the early neoclassical arsenal.[2] The
labeling of neoclassical economics as marginalist was from this vantage
simply a mistake. While the rear-guard defenders of utility theory put up
little effective resistance, a nagging anxiety has persisted that something
was lost when marginal utilities and the smooth indifference curve were
dropped from the theoretical canon. One of my jobs will be to articu-
late this worry. We will see that the marginalist label captures part of the
truth: when individuals do not substitute the satisfaction of goods at specific marginal rates, they can instead be modeled by sets of such margins.

[2] See Hahn (1961) for example.

The theory of rational choice has in turn had to face a fresh set of tribulations – the pile-up of evidence that agents do not base their decision on unified orderings that rank all of their options. Rather than carrying on its own rear-guard struggle against behavioral economics, defenders of rationality would be better served by rethinking what a theory of rational choice is supposed to accomplish.

1.2 RATIONALITY IN ECONOMIC THEORY

The three views of decision-making do agree on one important point. Each theory classifies decisions as rational or irrational, not necessarily in the narrow axiomatic sense, but with the broader meaning that some but not all decisions an agent can take will serve that agent's goals and interests. When preferences are incomplete, some decisions can still be superior to others: an agent can succeed in forming some preference judgments. Each theory also assumes that agents will not undertake an action when a preferred action is available. Without this common ground, the dialogue in this book between theoretical camps would be impossible.

The two most frequent defenses of rationality argue that it provides reasonably accurate predictions of behavior and that competing theories that predict irrational actions, even if correct at a moment in time, are prone to failure as agents learn how to better serve their interests. Without passing judgment on these arguments, let me propose a third. Even if agents are bent on acting irrationally and disregard all attempts at persuasion, the determination of which actions serve their interests and which do not sets a research agenda. With a classification in hand, we can check empirically whether agents follow rational courses of action and how resistant to change their irrationalities are. When we come across an irrationality – an individual whose preferences are reversed by an immaterial redescription of options, a firm that refuses to adopt a technology that makes more money – does it become less likely over time? If not then an analysis of the irrationality should look for the constraints, both institutional and psychological, that prevent agents from correcting their errors. The most routine question in economics asks: Why has some apparent profit opportunity gone unexploited? Why for example don't perpetually overbooked restaurants charge more? Why did the British steel industry in the late 19th century stick with outmoded technologies?[3] The next

---

[3] See Kahneman et al. (1986), Becker (1991), and Karni and Levin (1994) on the first example and Temin (1966) and McCloskey (1973) on the second.

stage of research investigates whether new conventions and institutions emerge that can remedy the irrationalities, either with or without the cooperation of the irrational agents. For example, dynamically inconsistent agents may be unable to stop themselves from spending wealth that they had earlier decided to save for the distant future. Do savings options then appear that limit the opportunities for agents to thwart the plans laid down at earlier dates by their more prudent selves?[4]

This third argument will be more relevant for this book than the first two. I will argue that an absence of preference judgments will lead agents into behaviors that look irrational from the perspective of the classical axioms of rationality, for example, status quo bias and willingness-to-accept/willingness-to-pay disparities. Although these behaviors lead to intransitive revealed preferences, they in fact shield agents from harm when they have no preference judgments to guide them. So, if my argument is correct that an inability to compare options does not hurt agents or otherwise qualify as irrational then the agenda of economics should shift. Economists should stop trying to find out whether status quo bias will fade away when agents are given time for reflection: as an expression of rationality, there is no reason why it should. The soundness of this program however turns on the accuracy of my characterization of rationality.

A fourth and final argument in favor of rationality is that it brings diagnostic clarity. Economics analyzes the flaws of behavior and social institutions by first postulating an ideal world free of frictions, where the rational expectations and actions of agents lead to efficient outcomes, and then examining the effects of adding a candidate distortion to this hypothetical world. If, say, you want to argue that a pollution externality leads to inefficiency, your case will be more difficult if you assume in addition that agents act irrationally. With two sources of trouble, assignment of blame for the damage done can be ambiguous. The two malefactors can also offset each other: if agents irrationally underutilize a pollutant (from the point of view of their self-interest), they could unintentionally eliminate the inefficiency normally triggered by the externality. The same principles apply to individual decision-making. If you want to show that violations of independence in the theory of choice under uncertainty can expose agents to manipulation then you should not also assume that preferences are intransitive: those agents will already be manipulable.

---

[4] Laibson (1997).

But for this diagnostic method to work, the ideal world must portray the interests of agents accurately: otherwise the count of distortions will not be correct. So, once we relinquish the fiction that agents can always rank options and judge marginal trade-offs, the dangers and inefficiencies of economic life need to be recast. To analyze the world's many potential hazards – externalities, intransitive choices, missing markets, the incompleteness of contracts, asymmetries of information – one should not suppose that indifference curves are smooth or that preferences satisfy the classical axioms of rationality. For example, the explanation in Chapter 4 for why a rational agent must have transitive preferences does not and should not assume that agents have complete preferences: if it did then we would leave open the possibility that the drawbacks of intransitivity were an artifact of completeness. Conversely, a demonstration that incompleteness does no harm should not presuppose that agents violate those axioms such as the transitivity of preferences (as opposed to the transitivity of revealed preferences) that do serve their interests. To take a different example, I will argue in Chapter 8 that classical welfare economics offers workable advice only if preferences are complete; a more accurate characterization of the ideal frictionless world will thus expose the ineffectiveness of traditional policy advice.

These uses of rationality mark the difference between economics and those social sciences, such as psychology, that do without norms of behavior. An economic understanding of individuals and social institutions must go beyond how agents act and pose a pertinent set of counterfactuals. When agents violate a putative norm of rational conduct, we must ask if the agents would be better off if they instead complied with the norm, and if so, what is preventing them from doing so.

"The combined assumptions of maximizing behavior, market equilibrium, and stable preferences, used relentlessly and unflinchingly, form the heart of the economic approach...." These words of Gary Becker from 1976 leave the meaning of "maximizing" ambiguous. Does maximizing mean that, in a properly constructed economic model, agents pursue their interests? Or does it mean that each agent's goals are sufficiently unified that they can be assimilated into a single utility function? And if an agent maximizes a utility function, must that function display smooth trade-offs, as the utility functions in all of Becker's models do? If only the answer to the first of these questions is "yes" then this book hews to Becker's philosophy. The shading though will admittedly look different: preferences will be displaced from their position at the heart of economics and production becomes central.

1.3 THE IDEOLOGY AND SCOPE OF TRADE-OFFS

When economists advise governments or run universities, they are eager
to point out that decisions present trade-offs. Redistributions of income
bring tax distortions and hence inefficiency. Lower tuition comes at the
cost of increased faculty teaching loads. The lockdown that saves lives
from an infectious disease will choke off economic activity. This fixa-
tion – that trade-offs are the be-all and end-all of governance – provides
economics with its own distinctive ideology. Just as battlefield casualties
force a medic into triage decisions, life confronts us with hard choices.
Real economists are ready to tackle them.

The difficult decisions the world serves up are resolved in economics
by the differentiable preference trade-offs of the indifference curve. Thus
armed, the agents of economic models can identify a small class of solutions to the problems they face. This resolution made perfect sense in the
19th century when the differential calculus provided the lingua franca
of science. Enough time has passed, however, to allow economics to
acknowledge that agents do not always know how to compare and judge,
both on the margin and overall. Deciding whether to accept this fact may
be the ultimate hard choice for an economist.

Smooth preference trade-offs will be absent when different goods
appeal to an agent but the agent cannot identify a specific rate at which
increments of those goods can be substituted without benefit or loss.
These lapses from the neoclassical ideal come in two varieties. In the first,
an agent views some trade-offs of consumption as neither beneficial nor
harmful. Since these appraisals moreover will not depend on the exact
terms of the trade-off, they cannot be explained away as cases of indifference. For instance, a one unit sacrifice of good 1 might require at least
x additional units of good 2 to leave an agent at least as well off but a
gain of less than x units of good 2 might not harm the agent. As we will
see, incompleteness provides the only convincing account of these judgments. In the second, an agent might have classically rational preferences
but the agent's indifference curves are kinked. A one unit sacrifice of good
1 might again require x units of good 2 as compensation but an x unit
sacrifice of good 2 might not be remedied by a one unit gain of good 1.
In both cases, an agent will display an interval of margins or supporting
prices at some or all consumption options.

Not every pathology of preference theory indicates an inability to say
what one good is worth in terms of another. A telling case is provided
by lexicography, where an agent considers one good to be so superior to
a second good that any increase in the consumption of the former, no

matter how small, is superior to any increase in the latter, no matter how large. For example, let the bundle of two goods (x_1, x_2) be preferred to (y_1, y_2) if and only if $x_1 > y_1$ or $(x_1 = y_1$ and $x_2 \geq y_2)$. Although lexicography is the bad boy of utility theory – the preference is complete and transitive and yet has no utility representation[5] – a lexicographic agent *can* say what one good is worth in terms of another: there is no amount of good 2 the agent would accept for any amount of good 1. The market demand of such an agent, moreover, is identical to the demand of an agent with the differentiable utility $u(x_1, x_2) = x_1$ when prices are strictly positive.[6] A world of such lexicographic agents moreover would create no ripples; firms would not produce good 2 and it would cease to exist. Lexicography thus amounts to a decided trade-off. It is the undecided trade-offs that spell trouble for conventional economics.

You may walk away unconvinced, despite my efforts, that agents display ranges of marginal valuations rather than the single margins of smooth indifference curves and that such preferences pass the test of rationality. Intellectual debates on fundamentals are always prone to cycles of objection and rejoinder. But you ought to know what turns on your allegiance to the smooth textbook indifference curve. With smooth trade-offs, market prices will display less volatility and classical welfare economics will be able to generate usable policy recommendations. Your allegiance however will also mean that you must live with a stubborn discrepancy between your predictions and the reality of individual choice behavior. You will have trouble explaining why agents hold persistently to the status quo and why they so often conclude that their options include no dominant alternative.

Since the link between smooth trade-offs and their economic consequences will often be the implicit subject matter, many of the arguments in this book have a contingent or hypothetical character; the causal mechanisms at play are as important as the facts on the ground. For example, the goal of Chapter 7 is not that pricing is volatile, the point is that the best explanations of the incidence and logic of volatility rest on production rather than preferences. If you are skeptical of volatility, you should know what arguments best rationalize your position. For a second example, my assumption throughout the book that preferences (as opposed to revealed preferences) are transitive is not an empirical claim: it is made to

---

[5] Debreu (1954).

[6] This point is due to Richter (1966) though he gives this agent a more complicated utility function that fails to be differentiable.

isolate without any extraneous distortions the impact of incomparability and incompleteness.

The two varieties of preferences without smooth trade-offs mentioned in the previous section will be presented in two models, local incomparability and safety bias. They provide the centerpieces of Part I and appear in Chapters 3 and 5. In the chapter in between, you will find the case for the rationality of agents who are not always capable of comparing alternatives. The book's preference applications in Part I and economy-wide analyses of pricing and policymaking in Part II are built on this foundation.

The run-through below will outline the two main models and their connections to pricing and policymaking – which might otherwise be difficult to see. For readers interested in practical applications, the run-through also offers a theory-light path: read the synopsis below possibly joined to a sightseeing tour of Chapters 3 and 5, take a sample of the preference applications in Sections 4.3 and 6.3, and then jump to Part II. I have omitted from the run-through several topics, including the book's positive proposals for policymaking in Chapter 9, when the run-through provides a sufficient bridge.

A Puzzle

Jamie and Pat are deciding on a movie. Jamie says "You should choose since I am indifferent." Pat makes the same plea. Are these claims believable? Are the parties indifferent, as they claim, or are they waffling, unable to rank the available alternatives?

Classical consumer preferences rule out incompleteness, the inability of an agent to form a preference between some pairs of options. So if we infer from Jamie and Pat's conversation that neither holds a strict preference between some pair of movies, then the only remaining classical possibility is that they are indifferent. But indifference is a highly unlikely event. If a preference satisfies the textbook assumptions of continuity and increasingness, then the pairs of bundles that are indifferent form a low-dimensional subset of the space of all pairs of bundles: each indifference curve will be a "thin" subset of the positive orthant, a line (usually assumed to be convex) when there are just two goods. As a practical matter therefore we should rarely if ever see agents who are indifferent between alternatives. But since we see agents like our moviegoers all the time, the classical model cannot be correct.

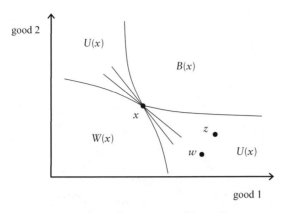

FIGURE 1.1 Locally incomparable preferences

Local Incomparability

To address this puzzle and other problems with the classical model, the agents most frequently encountered in this book will have a form of incomplete preferences where they cannot decide how much a small increment of a good is worth in terms of another good. Given any bundle x, the set of bundles one of our agents regards as weakly better than x, which I label $B(x)$, will display a kink at x. Equivalently, multiple price lines will *support* $B(x)$ at x, that is, $B(x)$ lies to the northeast of multiple price lines through x. The agent thus has an interval or band of margins. See Figure 1.1. Remarkably enough, kinks of this sort are intimately connected to incompleteness. If $B(x)$ displays a kink at x greater than some minimal size for every bundle x then under mild conditions the agent's preferences must be incomplete. So some bundles y will not land in either $B(x)$ or in $W(x)$, the bundles weakly worse than x, but in a third category $U(x)$ of bundles unranked relative to x.

Preferences that fit the pattern of Figure 1.1 – the presence for each x of multiple price lines that support $B(x)$ and that, in the vicinity of x, are contained in $U(x)$ – will be called *locally incomparable*. For such preferences, the $B(x)$ sets will frequently overlap as x varies, illustrated in Figure 1.2. And due to their incompleteness, locally incomparable preferences never have utility representations: a utility would place any bundle y in either $B(x)$ or $W(x)$ or both.

One way that locally incomparable preferences can arise is from *unanimity aggregation* where an individual holds several candidate preference relations to be reasonable and commits to a ranking of alternatives only when all of the candidates agree. For example, in Figure 1.1, each of the two segments of the boundary of $B(x)$ could be a portion of an

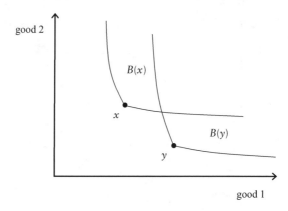

FIGURE 1.2 The overlap of better-than sets

indifference curve of a fully orthodox candidate preference: a bundle y then lies in $B(x)$ only if the two candidates unanimously back y over x.

Incompleteness and local incomparability can account for Jamie and Pat's interchange. A bundle is classically defined to be indifferent to x if it is contained in both $B(x)$ and $W(x)$. In Figure 1.1, x itself is the only such bundle but the bundles in $U(x)$, which are unranked relative to x, are plentiful. If in addition $B(x)$ and $W(x)$ change continuously as x varies then incompleteness is robust: when y lies in the interior of $U(x)$, an absence of preference will also hold for pairs near x and y. So if we reinterpret our couple's claims of indifference as an inability to form preferences then their actions, though they violate the classical model of consumer theory, can readily be explained.

Little turns on how the bundles in $U(x)$ are labeled, and we could instead declare each bundle in $U(x)$ to be indifferent to x. The drawback of this redescription is that the agent's preferences and specifically the agent's indifference relation will then fail to be transitive. For example, if z has slightly more of both goods than w and both lie in $U(x)$ then w will be indifferent to x and hence weakly preferred to x, x will be indifferent and hence weakly preferred to z, and yet z will be strictly preferred to w (assuming the preference is increasing). Letting $\succsim$ and $\succ$ denote weak and strict preference, the intransitivity $w \succsim x \succsim z \succ w$ has appeared. Since with this new preference we would face the chore of disentangling such intransitivities of indifference from the more significant intransitivities of strict preference, I will stick to the standard definition of indifference. The standard definition should also reassure you that the overlap of $B(x)$ sets in Figure 1.2 does not imply that the underlying preference is intransitive;

since the boundary of $B(x)$ need not contain any points indifferent to x besides x itself, an overlap does not lead to indifference curves that cross. Indeed incompleteness nearly snuffs out indifference: it turns out that x can be indifferent to only a negligible fraction of points on the boundary of $B(x)$.

Why is it important to keep track of whether preferences are transitive? Decades of tradition in economics have tied rational self-interest to preferences that satisfy the two classical axioms of rationality, completeness and transitivity. This unfortunate fusion, never backed up by rigorous argument, has misled generations of economists, students and teachers alike.

Failures of transitivity can inflict harm by leading agents through sequences of decisions that leave them with options worse than what they began with. The money pump – where an agent with the preferences $x \succ y \succ z \succ x$ will happily pay a small sum in each round of an endless sequence of exchanges of a worse for a better option – is only the most famous and extreme case of the damage intransitivity can wreak.

Incompleteness on the other hand does no harm if the preference judgments that agents can make satisfy transitivity. Agents can protect themselves from damaging sequences of trades simply by declining to swap options that they do not know how to order. As long as an agent does accept any offer of an alternative that is strictly preferred to the agent's current holding, the agent will not be led to an option worse than what the agent could have reached with a different trading strategy.

These conclusions bring to light the rational self-interest behind one of the enduring regularities of behavioral economics, sticking to the status quo. In Figure 1.1, z has slightly more of both goods than w but neither is ranked relative to x. A strategy of exchanging unranked options at will could lead the agent from z to x and then to w. Status quo bias will stop the agent from being ensnared by vetoing the first exchange.

The rationality logic behind status quo bias is visible however only if we treat choice and preference as different concepts. If the agent in Figure 1.1 follows the status-quo bias strategy of making exchanges only when offered a preferred alternative, the agent will sometimes choose x over z and sometimes choose z over x: it will depend on which is the status quo. The agent will similarly vacillate between x and w. On the revealed preference view that choice and preference are different names for the same phenomenon, an intransitivity has appeared: the agent has revealed a strict preference for z over w and indifference between w and x and between x and z. The same intransitivity arose when we labeled the options in $U(x)$ as indifferent to x and it underlies the skepticism of economists that agents will persist in status quo bias. But if we distinguish between preference and choice then we can see that the intransitivity that stems from status quo bias, far from inflicting harm, protects agents from destructive chains of decisions.

When preference is defined by an agent's judgments of well-being, self-interest will require those judgments to be transitive but not complete: an agent facing some pair of options might not be able to say which is better. And the intransitivity that accompanies status quo bias shows that a choice definition of preference will not rescue the completeness-cum-transitivity theory of rationality. An agent's revealed preferences must be complete – if x and z are unranked then x when it is the status quo will be revealed preferred to z – but they will fail to be transitive.

A locally incomparable agent exemplifies the status quo bias that accompanies incomplete preferences. Such an agent will have a band of marginal valuations, illustrated in the multiple price lines of Figure 1.1 that support $B(x)$. The steepest of these lines indicates that when facing a unit loss of good 1 the agent will require a large amount of good 2 as compensation, the flattest of the lines indicates that the agent will sacrifice only a small amount of good 2 for a unit gain of good 1. This differential response to gains and losses goes under several names, including loss aversion and the willingness-to-accept/willingness-to-pay disparity, and the differential also serves as a common definition of status quo bias. None of these classic patterns of behavioral economics need to be posited as ad hoc psychological facts: they stem from the demands of rationality when agents cannot judge trade-offs.

The agents with smooth indifference curves that appear in orthodox consumer theory, in contrast, will not display status quo bias or any of its cognates. If to begin such an agent has purchased positive amounts of all goods then he or she will necessarily want to make further trades if prior to consumption relative prices were to shift even slightly. Incompleteness therefore scores a second empirical success over the textbook indifference curve, beyond its better explanation of how frequently agents cannot strictly rank their options.

Rooting status quo bias in incomplete preferences also lets us dispense with the awkward psychological asymmetry where the pain of losses inherently cuts deeper than the pleasure of gains. Suppose that unanimity aggregation lies behind Figure 1.1 with the two halves of the boundary of $B(x)$ representing portions of the indifference curves of two candidate preferences. The simplest way for this agent to unanimity aggregate is to see if a change relative to x benefits the candidate preference that is most pessimistic about the change: if this candidate preference approves the change then so will the other candidate. So if the change is a loss of good 1 and a gain of good 2, the agent can let the candidate with the steeper indifference curve make the decision and if the change is a gain of good 1 and a loss of good 2, then the candidate with the flatter indifference curve can make the call. This delegation amounts to an optimization technique, not an impulsive reaction to losses.

Safety Bias
When agents cannot judge trade-offs, they can turn to many ways of making decisions – unanimity aggregation is just one possibility. An agent facing a difficult choice can take a cautious approach by letting the decision be settled by a worst-case assessment of each option. To this end, the agent can deploy a set of *welfare functions,* each of which assesses all of the agent's options. The worst case for an option x will be given by the smallest of these welfare assessments and the agent when facing a pair of options will choose the option with the greater worst-case assessment; these rankings of the pairs in turn define an entire preference relation. When one of the agent's welfare functions fails to provide the worst-case assessment for either of two options x and y, then that function is irrelevant to the agent's preference between x and y. So, in contrast to unanimity aggregation, the present preferences do not require unanimous agreement.

When the agent's assessments all agree on the welfare level of an option x then x guarantees that welfare level: x is *safe.* Since different movements away from x can affect which welfare function delivers the worst-case assessment, the agent's better-than set $B(x)$ will be kinked at x: a set of margins or price lines will support $B(x)$ at x. In contrast to local incomparability, however, the multiplicity of supporting prices occurs only at the safe consumptions rather than at every consumption. The agent's decisions will therefore be biased in favor of safe options.

In intertemporal choice, for example, an agent who is unsure how to trade-off consumption at different dates might consider, for each time t, a welfare function that equals time-t consumption x_t to provide one of the reasonable assessments. The minimum coordinate of a bundle $x = (x_1, \ldots, x_T)$ would then be the agent's worst-case assessment of x and the agent when choosing between two options would select the bundle whose minimum coordinate is greater. The safe consumptions would then consist of the constant bundles – the $45°$ line when there are two periods.

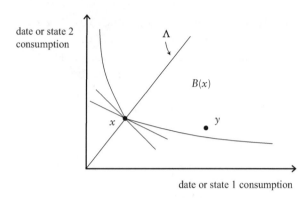

FIGURE 1.3 Safety bias

To see with two periods that a kink in $B(x)$ occurs when $x_1 = x_2$, fix date 1 consumption at $\bar{x}_1$ and increase x_2 from 0. The worst-case assessment then begins at 0, increases with x_2, and plateaus at $x_2 = \bar{x}_1$ when the welfare function that gives the worst-case assessment switches from x_2 to x_1. A kink in $B(x)$ therefore occurs at $(\bar{x}_1, \bar{x}_1)$.

This Leontief-style example is extreme for clarity's sake. An agent could well regard a ray of time-varying consumption bundles to be safe – social conventions might convince the agent that consumption must increase over time to qualify as safe. An agent would also be likely to accept some intertemporal trade-offs and prefer a nonsafe y over a safe x when the gains that come with y at some dates sufficiently outstrip the losses at other dates. These possibilities are pictured for the two-period case in Figure 1.3, where the preferences arise from two welfare functions and Λ is a ray of safe bundles. Each of the two parts of the lower boundary of $B(x)$ is a portion of an indifference curve of one of the two welfare functions and, since the two parts meet at a point on Λ, the two welfare functions assign the same welfare number to the two indifference curves. As in the Leontief case, kinks occur along the ray because as a path of consumption crosses the ray the welfare function that gives the worst-case assessment switches.

In choice under uncertainty, an agent might be unsure which subjective probability distribution to employ. Each distribution in some set of distributions the agent deems reasonable would then define an expected utility function that can serve as a welfare function and the worst-case assessment of an option x would be the minimum of these expected utilities when evaluated at x. Consumption constant across states of the world will then form a safe pattern; with two states, the ray Λ of safe bundles in Figure 1.3 would be the $45°$ line.

For both intertemporal and uncertain choice, multiple rays of safe consumption are also possible.

An agent with rays of safe bundles along which the agent's indifference curves are kinked and supported by multiple prices will be called *safety biased* – whether or not the psychological backstory of making the worst-case assessment as beneficial as possible holds. Although an inability to make preference judgments is the most prominent source of safety bias, there can be other origins, for example, complementarities in consumption. The left and right shoes that motivate Leontief utilities provide a textbook example though the vertical and horizontal stretches of Leontief indifference curves will not hold in any important case of safety bias in this book. One goal will be to show that complementaries are not as innocuous as economists have been trained to believe.

Welfare Economics and Volatility
Local incomparability and safety bias will drive the economy-wide applications in Part II of the book.

In welfare economics, the omnipresent kinks of local incomparability imply that an agent has a range of valuations of one good in terms of another. So if, for example, good 1 in Figure 1.1 is a public good and good 2 is the agent's private consumption, the kink in $B(x)$ implies that the agent would sacrifice only a little private consumption to scale up the public good a notch and would demand a lot of private consumption to take it down a notch. When these gaps are summed across agents, there will be a large band of aggregate marginal valuations of the public good. So if the marginal cost of the public good in terms of private consumption falls into this band, classical welfare criteria will offer only limited help to a government deciding how much of the public good to construct: both large and small quantities will qualify as efficient.

A similar policy paralysis besets the economy as a whole. Due to the second welfare theorem, if an allocation of goods $x = (x^1, \ldots, x^I)$ among I individuals is Pareto efficient then a common price vector will support each agent i's better-than set at x^i. Under local incomparability however a band of vectors can typically serve as supporting prices. If moreover this band moves continuously as the allocation changes and the band has maximum dimension, then for allocations near x each agent i's better-than set will typically continue to be supported at i's new allocation by a common price vector. The first welfare theorem therefore implies that the new allocation will also qualify as efficient. Similarly, when an allocation x is Pareto efficient and the economy subsequently undergoes a small change to the modeling environment, perhaps a small externality, the price vector that initially supported the agents' better-than sets at x will usually continue to do so; the change will therefore call for no policy response. The discriminatory power of economic policy advice thus leaches away.

In early neoclassical economics, the differentiable utility function underlay the stability of prices: small exogenous changes to endowments or technology will typically lead to a small response in the marginal rates of substitution that hold in equilibrium and thus in equilibrium relative prices. With safety-biased preferences, on the other hand, the kinks in indifference curves undermine this argument: small endowment changes in the vicinity of a kink will now force large changes in supporting price lines. Relative prices will consequently be volatile. Modern general equilibrium theory has countered that it is exceedingly unlikely that endowments land at just the points that allow agents to consume in the neighborhood of indifference-curve kinks. The kinks however are attractors. In their presence, an intertemporal investment in a future consumption good will earn a future utility return that fails to vary smoothly as a function of current consumption forgone: the rate of return will fall discontinuously as the production of the future consumption good places agents along their safe rays. Investment can therefore propel an economy to the endowment points where agents do consume at indifference-curve kinks. The volatility scenarios will then play out: small endowment changes in the future will drive substantial movements in relative prices.

1.5 CONVENTIONS, DEFINITIONS, AND AVOIDING MATH

Mathematical models supply the alpha and omega of this book and many Greek letters in between, but the synopsis above and the preference applications in Sections 4.3 and 6.3 allow a math-avoiding route to Chapters 8 through 10 on policymaking, where the models are more concrete and self-contained. Discovering the intersections of mathematics and economic content, where a formal model quietly imports a vision of human nature, is one of the pleasures of economic theory. But not necessarily on every occasion.

The initial sections of most chapters provide informal summaries of the models to follow and, in the second half of the book, earlier-in-the-chapter partial equilibrium treatments are lighter going that later-in-the-chapter general equilibrium models. When a section or displayed example bears obvious mathematical warning signs, you may drive by. If you are not well-versed in general equilibrium theory, portions of Chapter 7 invite skimming: I could not in this case shepherd the math into skippable chunks.

Many proofs will be found in the Appendix rather than the body of the text.

The items below lay out the notation used in this book. While most of these definitions will be repeated along the way, this list can serve as a backup.

In models with goods, there will when possible be L goods and I agents, the agents will consume nonnegative bundles, subscripts will denote goods, and superscripts will denote individuals. So agent i's consumption of goods will normally be a vector of L real numbers $x^i = (x^i_1, \ldots, x^i_L) \geq 0$. Both L and I will always be finite.

For any two vectors of n real numbers x and y, $x \leq y$ holds if $x_i \leq y_i$ for all i, $x < y$ holds if $x \leq y$ and $x \neq y$, and $x \ll y$ holds if $x_i < y_i$ for all i. Greater than inequalities are defined analogously.

Preferences will often be expressed as binary relations. A binary relation $\succsim$ on a set X is *complete* if, for all $x, y \in X$, either $x \succsim y$ or $y \succsim x$ (or both); *transitive* if, for all $x, y, z \in X$, $x \succsim y$ and $y \succsim z$ imply $x \succsim z$; *asymmetric* if $x \succsim y$ implies not $y \succsim x$; *reflexive* if, for all $x \in X$, $x \succsim x$; *incomplete* when $\succsim$ is not complete; and *classically rational* if $\succsim$ is complete and transitive. When a binary relation $\succsim$ is incomplete and neither $x \succsim y$ nor $y \succsim x$ holds then x and y are $\succsim$-*unranked* or $\succsim$-*unrelated* and I sometimes then write $x \perp y$. If either $x \succsim y$ or $y \succsim x$ (or both) then x and y are $\succsim$-*related*.

Given a binary relation $\succsim$ on X that is interpreted as a preference, the *strict preference* $\succ$ is defined by $x \succ y$ if and only if $x \succsim y$ and not $y \succsim x$, the *indifference relation* $\sim$ is defined by $x \sim y$ if and only if $x \succsim y$ and $y \succsim x$. If neither $x \succ y$ nor $y \succ x$ hold then (in Chapter 6 only) I will write $x \sim^* y$, which need not imply $x \sim y$.

A preference relation $\succsim$ on X is *represented by a utility function u* from X to $\mathbb{R}$ if, for all $x, y \in X$, $x \succsim y$ if and only if $u(x) \geq u(y)$.

When the set of consumption possibilities consists of bundles of goods, $X = \mathbb{R}^L_+$, I will normally assume that preferences and utility functions are increasing, though utilities will on occasion be weakly increasing to admit convenient illustrations. Increasingness can usually be weakened considerably, for example to local nonsatiation. Given $X = \mathbb{R}^L_+$, a preference relation $\succsim$ is *increasing* if, for all $x, y \in X$, $x > y$ implies $x \succ y$; *weakly increasing* if, for all $x, y \in X$, $x \gg y$ implies $x \succ y$; *convex* if, for all $x \in X$, $B(x) = \{y \in X : y \succsim x\}$ is a convex set and *strictly convex* if $B(x)$ is a strictly convex set, that is, for all $y \neq z$ and $0 < \alpha < 1$, $\alpha y + (1 - \alpha)z$ lies in the interior of X; *locally nonsatiated*, if for all $x \in X$ and all $\varepsilon > 0$, there is a $y \in X$ such that $\|y - x\| < \varepsilon$ and $y \succ x$; and *smooth* if $\succsim$ can be represented by a differentiable function u.[7] A function u from X to $\mathbb{R}$ is *increasing* if, for all $x, y \in X$, $x > y$ implies $u(x) > u(y)$ and is *weakly increasing* if, for all $x, y \in X$, $x \gg y$ implies $u(x) > u(y)$.

If x and y are two vectors of n real numbers, then $x \cdot y$ denotes the dot or inner product $\sum_{i=1}^{n} x_i y_i$. Unless clarity demands an exception, I will omit the bounds in sums: so $\sum_i x_i$ rather than $\sum_{i=1}^{n} x_i$.

The set $B(x)$ above, sometimes denoted $B_{\succsim}(x)$, is the *better-than set* of the binary relation $\succsim$ at x. A $p \in \mathbb{R}^L$ *supports* $B(x)$ at x if $p \cdot (z - x) \geq 0$ for all $z \in B(x)$.

Let f be a function from $\mathbb{R}_+^L$ (or some other convex set) to $\mathbb{R}$. If f is differentiable then $D_{x_i}f(x)$ will denote the partial derivative of f with respect to its ith argument evaluated at $x = (x_1, \ldots, x_n)$ and $Df(x)$ will be the vector of these partial derivatives. When $L = 1$ (the domain of f is $\mathbb{R}_+$) then $D_+f(x)$ or $D^+f(x)$ will denote the right derivative of f evaluated at x, and $D_-f(x)$ or $D^-f(x)$ will denote the left derivative. The function f is *concave* if, for all x and y in $\mathbb{R}_+^L$ and all $0 \leq \alpha \leq 1$, $f(\alpha x + (1 - \alpha)y) \geq \alpha f(x) + (1 - \alpha)f(y)$. If $\geq$ is replaced by $\leq$ in the last inequality then f is *convex*. The function f is *strictly concave* if, for all $x \neq y$ and all $0 < \alpha < 1$, $f(\alpha x + (1 - \alpha)y) > \alpha f(x) + (1 - \alpha)f(y)$. If $>$ is replaced by $<$ in the last inequality then f is *strictly convex*.

---

[7] Debreu (1972) provides a condition on preferences that implies the existence of such a representation.

PART I

TRADE-OFFS AND RATIONALITY

2

The Rise and Fall of Utility as an Ordering Principle

2.1 IN THE BEGINNING

Natura non facit saltum. (Nature does not jump.)
Alfred Marshall, motto of *Principles of Economics*

People make decisions for reasons even in economic life. In the psychology that launched neoclassical economics, those reasons were crude. A good k delivers an amount of pleasure or utility represented by an increasing and differentiable function u_k of its quantity x_k, and an agent's total satisfaction equals the sum of the utilities of all of the pleasure-providing goods $\sum_k u_k(x_k)$. An agent with an extra dollar of income should seek out and purchase whatever good can generate the greatest increment of pleasure when the dollar is spent on it. In this account, the utilities of goods and the summing of utilities are not merely tools that summarize an agent's choices. They are *ordering principles* that indicate how a self-interested agent should choose: good k should be assessed using u_k and the pleasure delivered by different goods should be summed. Agents in fact can make consumption mistakes. A good might not turn out to generate as much pleasure as an agent anticipated, though a rational agent will correct these errors in time. An agent consequently cannot be perpetually stumped as to which good or goal to pursue. Early neoclassical consumers thus resemble our current view of firms: they have objectively correct actions though they sometimes fail to perform them.

The advice-giving function of utility theory explains why the early neoclassical economists linked pleasure-seeking to the additive separability assumption that an agent's total utility equals the sum of individual-good utilities. While hedonism and additive separability can be untangled –

non-pleasure magnitudes can be added and the consumption of one good can affect the pleasure of another – together they point out simple paths to utility improvements. If after a consumption experiment with goods 1 and 2 an agent discovers that good 1's marginal utility per dollar exceeds that of good 2, then the agent will know to replace part of his or her good-2 consumption with good-1 consumption. Additive separability ensures that this compartmentalization will work: the loop from consumption experiment to utility feedback will lead an agent to successful adjustments. But if the utility of a good cannot be detached from the entire stream of goods consumed at various dates and under various contingencies, then the feedback would be attenuated: an agent would have to wait until the consumption stream played out to see the utility result. Suppose for example that satisfaction trade-offs today are affected by consumption next year; a utility improvement today then cannot be found independently of next year's search for improvements. The early neoclassical economists therefore shied away from utility functions that apply to elaborately defined actions: consumers would not know how to discover them.

A more disorienting feature of early utility theory is that it is not always rational for an agent to select the available option that delivers the greatest utility, a contrast to our long custom of thinking that greater utility is shorthand for what is rational to choose. According to the early neoclassical economists, utility comparisons show only how to decide between options that can be reduced to various quantities of pleasure – for example, foods and other material comforts – and not the alternatives that involve a "higher rank" of feelings – for example, what walk of life to pursue.[1] Neoclassical economics at its beginning offered a psychology of choice designed to apply only to a certain class of decisions.

Even before economists came to a formal theory of choice, mathematicians in the 18th century – only the Bernoullis are now remembered – invented expected utility to explain what gambles agents will agree to.[2] A Bernoullian agent is endowed with a utility function u for outcomes, which I will take to be consumption bundles. Let a lottery offer outcomes $x(1), \ldots, x(n)$ with probabilities $\pi(1), \ldots, \pi(n)$ respectively, where each $\pi(i) \geq 0$ and $\sum_{i=1}^{n} \pi(i) = 1$. The agent's expected utility for the gamble is then defined to equal $\sum_i \pi(i)u(x(i))$. To make the right choice between a pair of lotteries, the function u must be discovered and its mathematical

---

[1] Jevons (1871), 23–27.
[2] Bernoulli (1738) took care to credit his predecessors.

expectation must be calculated. Mistakes are again possible; the dazzle of a polished roulette wheel might trick an agent into error.

Both utilitarian psychology and Bernoullian expected utility theory can compare any pair of alternatives drawn from their respective domains. For the early neoclassicals, each bundle delivers a specific quantity of pleasure and hence for each pair of bundles at least one of the bundles is weakly superior to the other. Similarly for the Bernoullis: each gamble delivers a specific expected utility and so at least one out of each pair of gambles is weakly superior to the other. Ties moreover will be unlikely accidents: in the lottery case, for example, a small increase in the consumption of one of the goods for one of the positive-probability outcomes will raise the expected utility of a lottery and hence break any indifference with another lottery.

The early neoclassical economists assumed that utility functions are differentiable and elevated their derivatives – marginal utilities – to the forefront of their theory. One advantage, no doubt, was that calculus burnished their scientific credentials. The centrality of marginal utility went deeper, however, so deep that Marshall began his grand unification of 19th century economics by telling his readers that nature, which includes the pleasure that goods provide, does not make jumps. People come equipped with marginal utilities.

Differentiable utility functions lead to a decisiveness that goes beyond the mere ability to compare arbitrary pairs of alternatives. Agents with differentiable utilities can not only decide which alternative in a pair is better: they can also judge the exact rate at which to substitute goods. When trading goods 1 and 2 at some exchange ratio, a differentiable utility will increase or decrease at approximately the same rate whether the agent buys or sells a small of amount of good 1. Suppose a change Δx_1 in the consumption of good 1 exchanges for a change of $\rho \Delta x_1$ in the consumption of good 2, where ρ is negative. If u_1 and u_2 are differentiable functions, $x = (x_1, x_2)$ is the agent's initial consumption, and Δx_1 is small, then the change in the agent's utility will approximately equal

$$(Du_1(x_1) + Du_2(x_2)\rho)\, \Delta x_1.$$

This approximation holds whether Δx_1 is positive or negative: if a small Δx_1 leads to a utility change of δ then $-\Delta x_1$ leads to a utility change of approximately $-\delta$. The individuals imagined by the early neoclassical economists are not capricious.

Assuming that each u_k has strictly positive first derivatives, we can find the rate at which the agent trades off the satisfaction of goods by setting the expression above equal to 0 and solving for ρ. The result, $\rho^* = -\frac{Du_1(x_1)}{Du_2(x_2)}$, is also the slope of the agent's indifference curve and the agent's marginal rate of substitution at x. So, to leave the agent approximately indifferent following a change Δx_1, the agent's good 2 consumption must change by $\rho^* \Delta x_1$, regardless of the sign of Δx_1. The agent thus can identify an exact marginal valuation of one good in terms of another whether gain or losses are involved.

These conclusions do not hinge on additive separability. If the agent has just one utility u that is a function of all of the agent's consumption goods, then each derivative $Du_k(x_k)$ above can be replaced by the partial derivative $D_{x_k}u(x)$ and ρ^* will remain well-defined.

When the utility u defines a unique ρ^* for any pair of goods and any x, I will say that u (or the agent with the utility u) is *locally decisive*. This property holds when a utility function is differentiable but nondifferentiable utility functions can also have a unique marginal rate of substitution at every x.[3] Expected utility functions will be locally decisive when the utility function for outcomes in that model is differentiable and has strictly positive first derivatives.

Locally decisive agents are tailor-made to exchange goods. Whenever the price ratio for some pair of goods deviates even slightly from the corresponding ρ^* and the agent has a positive endowment of these goods, there will be a trade that benefits the agent. Marginal utilities thus provided an ideal starting point for a theory where the exchange of goods is the prototypical economic activity.

The differentiable utilities embraced by the economists of the late 19th century fit best with a physiological view of economic satisfaction. If we adopt Marshall's principle that nature does not jump, the rate at which utility responds to increments of a consumption good should converge as the increments becomes small; marginal utilities for goods will then be well-defined. Without such a basis in physiology, any claim that agents are locally decisive would have been questionable. In a symbolic view of economic welfare, for example, there would be no presumption that the magnitude of a gain will be comparable to the magnitude of a loss: gains might be a matter of course while losses might be humiliations. By rooting the drive for consumption goods in material pleasure, the early neoclassicals could present smooth utilities as nearly a corollary.[4]

Local decisiveness is no longer considered the signature of consumer optimization in economic theory though for many economists it still lies

---

[3] Neilson (1991).

[4] For the role of physics as a spur to the early neoclassicals, see Mirowski (1984).

at the heart of individual decision-making. The convexity of preferences and pared-down rationality assumptions took center stage in post-World War II economic theory: these were the assumptions pertinent to the existence of equilibrium and to the welfare theorems of general equilibrium theory. The differentiable utility function became an anachronism from this angle, a quaint holdover of the amateur inventors of neoclassical economics and their devotion to differentiation, now met by a smile of condescension. We will see, however, that marginal utility and the smooth indifference curve it underpins served a well-honed theoretical agenda. When applied to the nuts and bolts of economic analysis, the fine-grained decisiveness brought by differentiability plays a critical role: it precludes choice pathologies, irons out the volatility of market prices, and lays out the smooth relationship between choice and welfare that economics needs to discriminate among policy options.

Despite its theoretical conveniences, pleasure-seeking – with or without the added decisiveness of differentiability – offers a poor model of consumption choice even for material goods. To decide what to buy for dinner, agents may need to weigh the health advantages of a low-salt diet, the virtues of sustainable agriculture and organic produce, and even their fidelity to the dietary laws of their religion. Once they get home from the supermarket and think about their summer plans, they need to balance the relaxation of a family vacation against an addition to the children's college fund. Pleasure will have some role in these deliberations but only some. Consumption decisions are intertwined with the full complexity of human lives and cannot be boiled down to calculations of the intensity of satisfaction.

2.2 THE NEW TESTAMENT

Hedonism as a model of consumption survived into the 20th century but only barely: pleasure-seeking in Marshall's *Principles of Economics* (1890) and its many revisions was watered down in comparison to the Jevons (1871) original, while on the continent, where hedonism had been an add-on to Walras (1874), the rejection was wholesale. Along with the disavowal of hedonism, the summing of good-specific utilities was also discarded. If goods cannot be understood solely as pleasure-delivery vehicles then it became difficult to see why the benefits of goods should be added or even what exactly add means. Following these retreats, utility theory no longer explained how agents find their way to maximizing decisions; it was therefore only a matter of time before consumers in neoclassical economics would be modeled by a new formal language.

Though the door might have opened to entirely new possibilities – perhaps where maximization does not underlie individual choice – the transformation of consumer theory would preserve much of the preexisting orthodoxy: it was the psychology of decision-making that would change, not the conclusion that agents optimize. Agents in the new vision would in fact not just optimize, they would choose "as if" they were maximizing utility functions.

The utility function finally loosened its hold on consumer theory in the 1930s. Hicks and Allen's work on indifference curves and ordinal utility and then Samuelson's experiments with binary relations showed that consumption decisions did not have to take utility or pleasure as their starting point.[5] Once von Neumann and Morgenstern laid down an explicit system of axioms on preference relations over lotteries in 1947, the path to a new orthodoxy was paved: preferences were now the primitive.

The movement became more ambitious as it progressed. Hicks had stuck to the older program of laying down psychological laws, though the laws now dealt more modestly with which combinations of goods left an agent better or worse off rather than with quantities of pleasure. But psychological assumptions on preferences rapidly evolved into axioms of rationality; the theory of choice that would coalesce and become dominant would ultimately claim to characterize the very nature of rationality.

The basic object of the theory as it consolidated in the 1950s was – and today remains – a preference relation, which we denote by $\succsim$, a binary relation on a domain of consumption alternatives, with $x \succsim y$ carrying the interpretation that the agent weakly prefers x to y and will therefore accept x when offered a choice between x and y. Strict preference $x \succ y$ is defined to obtain when $x \succsim y$ holds but $y \succsim x$ does not hold. According to its proponents, $\succsim$ comes close to being a direct representation of how agents behave and the decisions they make, which is what economists in this view ought to care about.

The characterization of rationality that preference relations allow is remarkably simple: only two assumptions are needed, completeness and transitivity. A preference $\succsim$ is *complete* if, for every pair of alternatives x and y, either $x \succsim y$ or $y \succsim x$ or both, and *transitive* if, for all triples x, y, and z, $x \succsim y$ and $y \succsim z$ imply $x \succsim z$. Completeness means that every pair of alternatives can be at least weakly ranked while transitivity ensures that the only chains of preference rankings that can cycle are chains of

---

[5] See Hicks and Allen (1934), Hicks (1939a), and Samuelson (1938).

indifference. I will call the combination of completeness and transitivity *classical rationality*.

What is striking in this picture of rationality is the dog that isn't barking. There is no mention of marginal utility or indeed of any derivative. Derivatives were casualties of the convex sets that swept economic theory in the 1950s. Convex preferences – where the bundles an agent prefers to a reference bundle form a convex set – did away with diminishing marginal utility; convex production sets replaced diminishing marginal productivity. The new vocabulary allowed the front-page results of general equilibrium theory, the existence of equilibrium and the link between equilibria and Pareto optima, to be stated and proved with great generality. These successes sealed the victory of classical rationality. For every item of economic theory the new era cared about – including rationality, equilibrium, and optimality – the smooth indifference curve appeared unnecessary.

The banishment of utility brought philosophical comfort as well. The objective character of pleasure-seeking – which implies that an agent's consumption choices are either right or wrong – fit badly with the liberal view of the individual as a locus of subjectively formed desires. By moving from pleasure to preference, economists could see the characteristic problem of society as a clash of competing individual goals over scarce resources rather than as the maximization exercise of a planner pursuing an objective target. As long as the desires of individuals are shaped independently rather than harmonized by social custom, there will be an allocation problem for markets to solve.

At a formal level, classical rationality comes close to generalizing a utility description of agents. It is easy to confirm that the preferences that a utility u represents – the $\succsim$ defined by $x \succsim y$ if and only if $u(x) \geq u(y)$ – are necessarily complete and transitive. Conversely, classical rationality nearly implies that a preference has a utility representation. If the domain of alternatives is finite or countable, completeness and transitivity do guarantee the existence of utility representation but for larger domains an additional order-density condition is needed.[6]

Classical rationality thus delivers the behavior of utility maximization without the embarrassment of pleasure-seeking as a theory of motivation. The existence of utility representations for classically rational preferences

---

[6] The order-density condition requires that there is a finite or countable subset S of the domain X such that for each pair $x, y \in X$ with $x \succ y$ there is a $z \in S$ such that $x \succsim z \succsim y$. See, for example, Fishburn (1970b).

does not however imply that the representations are determinately pinned down: if u represents $\succsim$ and f is an increasing function from real numbers to real numbers then the composition of functions $f \circ u$ also represents $\succsim$.

In the world of post-World War II economics, these facts were taken to nail shut the case against letting utility be the foundation for decision theory, as it had been for the early neoclassical hedonists. If $\succsim$ is represented by a function u, the statement $u(x) \geq u(y)$ adds nothing to the statement $x \succsim y$. Since no inference can be made from $u(x) \geq u(y)$ beyond $x \succsim y$, the specific numbers provided by the function u convey no further meaning.[7] For example, if $x \succ y$ then for any number $n > 0$ there is a utility representation v of $\succsim$ where the utility difference $v(x) - v(y)$ equals n. Even the existence of a utility representation for a preference, notwithstanding its mathematical convenience, carries no significance beyond its implication that $\succsim$ is complete, transitive, and order-dense.

The overthrow of utility theory would have been an unqualified triumph if the only role for utility had been to summarize preferences. But as we have seen utility maximization served as a psychological process that explained to the economists of the 19th century how and why agents come to make well-defined and reasonably stable decisions. The new consensus ought therefore to have explained why agents will normally comply with the axioms of classical rationality. Just as the early neoclassical view of decision-making had been built on the ordering principles of pleasure-seeking and the summation of utilities, assumptions on preferences need comparable foundations.

Economic theory has not been able to fill this void: it cannot explain why rational agents should always be able to form preference judgments. If we free agents from the mandate of pleasure-seeking and grant them the right to pursue goals of their own making, then we must also allow them to end up with multiple goals they cannot integrate. Incomplete preferences will be the result. With no link between the rules of classical rationality and the self-interest of agents, those rules will be a poor predictor of behavior – though it took until the 1980s before the empirical project of rational choice theory began to collapse.

There have been attempts to justify the axioms of classical rationality but they have been relegated to the periphery of the subject: most official defenses of preference theory simply point to the behaviorist position that preferences impose assumptions directly on the choices an agent makes when facing pairs of alternatives. Deeper explanations are unscientific or

---

[7] See for example Arrow (1963, p. 17).

unnecessary. It is revealing that foundations nevertheless have been set forth and I will consider these proposals in Chapter 4.

It is not a defense of early neoclassicism to acknowledge that it met a certain theoretical ideal. Economic agents, as imagined by the founders, knew how to go about their business. By measuring and summing the utilities of goods, weighted as needed by known probabilities, these agents could compare any pair of bundles, and by equating the marginal utility per dollar of their expenditure on each good, they could figure out which bundles to choose. The theoretical closure brought by these guidelines may explain why such a manifestly inaccurate account still holds sway over economists; the inability of subsequent work to provide replacement ordering principles lends the old-time religion a continuing appeal.

2.3 PREFERENCE FORMATION UNDER UNCERTAINTY

Expected utility theory underwent an overhaul later in the 20th century comparable to the transition from hedonism to ordinal preference theory. In the Bernoullian theory, a lottery assigns a specific probability $\pi(i) \geq 0$ to each outcome $x(i)$. But in virtually every economic decision, the probabilities of outcomes have no external, objective definition. Owning a share in a firm, investing in a new technology, and choosing a career all have outcomes that are not only uncertain but difficult even to list. To specify the outcomes relevant for a share in a firm, you would need to know how the firm's industry could evolve, how tastes and perhaps fashion could change, how the regulations the firm is subject to could be shaped by political developments, and so on, a list not too different from an inventory of all possible futures of the ambient society. If you could create such a list of outcomes, each item on the list would be detailed and idiosyncratic, and there would be no obvious way to assign probabilities to them. Indeed, it takes some work to find an example outside of a casino where the outcomes of decisions can be linked to objective probabilities. Even the probabilities of prizes in state-run lotteries require judgments about the actions of others: players cluster in their selections of numbers and the payout to a number is divided by the number of selectors.

The subjective or Bayesian theories of choice under uncertainty that arose in response to this problem do without objective probabilities. They instead specify as exogenous data only the outcomes a decision-maker can encounter, perhaps sums of money or streams of consumption, and an exhaustive list of "states of the world."[8] Each state stipulates how all uncertainty about the world is resolved; it must specify a realization of all pertinent facts about the world at all relevant dates. In a model of a firm's shares, for example, a state must be detailed enough to specify the firm's future path of dividends and, since beliefs affect stock prices, for every date each agent's beliefs about the dividend paths that succeed that date, each agent's beliefs about other agents' beliefs, and so on. Even routine decision-making will require intricate states: to decide on a vacation, a state will have to identify, for each destination, the realization of the weather during the course of the holiday, the amenities available, its ambience and milieu, and so on, including possibly the realization of how the decision-maker will react to novel experiences.

An option for a decision-maker, usually called an *act*, specifies for every state an outcome that is sure to occur at that state. In a model of a firm's shares, an act might specify for each state the stream of returns that stem from owning a share. A preference relation $\succsim$ is defined over acts and the subjective probabilities that an agent implicitly holds are derived from $\succsim$.

To compare the objective and subjective theories, we can recast the objective Bernoullian theory in the language of states, outcomes, and acts. Consider an agent pondering whether to buy an umbrella. Let there be just two states – rain or not rain – and let an act specify, for each state, an outcome of whether the agent is dry d or wet w and the agent's non-umbrella consumption x. In the Bernoullian version of the model, probabilities are exogenous, π_r for rain and $1 - \pi_r$ for not rain. With these data, an act reduces to a lottery since a probability is attached to each outcome that can obtain with the act: buying an umbrella leads to the certain outcome of being dry and a smaller consumption x_s while not buying an umbrella leads to being wet with probability π_r, dry with probability $1 - \pi_r$, and to a larger consumption x_l. An agent can determine the better act from π_r and a utility function u on outcomes that indicates the agent's feelings about being wet or dry and the pleasures of goods. Buying the umbrella is an optimal decision if and only if

$$u(d, x_s) \geq \pi_r u(w, x_l) + (1 - \pi_r)u(d, x_l).$$

In a subjective theory, the agent must again choose whether to buy the umbrella and both decisions can continue to be understood as acts. But

---

[8] The classic references are Savage (1954) and Anscombe and Aumann (1963).

now the agent must decide on a preference without knowing the probability π_r. The theory instead posits a preference $\succsim$ for the agent that orders each pair of acts. The probability π_r and utility u still make an appearance but now they are inferred from $\succsim$. For example, if the agent prefers buying the umbrella to not buying the umbrella, then the π_r the agent implicitly holds and the u the agent implicitly uses to value outcomes must satisfy the above inequality. Much of the work of Bayesian decision theory involves specifying assumptions on $\succsim$ and indirectly on the set of states or domain of outcomes that will pin down unique subjective probabilities of the states for the agent. An observer can then in principle deduce these probabilities from an agent's preferences – though now the probabilities will indicate the agent's beliefs and lack objective standing.

The striking claim of subjective theories is that agents will have a preference judgment for any pair of acts, even though they lack the ordering principles that in the Bernoullian objective theory helped them figure out what to prefer: the probabilities and the prespecified utility function are missing. This assumption of completeness brings theoretical closure: agents will be able to make characteristic economic decisions and their choices can be read as optimizing. In the case of shares, for example, an agent's preferences will determine the quantity of shares the agent will hold at various prices and there will be a prima facie case that those trading decisions will promote the agent's welfare.

But how will agents come to judgment in the absence of the probabilities their Bernoullian predecessors relied on? In some settings, agents may be able to form their own assessments of the likelihood of an event and then use those assessments to form preferences. If you know the past returns of a financial asset and believe the future will resemble the past then you may have enough information to determine if buying the asset will serve your interests. But if you lack information from the past or are unsure that the future will be like the past or if you face unfamiliar events, you may not be able to assess the likelihood of states with any precision. The result can be that you will identify only a set of probability distributions and will be unable to form preference judgments between some options – whether for complex decisions like trading a stock or quotidian decisions like buying an umbrella.

The agents of subjective decision theory must not only form preferences without objective probabilities to guide them, they must also build state spaces for themselves. Objective theories either present agents with lotteries that specify probabilities for outcomes or, if they employ states of the world and acts, they present agents with a list of states as part of the definition of the acts. At first glance, subjective theories would appear to follow the latter path: subjective theories formally take the state space to be exogenous and the agent's contribution is only to supply a preference relation over acts. But subjective theories of decision must confront the objection that agents will typically will not know with certainty what outcome an act leads to at some states. The unanimous response of subjectivists has been that any agent who lodges this complaint should use states defined with greater precision. When Savage told his famous story of an agent deciding whether to add an egg that might be rotten to an omelet, he acknowledged that the agent might not know whether a rotten egg would ruin the dish. The solution, Savage claimed, was for the agent to use a more refined state space that distinguishes between states where rotten eggs ruin omelets and states where they do not.[9] So, even though the set of states is formally exogenous, an agent implicitly builds that set. Savage chose his example artfully: agents may well be able to figure out that they should distinguish between various theories of the impact of rotten eggs. But they may not have as much luck defining states so minutely that a stock's payout conditional on a state is unambiguous.

If moreover agents do succeed in specifying an exhaustive list of precisely-defined states, they will likely find the task of forming preferences over acts to be even more difficult: if you cannot implicitly assign probabilities to various stock returns then you are unlikely to be able to assign probabilities to the various economic theories of what determines stock prices. If agents fail at either of these two junctures – either in specifying states or in building preferences over the acts thereby defined – they will not be able to arrive at preference judgments over the options they face.

Some formulations of subjective expected utility theory excuse agents from the task of creating an exhaustive set of states of the world. Agents can instead bundle together the states that lead to the same pertinent outcomes, thus providing what amounts to a lottery formulation of subjective theory.[10] In the case of a stock with a random dividend, an agent might fuse all states that lead to the same path of dividends and future stock prices. But this simplification will not help agents that could not form a state space to begin with. If agents do not know why the pertinent outcomes arise – because they have not created a list of the underlying

---

[9] Savage (1954), p. 15.
[10] Maskin and Tirole (1999).

states – it will become even harder for them to assess the likelihoods they need to form preference judgments. On top of being unsure of the likelihoods of the scenarios that determine stock prices, they would not even know the scenarios for which they need to form likelihoods.

While I have drawn the contrast between the Bernoullian, hedonistic version of objective expected utility theory and a subjective theory, a similar story can be told for the transition from the objective von Neumann-Morgenstern theory, which was not hedonistic, to a subjective theory. For both transitions, agents lose information about probabilities and states but emerge nevertheless with well-defined preferences.

2.4 EASY VERSUS DIFFICULT DECISIONS

The agents of present-day economic models must form preferences over alternatives vastly more complicated than the options their early neoclassical ancestors faced. No sensory psychology can tell agents how to compare acts that deliver intertemporal streams of benefits at subjectively defined states. So, at just the point when the psychological rationale for why agents can form preferences became problematic, the decision-making demands that economic models place on individuals soared. Completeness can perhaps maneuver around one of these obstacles, but it cannot escape both.

The challenges of optimization have led many social scientists to conclude that decision-making complexity is the main barrier that prevents agents from reaching the heights of classical rationality. When handed a complicated decision, agents cannot figure out which option best serves their ends. If agents try to proceed by treating optimization itself as a cost to be weighed against the benefit of an immediate decision, they will face an even more complex decision problem; and any dogged pursuit of this strategy will lead to an infinite regress.[11] The complexity view lets one cling to the vestige that agents at least always have a preference between options, even though sometimes they do not know what that preference is. No less a critic of neoclassical economics than Herbert Simon embraced this stance.[12] It is however ultimately an act of faith, unsupported by argument, to suppose that these ghosts exist.

---

[11] Savage was well aware of comparable regresses. See Savage (1954, chapter 3) and also Radner (1968).

[12] See Simon (1978, 1979), Conlisk (1988), and Winter (1971).

There are many decisions where agents can come to a clear judgment. Some choices, particularly repeated discrete decisions, agents eventually learn to make by rote; most people can readily name their favorite restaurants, the neighborhoods where they would like to live. Agents also prefer smaller prices for what they buy and better-paying work, all else being equal. Other decisions may become clear-cut following deliberation, for example by figuring out how to break down goods into their component attributes. If one car protects drivers against likelier accidents while a second car protects against rare accidents, then a buyer who has done the research will prefer the first car, all else being equal. Opting for the cheaper or the better-paying or the safer alternatives are easy decisions because they deliver more of something agents desire without a sacrifice of competing goals.

But the straightforward judgment calls are often wrapped up with more difficult decisions – the trade-offs and specifically the marginal trade-offs. How much more should you pay to drive home in a car that is 1% less likely to kill you and your family? It is difficult to invoke an ordering principle that will supply you with the answer.

These simple examples yield some obvious lessons. Decisions subject to ordering principles should not be confused with decisions where agents struggle to find guidance. And the resolute preferences that rule over the first class of decisions do not provide evidence for the existence of preferences for the second class. I will not stake a stand on which class is more prevalent or important; but economics could make unequivocal progress simply by calling upon preferences only when they exist and disentangling the judgments that agents do know how to make from those they cannot assess.

3

Incomplete Preferences, Global and Local

One reason an agent can be unable to form preference judgments is that many different ways of valuing goods provide a plausible basis for decision-making. These macroscopic sources of incompleteness, which I will represent by competing "candidate" preference relations or utility functions, will normally undermine an agent's ability to pin down the marginal rate at which goods can be substituted without benefit or loss: an agent that cannot make the big decisions will typically also be unable to judge the marginal trade-offs and valuations. It is the margins moreover that matter for economic analysis. The remainder of the book will show the consequences for the willingness of agents to trade, for price determination, and for the optimal allocations of goods. This agenda will vindicate the early neoclassical emphasis on margins. Where the early neoclassicals went wrong lay in the additional claim that an agent's preference trade-offs between goods reduce to a single marginal rate rather than forming an interval.

3.1 UNANIMITY AGGREGATION

In early neoclassical psychology, the direct experience of consumption reveals to agents the marginal utilities that will guide them to optimal decisions; mental calculation need not play any role. But if goods do not bring quantities of homogeneous pleasure, consumption experiments might not be of much help. An agent can coherently report that goods 1 and 2 both have advantages and that it is difficult to say whether a swap at some rate brings a net gain. Suppose you are deciding between an afternoon of either rest and relaxation or invigorating exercise. Though

43

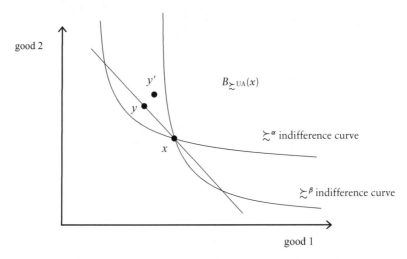

FIGURE 3.1 Incompleteness arising from two candidate preferences

drinking a pint of Guinness and going for a swim both bring pleasure, a quantitative comparison will not issue a verdict. Diverse types of pleasure are involved and different views of the merits of the activities – even of what sort of life to lead – may be at stake.

Suppose an agent judges two candidate preferences $\succsim^{\alpha}$ and $\succsim^{\beta}$ to be reasonable, where an option $x = (x_1, x_2)$ is a bundle of two goods. Let $\succsim^{\alpha}$ and $\succsim^{\beta}$ be as orthodox as possible with differentiable and concave utility representations u^{α} and u^{β}. The preferences $\succsim^{\alpha}$ and $\succsim^{\beta}$ will then feature smooth indifference curves, but they may display different marginal rates of substitution at every bundle x. For example, with the differentiable utilities defined by $u^{\alpha}(x) = \underline{\gamma} u_1(x_1) + u_2(x_2)$ and $u^{\beta}(x) = \overline{\gamma} u_1(x_1) + u_2(x_2)$, where $0 < \underline{\gamma} < \overline{\gamma}$, u^{α} places a smaller relative weight on good 1 than does u^{β} and hence the two utilities generate different marginal rates of substitution at every x. Each candidate preference offers one resolution of the conflicting views of goods that pull at the agent and the marginal utilities of its utility representation offer one way to evaluate small consumption changes. But unlike an unwavering individual with well-defined marginal utilities, the conflicted agent taken as a whole need not be locally decisive.

One indifference curve for each candidate preference is depicted in Figure 3.1. If the agent holds bundle x and ponders a switch to y, how should the alternatives be evaluated? If the agent were committed to the $\succsim^{\alpha}$ preference, then y would bring an improvement but with the $\succsim^{\beta}$ preference y would bring a loss. If the agent thinks both preferences are reasonable, the agent could decide that an overall preference judgment holds between two options only when both candidate preferences agree; these are the comparisons where the agent can make an unambiguous comparison of welfare or well-being. For two bundles *a* and *b*, the agent would then declare *a* to be better than *b* only if both candidate preferences judge *a* to be superior to *b*, declare *a* to be worse than *b* only if both candidates judge *a* to be inferior than *b*, and otherwise declare no preference between *a* and *b*.

Definition 3.1 *Given n candidate preferences* $\succsim^1, \ldots, \succsim^n$, *the unanimity aggregation* $\succsim^{\mathrm{UA}}$ *of these candidates or of the utilities that represent them is defined by* $a \succsim^{\mathrm{UA}} b$ *if and only if* $a \succsim^i b$ *for* $i = 1, \ldots, n$.

So $x \succsim^{\mathrm{UA}} y$ holds when all of the agent's candidates preferences agree that *x* is at least weakly better than *y*. Unanimity aggregations will normally be incomplete: they will not declare a preference ranking between some pair of alternatives, such as *x* and *y* in Figure 3.1. As with any incomplete preference relation, such a unanimity aggregation will not have a utility representation.

Formally, a preference $\succsim$ is *incomplete* if there exists a pair of alternatives *a* and *b* such that neither $a \succsim b$ nor $b \succsim a$ obtains and I will then say that *a* and *b* are $\succsim$-*unranked* or $\succsim$-*unrelated*. I will use similar language for the strict preference relation $\succ$ derived from a preference $\succsim$, that is, the binary relation defined by $a \succ b$ if and only if $a \succsim b$ and not $b \succsim a$. So *a* and *b* are $\succ$-*unranked* if neither $a \succ b$ nor $b \succ a$ holds. When *a* and *b* are $\succ$-unranked, either no preference obtains between the options (*a* and *b* are also $\succsim$-unranked) or they are indifferent (both $a \succsim b$ and $b \succsim a$ hold). Incompleteness thus differs from indifference. I will consider the rationale for this distinction in Chapter 6.

When an agent with incomplete preferences – perhaps a unanimity aggregator – faces unranked options, nothing in the abstract theory of preference can tell us how the agent will make a one-time choice. The agent must then turn to other criteria, perhaps related to the particular setting of a decision problem. A similar indeterminacy of choice appears when textbook consumers face indifferent options. But for unanimity aggregations and other important cases of incompleteness, alternatives that are not preference-ranked will be far more common and conspicuous than indifferent options in classical consumer theory; incomplete preferences can generate a great abundance of unranked alternatives.

The only ironclad rule for a self-interested agent with incomplete preferences facing a finite set of alternatives is that the agent should not choose a dominated option: if $x \succ y$ and both *x* and *y* are available

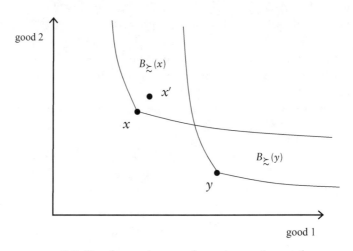

FIGURE 3.2 Two better-than sets for an incomplete preference

then the agent should not choose y. An agent with complete preferences should of course obey the same rule. The principal behavioral differences between complete and incomplete preferences come out only when agents face sequences of linked decisions: agents that cannot rank all of their alternatives must then avoid arbitrary exchanges of unranked options, as we will see in Chapter 4.

The geometry of unanimity aggregation and incomplete preferences differs from the pictures economists grow up with. Given a preference $\succsim$, possibly a unanimity aggregation, let $B(x)$ denote the set of bundles that are $\succsim$-better than x: $B(x) = \{z : z \succsim x\}$. When the underlying preference $\succsim$ is in doubt, I will write $B_{\succsim}(x)$. Since with unanimity aggregation $y \succsim^{\mathrm{UA}} x$ holds only if each candidate $\succsim^i$ has $y \succsim^i x$, a typical $B_{\succsim \mathrm{UA}}(x)$ will display a kink, as in Figure 3.1.

The better-than sets for a single preference $\succsim$ will usually overlap when $\succsim$ is incomplete. For example, for an increasing (more is better) preference $\succsim$, if x and y are $\succsim$-unrelated and x' is an improvement to x that increases the quantity of each good and x' is also $\succsim$-unrelated to y, then $B_{\succsim}(x)$ and $B_{\succsim}(y)$ cannot coincide. The overlap between the sets can be substantial, as in Figure 3.2. Do not confuse the overlaps in Figures 3.1 and 3.2: the first is an overlap of better-than sets for different candidate preferences and the second is an overlap of better-than sets for a single preference $\succsim$, where $\succsim$ could be a unanimity aggregation.

The overlap of better-than sets that comes with incomplete preferences is not a sign of intransitivity. As long as y is not in $B_{\succsim}(x)$ and x is not in

$B_{\succ}(y)$, the sets $B_{\succ}(x)$ and $B_{\succ}(y)$ do not imply the existence of a triple $a \succsim b \succsim c$ that a test of transitivity requires. In fact, a unanimity aggregation must be transitive if the candidate preferences are transitive. It follows that a bundle on the lower boundary of a better-than set $B_{\succ}(z)$ need not be indifferent to z. To illustrate, let the $\succsim$ in Figure 3.2 be transitive as well as increasing and suppose, to the contrary, that for any bundle z each point on the lower boundary of $B_{\succ}(z)$ is indifferent to z. Since the transitivity of $\succsim$ implies that the indifference relation of $\succsim$ is transitive and since the lower boundaries of $B_{\succ}(x)$ and $B_{\succ}(y)$ intersect, all of the bundles on both boundaries would have to be indifferent – and Figure 3.2 would then contradict the increasingness of $\succsim$.[1] We will see in Chapter 6 that incompleteness nearly drives indifference to extinction.

3.2 LINES OF INCOMPARABILITY

A unanimity aggregator considers multiple preference relations or utility functions to provide reasonable rankings of the agent's options. While each candidate preference is authoritative in isolation, when applied jointly many pairs of alternatives will fail to be preference-ranked. This global source of incompleteness will almost always generate a multiplicity of marginal or local valuations: unanimity aggregators will display kinked better-than sets. For the unanimity aggregation $\succsim^{UA}$ in Figure 3.1, the kink in $B_{\succ^{UA}}(x)$ implies there are multiple lines that intersect x, for example through y and y', such that bundles near x along these lines are $\succ^{UA}$-unranked relative to x, where $\succ^{UA}$ is the strict preference derived from $\succsim^{UA}$. The qualification "near" is needed since bundles that lie sufficiently far from x may once again be $\succ^{UA}$-ranked relative to x, as in Figure 3.1.

The lines that intersect x and y or x and y' are examples of what I call *lines of incomparability*. Given a preference $\succsim$, which does not have to be a unanimity aggregation, a line of incomparability through x is defined by the property that all bundles on the line near x are $\succ$-unranked. When there are more than two goods, the lines are actually planes or hyperplanes.

A preference $\succsim$ as a whole will be locally incomparable if, for each alternative x, there is more than one line of incomparability through x. Lines of incomparability abound for a locally incomparable preference: any line between two lines of incomparability will also form a line

---

[1] On the necessity of such failures of continuity for incomplete preferences, see Schmeidler (1971) and Gerasimou (2013).

of incomparability under mild conditions. The next section will provide more formal definitions.

A locally incomparable preference $\succsim$ will normally be incomplete. To see why, suppose that $\succsim$ is in addition transitive and increasing and let y and y' be two bundles near x with $y' \gg y$ that lie on different lines of incomparability through x, as in Figure 3.1. By the definition of a line of incomparability, y and y' must be $\succ$-unranked relative to x. Since $y' \succ y$ due to increasingness, if, say, y were indifferent to x then transitivity would imply $y' \succ x$, which contradicts the fact that y' and x are $\succ$-unrelated. A similar argument shows that y' and x also cannot be indifferent. With strict preference and indifference ruled out, both y and y' must be $\succsim$-unranked relative to x: incompleteness obtains and indeed will be a common occurrence. This reasoning applies to the unanimity aggregation special case, $\succsim^{UA}$, when the candidate preferences are transitive and increasing since $\succsim^{UA}$ will then satisfy the same assumptions. As Figure 3.1 indicates, $\succsim$-unranked pairs of bundles are plentiful.

A locally incomparable preference $\succsim$, whether or not it arises from unanimity aggregation, always displays a set of margins: $B(x)$ will be kinked at x for every bundle x. It turns out that under mild restrictions the mere assumption that $B(x)$ has a kink exceeding some minimal size for all bundles x implies incompleteness. See Chapter 6 and Theorem 6.5.[2]

Local incomparability is loosely speaking the opposite of local decisiveness, the assumption of early neoclassical utility theory that indifference curves are smooth (Chapter 2). If an agent is locally decisive then for any bundle x there is exactly one line (or hyperplane as the case may be) through x such that the bundles on the line near x will closely approximate the agent's indifference curve. With local incomparability, in contrast, for any x there will be many lines on which the bundles near x are not strictly ranked relative to x. But local incomparability is not the negation of local decisiveness: a preference with indifference curves that are kinked at some points and smooth at other points will be neither locally decisive nor locally incomparable. Local incomparability is an extreme failure of local decisiveness: for *every* bundle x, there must be multiple lines of incomparability.

Local incomparability lays down the route by which incomplete preferences affect economic analysis. Consider the willingness to trade two goods of a locally decisive agent and a locally incomparable agent. For

---

[2] Schlee (2021) also provides a formal result in this vein.

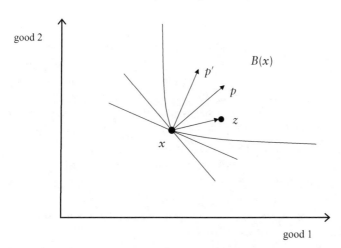

FIGURE 3.3 Multiplicity of supporting prices

the locally decisive agent endowed with x, there is exactly one trade-off rate at which the agent can exchange bundles while remaining approximately indifferent to x and hence at most one line through x that can contain no bundles superior to x. Since a line through x can be viewed as a budget line, the agent will exchange x for a better option when facing all budget lines but one. For a locally incomparable agent, on the other hand, there will be a continuum of trade-off rates at which the agent can exchange without encountering any options near x that are inferior or superior to x. Accordingly, as long as $B(x)$ is a convex set, there will be multiple budget lines through x that do not drive the agent to make exchanges, as in Figure 3.3. As measured by agents' willingness to trade, local decisiveness and local incomparability stand at opposite ends of the spectrum.

The link between local incomparability and economic inertia will occur repeatedly in this book. Locally incomparable agents show only a limited willingness to make substitutions: they will be more likely to stick with what they already have and it will be harder for policymakers to find efficiency improvements. These limitations on substitutability do not undermine the claim that equilibrium and optimality are governed by individual valuations on the margin. But these principles of marginalism will hold only if we drop the assumption that agents come prepackaged with unique preference trade-offs between goods and instead model agents by sets of margins.

The interpretation of lines of incomparability as budget or price lines leads to a convenient mathematical measure of the dimensional extent of an agent's set of margins. When preferences are convex and increasing, each line of incomparability through x is a price line that supports $B(x)$: the set $B(x)$ lies to the northeast of the price line.[3] Figure 3.3 depicts two such price lines. More formally, a price vector $p = (p_1, \ldots, p_L)$ for L goods defines the price line $\{w : p \cdot (w - x) = 0\}$ and p is the *normal* or perpendicular vector of the line.[4] If each $z \in B(x)$ satisfies $p \cdot (z - x) \geq 0$ then p and its associated price line *support* $B(x)$ *at* x, though "at x" will often remain implicit. So, if p supports $B(x)$ then any bundle z weakly preferred to x is at least as expensive as x or any other bundle on the budget line defined by p; $B(x)$ therefore cannot intersect the interior of the budget set defined by p.

With two goods, a normal vector has two coordinates and the line through x with the normal vector $p = (p_1, p_2)$ consists of the set of points $w = (w_1, w_2)$ such that

$$p \cdot (w - x) = p_1(w_1 - x_1) + p_2(w_2 - x_2) = 0,$$

and the requirement $p \cdot (z - x) \geq 0$ appears as

$$p \cdot (z - x) = p_1(z_1 - x_1) + p_2(z_2 - x_2) \geq 0.$$

When $p \cdot (z - x) \geq 0$, the angle formed by the vectors $z - x$ and p is acute. See Figure 3.3 where the vector $z - x$ is rooted at x and ends at z. Whether a p supports $B(x)$ is determined by its direction not its length: since $p \cdot (z - x) \geq 0$ implies $\lambda p \cdot (z - x) \geq 0$ when $\lambda > 0$, if p supports $B(x)$ and then so does any positive multiple of p.

Lines of incomparability and multiple directions for supporting price vectors do not appear discretely, in isolation from one another. Though Figure 3.3 displays just two supporting price lines with normals p and p', any positive linear combination of these prices – vectors $\lambda p + \mu p'$ where $\lambda, \mu \geq 0$ – will also support $B(x)$: if $p \cdot (z - x) \geq 0$ and $p' \cdot (z - x) \geq 0$ then $(\lambda p + \mu p') \cdot (z - x) \geq 0$. In the next section, we will see that for the preferences of interest the same conclusion holds for lines of

---

[3] Note that a supporting price line need not be a line of incomparability. For example, for a complete preference with strictly convex indifference curves a price line that supports $B(x)$ contains only x and bundles strictly inferior to x: the price line is not a line of incomparability.

[4] If $w = (w_1, \ldots, w_L)$ and $z = (z_1, \ldots, z_L)$ are two L-vectors, the dot product $w \cdot z$ is defined by $\sum_{i=1}^{L} w_i z_i$.

incomparability: if two price vectors define lines of incomparability then a positive linear combination of the price vectors also defines a line of incomparability. So between any two lines of incomparability lies another such line and indeed an entire interval of lines of incomparability: local incomparability leads to a wedge of directions along which bundles are not strictly ranked.

When there are two goods, the direction of a price vector p must land in a one-dimensional set and the direction can be associated with the slope of the price line orthogonal to p. Local incomparability then leads to a one-dimensional set of lines of incomparability. With more than two goods, however, the directions of lines of incomparability can vary along more than one dimension. The number of dimensions then measures the extent to which $B(x)$ is kinked.

At one extreme lie the locally decisive preferences favored by the early neoclassicals. The better-than sets $B(x)$ then fail to be kinked and for each x there can be at most one supporting price line or line of incomparability. The p's that define these lines therefore have a common direction, and if u is a differentiable utility that represents this preference then $Du(x)$ will point in this direction. A locally incomparable preference, on the other hand, will display a set of lines of incomparability whose dimension can vary from 1 to $L - 1$. The next section will explore in more detail the relationship between the number of dimensions and the extent of incompleteness.

Some multiplicity of supporting price lines – and thus a set of supporting price lines of positive dimension – is highly likely to appear with unanimity aggregation. If the coincidence occurs that each supporting price vector for each of the $\succsim^i$ used to build a unanimity aggregation $\succsim^{UA}$ points in exactly the same direction at some x, then only this direction will support $B_{\succsim^{UA}}(x)$. In all other cases multiple directions will support $B_{\succsim^{UA}}(x)$.

Proposition 3.1 *If $\succsim^{UA}$ is the unanimity aggregation of $\succsim^1, \ldots, \succsim^n$ and the price vector p^i supports $B_{\succsim^i}(x)$ then p^i also supports $B_{\succsim^{UA}}(x)$. Consequently, if two or more of the price vectors that support $B_{\succsim^1}(x), \ldots, B_{\succsim^n}(x)$ are not proportional then there are multiple directions for the price vectors that support $B_{\succsim^{UA}}(x)$.*

The proof is simply that if $y \succsim^{UA} x$ then y is in $B_{\succsim^i}(x)$ for each i and hence $p^i \cdot (y - x) \geq 0$. In the next section, we will see that for unanimity aggregations a multiplicity of supporting prices translates into a multiplicity of lines of incomparability.

3.3 A MODEL OF LOCAL INCOMPARABILITY

The aggregation of conflicting candidate preferences lays out one route to local incomparability. There are others. An agent might decide, without the intermediary of candidate preferences, that some directions of change are improvements while others are impossible to judge. The former would typically include the directions that increase the quantities of all goods while the latter would include some of the directions that trade off the consumption of goods and the different satisfactions they deliver. Local incomparability can also arise when an agent feels that the benefits of increases in consumption should be downplayed while the harm done by decreases is sizable. I will connect this psychology, a staple of behavioral economics, to local incomparability in Chapter 4.

A model of local incomparability in its own right proceeds directly to a preference that summarizes the conflicts that divide an agent. The analysis therefore begins with the zones demarcated by Figure 3.1 – the bundles preferred to x, the bundles that x is preferred to, and the bundles that are not ranked by $\succsim$ – rather than with an account of how these zones arise.

For a bundle (vector) of L goods z, let the vector's *length* be denoted $\|z\| = \left((z_1)^2 + \cdots + (z_L)^2 \right)^{\frac{1}{2}}$.

Given a preference $\succsim$ and its associated strict preference $\succ$, a bundle x, and a normal vector p, the set of bundles y such that $p \cdot (y - x) = 0$ is a *line of incomparability through* x if any bundle y in the set near x is $\succ$-unranked relative to x, that is, there is a $\varepsilon > 0$ such that x and y are $\succ$-unranked if y satisfies $p \cdot (y - x) = 0$ and $\|x - y\| < \varepsilon$. Under the assumptions I will impose, a p that defines a line of incomparability through x will support $B(x)$.

The formal definition of local incomparability will incorporate some background assumptions on preferences. Depending on the topic, some of these conditions can be relaxed but folding them into local incomparability will avoid distraction. For the record, a preference $\succsim$ is *increasing* if $x > y$ implies $x \succ y$ for all x and y;[5] *convex* if $B(x) = \{z : z \succsim x\}$ is a convex set for all x; and *reflexive* if $x \succsim x$ for all x.

Definition 3.2 *The preference $\succsim$, defined on bundles of L goods, is **locally incomparable** if it is increasing, convex, transitive, and reflexive and, for each $x > 0$, there is more than one line of incomparability through x.*

---

[5] For two n-vectors x and y, $x > y$ means $x \geq y$ and $x \neq y$.

Local incomparability entails widespread incompleteness: when multiple lines of incomparability intersect a bundle x, almost all of the bundles near x that are on or between these lines will be $\succsim$-unrelated to x. So although the bundles on a line of incomparability through x can in principle be indifferent to x, most of the bundles near x will not be: they will instead be preference-unranked relative to x. In fact, by choosing appropriate combinations of goods to place on the coordinate axes, a locally incomparable preference $\succsim$ will always generate a picture like Figure 3.1 (as the proof of Theorem 3.2 in the Appendix indicates).

If two lines have normals p and p' then a *positive linear combination* of the lines will be the line with normal $\lambda p + \mu p'$, where $\lambda, \mu > 0$; it will lie between the lines with normals p and p'.

Theorem 3.2 *If $\succsim$ is locally incomparable then, for each $x > 0$, each line of incomparability through x, and almost every y on the line, each bundle on the line segment between y and x sufficiently near x is $\succsim$-unranked relative to x.[6] Moreover any positive linear combination of the normal vectors of two lines of incomparability forms another normal vector of a line of incomparability.*

The local incomparability requirement that there are lines on which all points near x are $\succ$-unranked relative to x is stronger than necessary for many purposes in this book. We could instead require only that for each line of incomparability there is an orthant of $\mathbb{R}^L$ such that if y is on the line and is near x and if $y - x$ lies in that orthant then y is $\succ$-unranked relative to x. In the two-good case, for example, it might be that only those y's on a line of incomparability through x that are both near x and to the northwest of x are $\succ$-unranked relative to x. There could at the same time be other lines of incomparability through x such that, on these lines, only bundles near x and to the southeast of x are $\succ$-unranked relative to x. The entire set of $\succ$-unranked bundles could then border $B(x)$ but not be affine in any neighborhood of x.

The extent of incompleteness can be measured by the prices that define a preference's lines of incomparability. As we have seen, a single line of incomparability through a bundle x need not indicate that the underlying preference displays any incompleteness. But each further line of incomparability betrays an inability to judge a trade-off in some direction of

---

[6] That is, there is a $\delta > 0$ such that for all $0 < \alpha < \delta$ the bundles x and $\alpha y + (1 - \alpha)x$ are $\succsim$-unranked. "Almost every" is defined by Lebesgue measure on the line of incomparability.

change from x. To associate each line of incomparability with a single normal vector, we must take into account that a normal can be rescaled without changing the line or hyperplane it generates: λp defines the same hyperplane as p if $\lambda \neq 0$. By setting the length of p equal to an arbitrary positive number, $\|p\| = 1$, in which case p is *normalized*, we remove this multiplicity without losing any of the hyperplanes that normals can define.

The dimension of the set of normalized price vectors p that support $B(x)$ determines the number of independent directions along which $B(x)$ displays a kink at x and, when each p also defines a line of incomparability, the number of independent hyperplanes through x along which a preference cannot decide trade-offs relative to x.[7] With smooth preferences – those that can be represented by a differentiable utility function – a single normalized price vector supports each $B(x)$. The set of normalized supporting prices therefore has dimension 0: there are no directions along which $B(x)$ is kinked. In the two-good cases of local incomparability pictured in Figures 3.1 and 3.3, the normalized supporting prices have dimension 1, the maximum possible since each of the two goods can be traded-off against only one other good. With L goods, the maximum dimension of the normalized supporting prices is the number of goods less one, $L - 1$. If for a locally incomparable preference $\succsim$ the prices that support $B(x)$ at x has dimension $L - 1$ for all x, I will say that $\succsim$ is *maximally locally incomparable*.

A unanimity aggregation $\succsim^{\mathrm{UA}}$ of m or more candidate preferences, where $m \leq L$, will for each x typically lead to a set of dimension at least $m - 1$ of normalized price vectors that both define lines of incomparability and support the better-than set of $\succsim^{\mathrm{UA}}$ at x. When $m = L$ the dimension reaches its ceiling of $L - 1$ and then, under the assumptions of the following Theorem, the preference that results will be maximally locally incomparable. The proof is in the Appendix.

Theorem 3.3 *Suppose (1) $\succsim^{\mathrm{UA}}$ is the unanimity aggregation of $\succsim^1$, $\ldots, \succsim^n$, (2) each $\succsim^i$ is convex, increasing, and smooth and (3) for any x, there are $m > 1$ linearly independent price vectors such that each supports one of the $B_{\succsim^i}(x)$. Then $\succsim^{\mathrm{UA}}$ is locally incomparable and for any x there is a $(m - 1)$-dimensional set of normalized price vectors that define lines of incomparability through x and support $B_{\succsim^{\mathrm{UA}}}(x)$.*

---

[7] The dimension of a set $S \subset \mathbb{R}^L$ is the dimension of the smallest translated linear subspace that contains S (the affine hull of S).

3.4 THE MULTIPLE-PRIORS MODEL OF INCOMPLETENESS

When facing an uncertain decision, an agent deprived of objective probabilities may deem a set of probability distributions rather than a single distribution to offer a reasonable description of his or her beliefs (Section 2.3).[8] Each distribution in such a set will define a distinct expected utility function and candidate preference. If the agent resolves this impasse via unanimity aggregation, the incomplete preferences that result provide an elegant example of the model of local incomparability in Section 3.3. In this setting, local incomparability will mean that an agent cannot decide at what rate to trade off both state-contingent goods and goods where delivery does not vary by state but whose appeal is influenced by the state.

In the subjective theories that succeeded the Bernoullis and von Neumann and Morgenstern, agents have preferences over acts, that is, functions that assign one outcome to each state. Agents no longer begin with probability distributions: the distribution that an agent implicitly holds is derived from the agents' preferences over acts. For example, we can deduce the probability the agent assigns to the three weather states "rainy," "snowy," and "dry" by examining the agent's preferences among acts that offer various quantities of goods and even lotteries over goods at each of these three states. But, as we saw in Section 2.3, an agent may not be able to form such preferences and the limited preferences the agent can form might pin down only a set of probability distributions. Even if the agent can implicitly assign an exact probability to one of the states, he or she might still assign a range of probabilities to the other states. So if, say, the agent assigns probability $\hat{\pi}_d \geq 0$ to dry and the interval of probabilities $[\underline{\pi}_r, \overline{\pi}_r] \subset [0, 1]$ to rain, where $\hat{\pi}_d + \overline{\pi}_r \leq 1$, the agent would consider any probability distribution $(\pi_r, 1 - \hat{\pi}_d - \pi_r, \hat{\pi}_d)$ such that π_r lies in $[\underline{\pi}_r, \overline{\pi}_r]$ to be legitimate. The agent then has multiple priors and multiple expected utility functions. If a preference judgment must be approved by all of the expected utilities, the agent's preferences will be incomplete.

To build a general model, let $\Omega = \{1, \ldots, S\}$ be the set of states. The agent's set of probability distributions or priors will be given by $\Pi \subset \Delta \equiv \{\pi \in \mathbb{R}_+^S : \sum_{\omega \in \Omega} \pi_\omega = 1\}$ and the outcome for the agent at a state ω will be a ℓ-vector of goods x_ω that the agent consumes at ω. An act is then a

---

[8] Among the many disciplines that sometimes describe agents by sets of probabilities, the literatures in philosophy and statistics are most relevant to this book. I will not attempt to summarize this work but see Levi (1980, 1986) and Walley (1991).

consumption bundle $x = (x_1, \ldots, x_S)$ with ℓS entries. Let the agent have a concave and increasing utility function u that reports the utility $u(x_\omega)$ that act x delivers at state ω. When Π contains multiple distributions, the agent can calculate expected utilities in a variety of ways: for each $\pi \in \Pi$, there is a distinct expected utility function $E_\pi u$ defined by $E_\pi u(x) = \sum_{\omega \in \Omega} \pi_\omega u(x_\omega)$ for each bundle x.

A plausible preference for the agent is the unanimity aggregation $\succsim$ of the candidate preferences that are represented by the $E_\pi u$ such that $\pi \in \Pi$. The preference $\succsim$ was famously axiomatized by Bewley (1986), drawing on Aumann (1962, 1964). Formally, x weakly is preferred to y when each $E_\pi u$ judges x to be at least as good as y:

$$x \succsim y \text{ if and only if } E_\pi u(x) \geq E_\pi u(y) \text{ for each } \pi \in \Pi.^9$$

So no preference between x and y obtains when there are $\pi, \pi' \in \Pi$ such that $E_\pi u(x) \geq E_\pi u(y)$ and $E_{\pi'} u(y) \geq E_{\pi'} u(x)$ and at least one of these inequalities is strict. The same preference $\succsim$ arises if the set of probabilities is instead the convex hull of Π: if $E_\pi u(x) \geq E_\pi u(y)$ and $E_{\pi'} u(x) \geq E_{\pi'} u(y)$ for $\pi, \pi' \in \Pi$ then $E_{\alpha\pi+(1-\alpha)\pi'} u(x) \geq E_{\alpha\pi+(1-\alpha)\pi'} u(y)$ for any $0 \leq \alpha \leq 1$. We can therefore assume without loss in generality that Π is convex.

Each $\pi \in \Pi$ and x defines a set of bundles that $E_\pi u$ judges to be superior to x, $B_\pi(x) = \{z : E_\pi u(z) \geq E_\pi u(x)\}$, and the set of bundles that is $\succsim$-preferred to x is the intersection $B_\succsim(x) = \bigcap_{\pi \in \Pi} B_\pi(x)$. If Π contains more than one probability distribution then, for every x, $B_\succsim(x)$ is kinked and $\succsim$ is locally incomparable. When u is differentiable, these conclusions follow from Theorem 3.3 since, due to the concavity of the u, each $B_\pi(x)$ is convex and supported by the price vector $(\pi_1 Du(x_1), \ldots, \pi_S Du(x_S))$. As a consequence, when Π contains more than one distribution, multiple linearly independent price vectors will support the $B_\pi(x)$ sets.

Theorem 3.4 *If Π contains more than one probability distribution then the unanimity aggregation $\succsim$ of the $E_\pi u$ defined by $\pi \in \Pi$ is locally incomparable and, for every x, there is a set of normalized price vectors P of positive dimension such that each p in P will support $B_\succsim(x)$ at x and define a line of incomparability through x.*

---

[9] The Aumann and Bewley models are cast abstractly. My treatment follows the emphasis in Rigotti and Shannon (2005) on the kinked better-than sets that obtain when the Bewley model is joined to standard economic consumption goods.

When Π is sufficiently diverse, the supply of price vectors that support the $B_\pi(x)$ will be ample and $B_\succ(x)$ will be kinked along at least as many dimensions as the number of states allows, $S - 1$.

The upshot of Theorem 3.4 is that when agents hold multiple probability distributions to be reasonable and turn to unanimity aggregation, they will not know how to trade off some of the state-contingent goods. Each $B_\succ(x)$ will closely resemble the better-than sets in Figures 3.1 and 3.3. If u is differentiable, only one price line will support each $B_\pi(x)$ and $B_\succ(x)$ will lie to the northeast of each of these price lines: since $B_\succ(x) = \bigcap_{\pi \in \Pi} B_\pi(x)$, any price vector that supports one of the $B_\pi(x)$ must also support $B_\succ(x)$. And, since each $B_\pi(x)$ is convex, $B_\succ(x)$ will be convex as well.

To illustrate, suppose there are three states, one good per state, and the agent adopts the weather probabilities introduced earlier. A preference of y over x requires

$$\pi_r u(y_r) + \pi_s u(y_s) + \pi_d u(y_d) \geq \pi_r u(x_r) + \pi_s u(x_s) + \pi_d u(x_d)$$

to hold for all $(\pi_r, \pi_s, \pi_d) \in \Pi = \{(\pi_r, \pi_s, \hat{\pi}_d) \in \Delta : \pi_r \in [\underline{\pi}_r, \overline{\pi}_r]\}$. The inequality above is satisfied for all $\pi \in \Pi$ if and only if it is satisfied for $(\underline{\pi}_r, 1 - \hat{\pi}_d - \underline{\pi}_r, \hat{\pi}_d)$ and $(\overline{\pi}_r, 1 - \hat{\pi}_d - \overline{\pi}_r, \hat{\pi}_d)$. The bundles preferred to a reference bundle x are thus formed by the intersection of two conventional better-than sets and will display a kink at x: the agent does not know at what rate to trade off x_r vis-à-vis x_s. In this case, Π is not maximally diverse and hence the dimension of the normalized price vectors that support $B_\succ(x)$ equals 1, less than the maximum possible (which is 2, one less than the number of states). To see that the supporting prices form a 1-dimensional set, we may view any probability in Π as a convex combination of the probabilities $(\underline{\pi}_r, 1 - \hat{\pi}_d - \underline{\pi}_r, \hat{\pi}_d)$ and $(\overline{\pi}_r, 1 - \hat{\pi}_d - \overline{\pi}_r, \hat{\pi}_d)$.[10] A supporting price vector is then defined by feeding any (π_r, π_s, π_d) in this one-dimensional family of probabilities into $(\pi_r Du(x_r), \pi_s Du(x_s), \pi_d Du(x_d))$.

Multiple priors link up with the initial unanimity aggregations of Section 3.1 where an agent considers multiple preference relations over certain consumption bundles to be reasonable. Suppose an individual at state ω consumes a bundle of two goods $x = (x_1, x_2) \geq 0$ that does not vary by state (where I now revert to letting the subscript of x_i indicate a good rather than a state). Let the first good's benefit be governed by an

---

[10] That is, the probabilities $\alpha(\underline{\pi}_r, 1 - \hat{\pi}_d - \underline{\pi}_r, \hat{\pi}_d) + (1 - \alpha)(\overline{\pi}_r, 1 - \hat{\pi}_d - \overline{\pi}_r, \hat{\pi}_d)$ such that $0 \leq \alpha \leq 1$.

uncertain psychological parameter with a realization γ_ω that varies with the state, and let the agent's utility, which is now dependent on the state, be given by

$$v_\omega(x_1, x_2) = \gamma_\omega v_1(x_1) + v_2(x_2).$$

The agent again has multiple probability distributions given by Π, for each $\pi \in \Pi$ there is a corresponding candidate utility $E_\pi v$ defined at each x by

$$E_\pi v(x) = \left(\sum_{\omega \in \Omega} \pi_\omega \gamma_\omega\right) v_1(x_1) + v_2(x_2),$$

and $x \succsim y$ obtains if and only if $E_\pi v(x) \geq E_\pi v(y)$ for all $\pi \in \Pi$. The indifference curves for different candidate utilities will overlap, which implies that the set of state-independent bundles that are $\succsim$-preferred to an arbitrary x will be kinked. The overlap also indicates that $\succsim$ is incomplete and that local incomparability obtains. This model is in fact a rewrite of the toy example at the beginning of the chapter. Each candidate utility for the agent in that example took the form $\gamma u_1(x_1) + u_2(x_2)$, while in the present model the utilities have been replaced by expectations of the form $\left(\sum_\omega \pi_\omega \gamma_\omega\right) v_1(x_1) + v_2(x_2)$. The interpretations of the coefficients γ and $\sum_\omega \pi_\omega \gamma_\omega$ differ a little but they are functionally interchangeable. In both cases, the set of state-independent consumption bundles that is better than a reference bundle will equal the intersection of the better-than sets that hold for the agent's candidate preferences. Even when the latter sets are as nice as can be, unanimity aggregation will lead to a locally incomparable preference.

So under uncertainty the kinks in the better-than sets of unanimity aggregations do not require goods to be state-dependent. Kinks also arise when agents can consume only bundles that do not vary by state.

3.5 CONCLUSION

For the broader agenda of this book, the probability particulars of the Bewley model matter little. Though an agent's inability to make sharp probability judgments is a prominent special case, preference incompleteness has many potential sources. For an agent to be systematically unable to pin down trade-offs among goods, what matters is first that better-than sets display a nontrivial multiplicity of supporting prices and second that this multiplicity is ubiquitous and arises at every bundle.

4

The Rationality of Choice

When economics abandoned pleasure-seeking as the motive for decision-making, it lost its default explanation of why preferences should satisfy the completeness and transitivity assumptions that define classical rationality. That loss does not mean that replacement explanations cannot be found. The modern era of preference and decision theory does offer a defense of classical rationality; it has not been a prime arena for research but the account is there. If this analysis were sound, the triumph of preference theory over early neoclassical utility theory would be complete. Since classical rationality nearly implies that preferences have utility representations, preference theory could not only generate the same choice behavior as a utility-based theory, it could also explain when and why agents can be modeled by utility functions: it would outdo hedonism on its own turf.

The attempt to provide utility-free foundations for classical rationality has not in fact succeeded. If agents follow as simple a rule as sticking to the status quo when facing alternatives they cannot rank, they will fail to satisfy the axioms of classical rationality but no harm will come to them as a result. In fact, status quo maintenance has the stronger claim to the title of rationality. If agents want to base their decisions on preferences but do not arrive in the world with those preferences hard-wired, then they must construct them, a costly endeavor; it would be less burdensome to refuse all trades until offered an alternative known to be superior. Agents who stick to the status quo are rationally and efficiently pursuing their interests.

The grip of the axioms of classical rationality has been so strong that even psychological theories of status quo maintenance have clung to those axioms. The commitment to classical rationality has forced these theories onto the convoluted path of positing a separate and largely unobservable preference relation for every decision, a modeling decision that severs the connections among the decisions that agents make through time and breaks with the behaviorist foundations of ordinal preference theory. But economic theory does not have to throw out the baby with the bath water; by recognizing that agents sometimes do not form preference judgments, economics can preserve the unity of an individual's decisions and uncover the rationality design behind those decisions.

4.1 FOUNDATIONS FOR CLASSICAL RATIONALITY

The arguments for classical rationality devised in the second era of neoclassical economics changed the definition of preference. An agent's preference between two options no longer identified which alternative the agent believes will be more enjoyable, it would now indicate which option the agent will choose. There was no other obvious definition to turn to. Economics had rejected not just pleasure-seeking but the entire project of finding origins for preferences. And for good reason: the alternative ordering principles agents might turn to will not be comprehensive enough to order every pair of options. Classical rationality therefore stands or falls with the choice definition of preference; no substitute psychology will come to the rescue.

The redefinition of preference as choice suggests an obvious argument for why preferences should be complete. Agents can be forced to choose between two options if they face the threat of ending up with an obviously inferior choice, for example nothing, if they refuse to decide. At least one of the alternatives must then be accepted and is, in Paul Samuelson's language, revealed to be preferred to the other alternative.

With the case for completeness seemingly secure, a defense of classical rationality turns on whether preferences, defined as forced choice, should satisfy transitivity. Sometimes the argument in favor of transitivity has gone no further than a claim that agents choose consistently.[1] When something more substantial is needed, economic theory has argued that failures of transitivity will lead agents through sequences of decisions to outcomes they regard as inferior. Intertemporal self-interest in this view therefore requires agents to form transitive preferences.

To pursue this combination of arguments, let the revealed preference relation R indicate that an agent chooses one alternative when another

---

[1] See Arrow (1951a), Chapter 2.

is available: option x is *revealed preferred* to option y or xRy when an agent accepts x from a set of possibilities that contains both x and y. Formal derivations of R usually begin with a *choice function* c that specifies a nonempty set of options $c(A) \subset A$ that an agent will accept from a choice set A. Let the domain of c include all pairs of options. Given c, the revealed preference relation R is defined by xRy if there is an A in the domain of c such that $x \in c(A)$ and $y \in A$, that is, a choice set containing y from which x is one of the chosen options. Since c specifies for any $\{x, y\}$ that at least one of x and y is chosen, R must be complete. Choice functions thus deliver half of the classical rationality package.

An argument for transitivity must introduce a sliver of welfare content into R: otherwise we would never be able to infer that an agent's choices can lead that agent to harm. Define x to be *strictly revealed preferred* to y or xPy if xRy and not yRx: x is sometimes chosen when y is available while y is never chosen when x is available. When xPy holds, it is reasonable to infer that the agent believes x is a better choice and will deliver greater welfare than y. This dose of psychological interpretation is modest: xPy holds only when an agent is determined to avoid y whenever x is available.

This hybrid concept – the choice definition of preference salted with a welfare inference – allows us to ask if an intransitive R is a sign of irrationality: will such agents make sequences of decisions that lead from better to worse options? Suppose we confront an agent with a sequence of choice sets where at each stage at least one of the agent's current choices will be passed on to the next choice set. When the sequence comes to an end, the agent's actual consumption is drawn from the agent's final set of selections. The agent can then guarantee any option encountered along the way by choosing that option alone and refusing all offers to switch. For now, it will be enough to consider just two-stage sequences of choice sets, labeled A^1 and A^2. The right to hold onto a selection from A^1 then formally means that some option is in both $c(A^1)$ and A^2 and the agent will be manipulated if, in addition, there is a $z \in A^1$ and $x \in c(A^2)$ such that zPx.

Now suppose that R is intransitive. Since R is complete, there must be alternatives x, y, and z such that xRy, yRz, and zPx.[2] Since yRz, there must be a choice set that contains z from which the agent chooses y.

---

[2] A failure of transitivity by itself implies only that there exist x, y, and z such that xRy, yRz, and not xRz. But given the completeness of R, not xRz implies zRx which is the definition of zPx.

Let this choice set serve as A^1, the first choice set the agent confronts. Consistent with the agent's right to hold on to one of his or her selections from A^1, we can then ask the agent to choose from any choice set that contains y. Since xRy, there is an A^2 that contains y from which the agent chooses x. The agent can therefore end up with x, an alternative the agent feels is strictly worse than z, which the agent could have selected and held. Call a choice function *manipulation-free* if we cannot dupe the agent in this way, that is, if there do not exist A^1 and A^2 in the domain of c and a triple of alternatives x, y, z such that $z \in A^1$, $y \in c(A^1)$, $y \in A^2$, $x \in c(A^2)$, and zPx. We have proved the following result.[3]

Theorem 4.1 *If a choice function is manipulation-free then its revealed preference relation is transitive.*

The classical theory of rational decision-making thus has a defense worthy of serious scrutiny. Theorem 4.1 notably rests on the assumption that an agent always chooses the same set $c(A)$ from A. This assumption looks innocuous, but it turns out to be remarkably powerful.

4.2 CHOICE WITHOUT PREFERENCE: STATUS QUO MAINTENANCE

At behaviorism's high water mark in the 1950s, economists would sometimes yield to fashion and claim that "the phrase 'x is preferred to y' means that 'if x and y were offered, x would be chosen.'"[4] In common language as well, the question "which do you prefer?" can sometimes mean "which would you choose?" But preference often indicates that an underlying rationale, a reason for a choice, is present. In economics, those reasons are usually agents' judgments of their welfare and will dictate their decisions. When however agents cannot judge which alternatives best promote their welfare, their choices cannot reflect nonexistent evaluations. As long as we dismiss the ruse that prefer is a synonym for choose, two different concepts are in play.[5]

The distinction is ancient. In the Euthyphro, Plato distinguished at length between what is good (or just or pious) and what the gods desire, or in our words what the gods would choose. It so happens that the gods desire the good and perhaps the good coincides exactly with what the

---

[3] The money pump of Davidson et al. (1955) is an early relative of this argument. See Cubitt and Sugden (2001) for a more recent treatment of the money pump.

[4] Arrow (1952).

[5] Sen (1973, 1997).

gods desire, but Plato warned that we should not *define* the good by what
the gods desire: if we did we could never determine the nature of the good
or figure out, when we do not know what the gods would choose, what
is good. Closer to home, John Stuart Mill in his essay "Utilitarianism"
argued for a difference between higher and lower pleasures – between
intellectual pleasures and the satisfactions of the imagination on one hand
and sensory enjoyment on the other. Like the economists who would
reject hedonism 75 years after he wrote his essay, Mill did not explain
how agents decide between these types of pleasure. He claimed instead
that we can distinguish between higher and lower pleasures by observing
the choices of those familiar with both types. It will come as no surprise
that in Mill's view the knowledgeable will opt for the higher pleasures.
Though Mill upheld a causal link between the hierarchy of pleasures and
what agents choose, the concepts do not coincide: one refers to agents'
goals, the other to agents' behavior. Agents moreover can make mistakes
or suffer from a weakness of will; observations of choice therefore do not
always mirror the pleasure hierarchy.

In both of these historical examples, the true goals of agents normally
match what they choose, though Mill may have been using the what-
agents-choose criterion to mask his inability to defend his position on
where our ultimate interests lie. Even for the knowledgeable however
the alignment of choice and preference will break down when an individual cannot figure out which goals should take precedence or how to
weigh competing goals. Individuals may be unable to answer the question
"what are my true interests?" or even know if the question has a definitive
answer. If they cannot construct ordering principles that tell them how to
evaluate the world's manifold satisfactions, they cannot join Mill in his
evasion: their preferences will be incomplete and they will have to make
choices by some other method.

For the remainder of this chapter, I will for brevity say that an agent
prefers alternative *a* over alternative *b* when the agent judges *a* to deliver
greater welfare or better serve the agent's interests than *b*.

When an agent's endowment or default consumption *x* forms the status quo and the agent is given a chance to switch to a preferred alternative
y, the agent will relinquish *x* and actively move to *y*. Conversely, an active
move to an alternative *y* is good evidence that an agent believes that he
or she will be better off with *y*. But when an agent with some status quo
option *x* faces an alternative *y* and cannot decide which is preferred, the
agent will likely turn down the offer. Though the agent has no preference, he or she then implicitly chooses *x* over *y*. If *y* on the other hand is

the status quo, the agent will likely refuse to switch to x.[6] For one-time decisions, agents could accept one of these offers without doing themselves any harm. In sequential settings, however, we will see that refusal is mandatory.

The choice behavior of an agent with incomplete preferences therefore cannot be described by a choice function, at least not in the classical form that specifies one set of selections $c(A)$ for every choice set A. When an agent cannot compare the welfare of two alternatives x and y the agent may well select x from $\{x, y\}$ on one occasion and y on another. Status quo maintenance displays just this pattern.

With the raw material of choice functions missing, conventional revealed preference relations are no longer defined. The defense of classical rationality provided by Theorem 4.1 therefore breaks down. For the goal of showing that an effective pursuit of one's interests requires revealed preferences to be classically rational, it is unclear how to undo the damage. Should we declare x to be revealed preferred to y when x is *always* chosen over y or when x is *sometimes* chosen?

Suppose we follow the first path and declare $x R^{AC} y$ to hold if, regardless of the status quo or other factors, the agent when facing a choice set containing both x and y never selects y without also selecting x. The choices of a status quo maintainer whose underlying preference $\succsim$ is incomplete will then lead to a R^{AC} that is incomplete. Indeed if the agent faces only pairs and follows the rule "choose z from $\{s, z\}$ when s is the status quo if and only if $z \succsim s$" then R^{AC} and $\succsim$ will coincide. To illustrate, let s and s' be two status quos, each associated with a better-than set of $\succsim$-preferred options the agent will choose over the status quo, and assume $\succsim$ is increasing. See Figure 4.1, a rewrite of Figure 3.2. As drawn, s and s' are both $\succsim$- and R^{AC}-unrelated: the agent will not switch to s' when s is the status quo and will not switch to s when s' is the status quo.[7]

The move from R to R^{AC} thus neuters the original completeness advantage of revealed preference relations: when an agent's preference judgments are incomplete, R^{AC} will be incomplete too. Assuming that

---

[6] For the connection between incomplete preferences and status quo bias as it is modeled in behavioral economics, see Mandler (1998), published as Mandler (2004, 2005). Masatlioglu and Ok (2005) also pursue this link.

[7] The kinks in the better-than sets play no role in this argument and are included only to suggest the better-than sets that arise with unanimity aggregation and local incomparability (Chapter 3). Recall from Section 3.1 and Figure 3.2 that $B_\succ(s)$ and $B_\succ(s')$ are not the better-than sets of two candidate preferences that could be unanimity-aggregated: they are two better-than sets of a single preference $\succsim$.

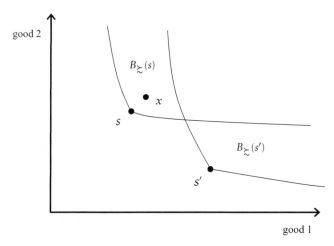

good 2

$B_{\succsim}(s)$

x

s

$B_{\succsim}(s')$

s'

good 1

FIGURE 4.1 Choice from multiple status quos

holding to the status quo does not lead an agent to any harm, a defense of classical rationality based on "always chosen" revealed preferences cannot succeed.

If we instead adopt a "sometimes chosen" definition of revealed preference and declare $xR^{SC}y$ to hold if there is merely some choice set that contains y from which x is chosen in some circumstances, then status quo maintenance will lead to an intransitive R^{SC}. In Figure 4.1, the agent will choose s from $\{s, s'\}$ when s is the status quo and choose s' from $\{s', x\}$ when s' is the status quo, but the agent will never choose s when x is available. Thus $sR^{SC}s'$ and $s'R^{SC}x$ but not $sR^{SC}x$, an intransitivity. The "sometimes chosen" path to a defense of classical rationality therefore also fails, assuming once again that status quo maintenance does not somehow lead agents into a danger we have not yet identified. A formal proof of the optimality of status quo maintenance will come in Section 4.4.

In light of these failures of revealed preference relations to satisfy both completeness and transitivity, our view of rationality must change. The vacillation that status quo maintainers display, that they choose different options on different occasions, serves their self-interest and requires no effort: their decisions are based solely on their actual preference judgments. Agents that try to obey the dictates of classical rationality when they cannot form preference judgments will have to manufacture fictitious preferences to guide their decisions, which would be costly. Self-interest thus clashes with the classical view of rationality. Presumably agents will let the former consideration prevail.

The overlap of the better-than sets in Figure 4.1 may set off the alarm bell that the underlying preferences are intransitive and that the agent is therefore manipulable. If the agent were willing to trade freely any pair of $\succsim$-unrelated options, he or she could indeed be led through a sequence of exchanges that in the end is harmful: a trade of x for s' and then s' for s will leave the agent with less of both goods. The great advantage of holding to the status quo is that these self-destructive sequences are blocked: a status quo maintainer will refuse both of these trades. A gap between choice and preference – sticking to x when offered s' even though the options are $\succsim$-unrelated – lets the agent stay out of trouble.[8]

4.3 BEHAVIORAL ECONOMICS VERSUS INCOMPLETE PREFERENCES

Sticking to the status quo is not usually seen as an optimizing strategy for agents with incomplete preferences; it is explained as an outgrowth of agents' instincts and habits or even hardwired by their psychophysics. As pioneered by the psychologists Kahneman and Tversky in prospect theory, individuals in this account do not rationally pursue a fixed set of goals through time. Their preferences instead change as a function of their reference or status quo points – typically their endowments of goods – and of how decision problems are framed.[9] Prospect theory brought forth a tidal wave of behavioral research in economics: the overarching agent of neoclassical economics, sovereign over his intertemporal demesne, has been replaced by a sequence of agents, one for each status quo point or moment of choice. The explanation of status quo maintenance offered by prospect theory and related models will serve as a proxy for this broader current of work.[10]

Prospect theory uses value functions to represent the agents that an individual becomes as the status quo changes. The functions report the effect on utility of a change in the consumption of a good relative to the status quo and are therefore defined on gains and losses of consumption. No change relative to the status quo leads to a value of 0. Once the status quo is fixed, the utility of changes given by the value functions for that status quo define a classically rational preference for the individual.

---

[8] The overlap of better-than sets does not in any event imply that $\succsim$ (or R^{AC}) is intransitive. See Section 3.1.

[9] See Kahneman and Tversky (1979, 1984) and Tversky and Kahneman (1991, 1992).

[10] According to Kahneman (2020), the value function from Kahneman and Tversky (1979) forged the path to behavioral economics.

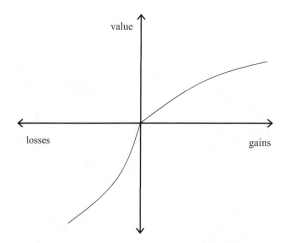

FIGURE 4.2 A behavioral value function

Value functions display two asymmetries. First, the marginal values of losses are strictly greater than the marginal values of gains (in absolute value) and therefore exhibit a kink or discontinuity of slopes at the origin. Prospect theory thus casts aside the differentiable indifference curves and local decisiveness of early neoclassical economics. Since the domination of losses over gains leads to loss-averse behavior, I will call the discontinuity of slopes a *loss aversion kink*. The second asymmetry is that the value of gains is concave while the value of losses is convex. A function that satisfies these properties, illustrated in Figure 4.2, will be a *behavioral value function*.

Behavioral value functions generate several signature results of behavioral economics – reference dependence, the endowment effect, status quo bias, and the willingness-to-accept willingness-to-pay (WTA-WTP) disparity, to name a few.[11]

Reference dependence is a joint effect of the gain-loss domain of value functions and their asymmetries: the evaluation of a single consumption level for a good can differ depending on whether that level arises from an increase relative to the status quo or a decrease. The other results express status quo bias in various ways and stem from the loss-aversion kinks. In the WTA-WTP disparity, for example, agents are willing to accept some sum of money for a good they own but are willing to pay only a much

---

[11] See Kahneman et al. (1990), Knetsch (1989), Knetch and Sinden (1984, 1987), Köbberling and Wakker (2005), Samuelson and Zeckhauser (1988), Sugden (2003), and Thaler (1980). As Kőszegi and Rabin (2006) argue, the status quo will often be the outcome agents anticipate rather than the outcome that has occurred in the past.

smaller sum for the same good when they do not own it.[12] In the Tversky and Kahneman (1991) interpretation, an individual's endowment of the good and of money determines the individual's reference point and thus the 0 point of his or her behavioral value function. The marginal value of a purchase of the good will therefore be small relative to the marginal value of a sale and consequently potential buyers of the good will frequently offer less money for the good than owners will accept. Compounding this effect, the behavioral value functions for money will assign a greater value to the money that could be spent on a purchase of the good than the value of the money that would be gained by a sale. For either or both reasons, it is difficult to push agents off their status quo points. Opportunities for trade are consequently limited.

Individuals with smooth indifference curves have well-defined marginal valuations that do not hiccup downward as a loss of a good is transformed into a gain. Agents in prospect theory not only show a hiccup due to their loss-aversion kinks but the hiccup recurs no matter where an agent's status quo or endowment is located. These discontinuities in agents' marginal valuations are closely related to the kinks in better-than sets that arise with local incomparability; the two accounts in fact predict the same choice behavior though the roads traveled differ markedly.

To derive the preferences and indifference curves that behavioral value functions generate, suppose for concreteness there are two goods. In the WTA-WTP disparity, the goods could be an item whose value is being assessed and money. For choice under uncertainty, the main focus of prospect theory, good i can be interpreted as consumption at a particular state of the world i.[13]

Let the status quo or endowment be $\bar{x} = (\bar{x}_1, \bar{x}_2)$ and suppose that for good i the agent has the behavioral value function u_i. If x_i is the agent's consumption of good i then $u_i(x_i - \bar{x}_i)$ is the value or change in the agent's utility when the consumption of good i moves from $\bar{x}_i$ to x_i.

Formally, u_i qualifies as a behavioral value function if $u_i(0) = 0$, the function is increasing, continuous, concave on gains, convex on losses, differentiable except at 0, and the marginal utility of a gain – the right derivative $D_+u_i(0)$ of u_i at 0 – is strictly less than the marginal utility of a loss – the left derivative $D_-u_i(0)$ of u_i at 0. See Figure 4.2.

---

[12] Carson (1997, 2012), Carson and Hanemann (2005), and Hausman (1993).

[13] The function u_i below would then be the product of an agent's change in utility for consumption at state i and the probability of state i.

In typical models, Tversky and Kahneman (1991) for example, an agent's total utility change equals the sum of u_1 and u_2. So, given the status quo or endowment $\bar{x}$, bundle $x = (x_1, x_2)$ is preferred to $y = (y_1, y_2)$ if

$$u_1(x_1 - \bar{x}_1) + u_2(x_2 - \bar{x}_2) \geq u_1(y_1 - \bar{x}_1) + u_2(y_2 - \bar{x}_2).$$

Once $\bar{x}$ has been fixed, the agent therefore has a well-defined preference between any pair of options. For the preferences that hold with $\bar{x}$, the options the agent prefers to $\bar{x}$ are found by replacing y above with $\bar{x}$. The agent when endowed with $\bar{x}$ therefore agrees to a move to x if

$$u_1(x_1 - \bar{x}_1) + u_2(x_2 - \bar{x}_2) \geq u_1(0) + u_2(0) = 0.$$

To find the agent's indifference curve through $\bar{x}$ for the preferences that hold with $\bar{x}$, let $x_2(x_1)$ equal the level of x_2 that leads to indifference between $(x_1, x_2(x_1))$ and $\bar{x}$ when x_1 is near $\bar{x}_1$. So $x_2(x_1)$ is defined by

$$u_1(x_1 - \bar{x}_1) + u_2(x_2(x_1) - \bar{x}_2) = 0.$$

Differentiating, this indifference curve has a slope $\frac{dx_2(x_1)}{dx_1}$ whose absolute value approximately equals $\frac{D_+u_1(0)}{D_-u_2(0)}$ when x_1 is slightly greater than $\bar{x}_1$ and $\frac{D_-u_1(0)}{D_+u_2(0)}$ when x_1 is slightly smaller than $\bar{x}_1$. See Figure 4.3. Since

$$\frac{D_+u_1(0)}{D_-u_2(0)} < \frac{D_-u_1(0)}{D_+u_2(0)},$$

the loss-aversion kinks in behavioral value functions translate into kinks in the indifference curves through the agent's endowment points. The prospect theory assumptions on value functions in fact gild the lily: to generate a kink in the indifference curve, the above inequality shows that it would be enough for just one of the u_i functions to display a gap between its left and right derivatives at 0.

While the prospect-theory preference that holds at any given endowment fails to be locally decisive, it will be classically rational. Prospect theory's grander departure from orthodoxy is reference dependence: an agent's preferences change with the endowment. Let x' be a new endowment and suppose that the u_i derivatives do not differ substantially as the endowment changes – as in the Tversky and Kahneman (1991) base case where each u_i is a linear function. If say x_1' is substantially greater than $\bar{x}_1$ and x' lies below the indifference curve in Figure 4.3, the indifference curve through x' (for the preferences that hold when x' is the endowment) will cross the original curve. A picture is unnecessary since, outside

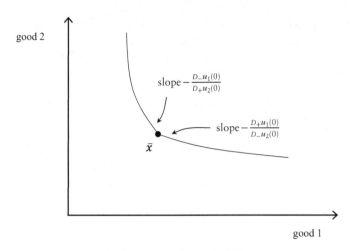

good 2

$$\text{slope} - \frac{D_-u_1(0)}{D_+u_2(0)}$$

$$\text{slope} - \frac{D_+u_1(0)}{D_-u_2(0)}$$

$\bar{x}$

good 1

FIGURE 4.3 A prospect-theory indifference curve

of how the bundles are labeled, it would replicate the incomplete preferences account of status quo bias in Figure 4.1: $\bar{x}$ and x' are comparable
to s and s'.[14]

This repeat of overlapping better-than sets is no coincidence: the
incomplete preferences and prospect theory explanations of status quo
bias have much in common. In both, an agent will stick to a bundle when
offered various alternatives but refrain from actively choosing the same
bundle when one of the alternatives forms the status quo. And in both,
better-than sets not only overlap, they will also be kinked, as long as the
incomplete preferences satisfy local incomparability.

The behavioral value functions at the heart of prospect theory chore-
ograph several moving parts: the loss aversion kink, the reference
dependence that comes with value functions defined on a domain of
gains and losses, concavity for gains, and convexity for losses. Each of
these apparently unconnected features must ultimately rest on a distinct
psychological mechanism. When incomplete preferences stem from unanimity aggregation, the same properties down to their details follow from
a single principle, that an individual's preferences are determined by the

---

[14] The only potential difference is visually undetectable. A set of $\succsim$-preferred bundles in
Figure 4.1 might not contain any bundles indifferent to the status quo along its boundary
besides the status quo itself, a possibility I will explain in Chapter 6. But a Kahneman-
Tversky better-than set can arise from a continuous preference and hence the curve in
Figure 4.3 – the boundary of the bundles preferred to $\bar{x}$ when the agent is endowed with
$\bar{x}$ – can consist solely of indifferent bundles.

candidate preference of the agent with the worst-case analysis of a change in consumption.

A unanimity aggregator declares a ranking between an alternative and the status quo when all of the individual's candidate preferences agree with that ranking. Although the individual views each candidate as reasonable at every point in time, it is only the candidate preference with the worst-case analysis of a change relative to the status quo that is relevant for the individual's bottom-line judgment. For a purchase of a good i, the worst case is given by the candidate preference with the most pessimistic assessment of greater consumption of i; if that candidate preference approves a purchase then so will the individual's other candidate preferences. For a sale, it is the candidate preference that is most optimistic about good i that provides the worst-case analysis. Unanimity aggregation thus boils down to a delegation system: let the candidate preference with the worst-case analysis of a change make the decision.

Putting utility curvature aside for a moment, consider a unanimity aggregator with candidate preferences represented by linear utilities. The status quo is again $\bar{x} = (\bar{x}_1, \bar{x}_2)$. Letting the utility of candidate j be $\alpha_1^j x_1 + \alpha_2^j x_2$, where each $\alpha_i^j > 0$, a change in consumption $\Delta x = (\Delta x_1, \Delta x_2)$ that is added to $\bar{x}$ will lead to a utility change for j of $\alpha_1^j \Delta x_1 + \alpha_2^j \Delta x_2$. Suppose the consumption of good 1 increases and the consumption of good 2 decreases, $\Delta x_1 > 0$ and $\Delta x_2 < 0$, and let $\alpha_i^{\min}$ and $\alpha_i^{\max}$ respectively be the minimum and the maximum of the α_i^j coefficients. The utility that uses $\alpha_1^{\min}$ to assess good 1 and $\alpha_2^{\max}$ to assess good 2 then provides the worst-case analysis: if this utility approves a change from $\bar{x}$ to $\bar{x} + \Delta x$,

$$\alpha_1^{\min} \Delta x_1 + \alpha_2^{\max} \Delta x_2 \geq 0,$$

then the individual's other candidate utilities will also approve the change. This inequality gives a sufficient condition for a change with $\Delta x_1 > 0$ and $\Delta x_2 < 0$ to be preferred to $\bar{x}$ and a necessary condition if $\alpha_1^{\min} x_1 + \alpha_2^{\max} x_2$ represents one of the individual's candidate preferences. Similarly, if the change to the status quo decreases the consumption of good 1 and increases the consumption of good 2, then the individual will prefer the change when

$$\alpha_1^{\max} \Delta x_1 + \alpha_2^{\min} \Delta x_2 \geq 0.$$

So a unanimity aggregator can optimize by assigning preference authority to different utility functions as the goods that undergo an increase or decrease in consumption vary.

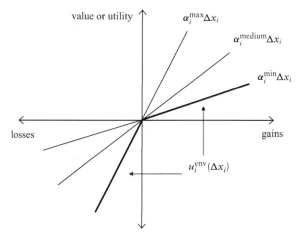

FIGURE 4.4 Linear candidate utilities that nearly lead to a behavioral value function

Figure 4.4 pictures $\alpha_i^j \Delta x_i$ for three candidates, where α_i^j equals α_i^{max}, α_i^{min}, and a value in between. The lower envelope in bold is the function

$$u_i^{env}(\Delta x_i) = \begin{cases} \alpha_i^{max} \Delta x_i & \text{if } \Delta x_i \leq 0 \\ \alpha_i^{min} \Delta x_i & \text{if } \Delta x_i > 0 \end{cases} .$$

Since the change in utility $\alpha_i^j \Delta x_i$ for good i reported by any candidate utility j will always be at least as great as $u_i^{env}(\Delta x_i)$, a move from $\bar{x}$ to Δx approved by $u_1^{env}(\Delta x_1) + u_2^{env}(\Delta x_2)$ will be approved by all the candidate utilities.

The kinks in the u_i^{env} imply that the better-than sets of the individual's preferences will also be kinked at $\bar{x}$. As is normally the case for unanimity aggregation, the preferences that arise are locally incomparable.

The u_i^{env} almost qualify as behavioral value functions. Since $\alpha_i^{min} < \alpha_i^{max}$, each u_i^{env} displays a loss-aversion kink. And given that the coefficient that multiplies Δx_i varies depending on whether Δx_i is positive or negative, reference dependence appears: the same quantity of a good will be evaluated differently depending on whether it is an increase or a decrease relative to the status quo. From this angle, both reference dependence and loss aversion are signs of rational calculation rather than its absence, but those signs can be read only if we recognize the continuity of an individual's preferences through time.

A unanimity aggregation of candidate utility functions can in fact deliver the whole gamut of behavioral value function properties, including concavity for gains and convexity for losses. Suppose for each i there

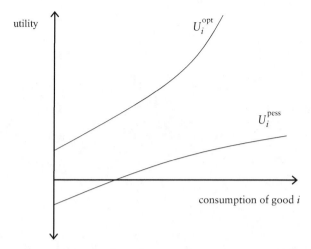

FIGURE 4.5 Optimistic and pessimistic candidate utilities

are two utilities for good i that an individual uses to construct candidate utilities over bundles, an optimistic utility U_i^{opt} and a pessimistic utility U_i^{pess}, each a function of total consumption of i rather than gains and losses. The optimism and pessimism labels stem from the following assumptions: the marginal utility of U_i^{opt} is greater than the marginal utility of U_i^{pess} at 0 and U_i^{opt} displays increasing marginal utility while U_i^{pess} displays diminishing marginal utility. So U_i^{opt} is more optimistic in that it starts out with a greater marginal utility than U_i^{pess} and the marginal utility difference can only grow wider as consumption increases. When consumption is uncertain, the optimistic utility holds consumption to be appealing enough to make risk attractive while the pessimistic utility is averse to risk. Formally, each U_i^{opt} is convex, each U_i^{pess} is concave, and $DU_i^{\text{opt}}(0) > DU_i^{\text{pess}}(0) \geq 0$. See Figure 4.5. I have capitalized the utilities to underscore that they, unlike the u_i, are functions of total consumption not of deviations from some status quo.

The candidate utilities themselves are given by one of the four possible sums $U_1^j + U_2^k$, where each superscript is either opt or pess. Call the agent an *optimism-pessimism aggregator* if bundle x is preferred to y if and only if all four sums of utilities agree that x is superior. We could add further candidate utilities for goods that are intermediate between optimism and pessimism, but only the extreme utilities will matter for unanimity aggregation (as in Figure 4.4 or in Section 3.4). See Mandler (2021).

The agent's preferences vis-à-vis the status quo can be represented more simply with just two functions which will turn out to be behavioral

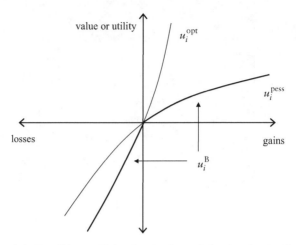

FIGURE 4.6　Candidate utilities that lead to a behavioral value function

value functions. We first return to the changes in utility from deviations from the status quo by normalizing the utility of good i to equal 0 at the status quo $\bar{x}_i$. Fixing $\bar{x}$ henceforth, set

$$u_i^{\text{opt}}(\Delta x_i) = U_i^{\text{opt}}(\bar{x}_i + \Delta x_i) - U_i^{\text{opt}}(\bar{x}_i),$$
$$u_i^{\text{pess}}(\Delta x_i) = U_i^{\text{pess}}(\bar{x}_i + \Delta x_i) - U_i^{\text{pess}}(\bar{x}_i),$$

for each i. See Figure 4.6. For an optimism-pessimism aggregator to recommend a move from $\bar{x}$ to $\bar{x} + \Delta x$, all four of the candidates must report a nonnegative change in utility: $u_1^j(\Delta x_1) + u_2^k(\Delta x_2) \geq 0$ must hold for each combination of opt and pess superscripts.

Now if $\Delta x_1 > 0$ then our assumptions on the marginal utilities and the utility normalization imply $u_1^{\text{pess}}(\Delta x_1) < u_1^{\text{opt}}(\Delta x_1)$. The change in each candidate's utility for good 1 must therefore be at least as great as $u_1^{\text{pess}}(\Delta x_1)$. Similarly if $\Delta x_1 < 0$ then $u_1^{\text{opt}}(\Delta x_1) < u_1^{\text{pess}}(\Delta x_1)$ and so the change in each candidate's utility for good 1 must now be at least as great as $u_1^{\text{opt}}(\Delta x_1)$. Figure 4.6 illustrates. As the evaluation of changes in good 2 consumption proceeds similarly, for any Δx a move from $\bar{x}$ to $\bar{x} + \Delta x$ that satisfies

$$\min\left[u_1^{\text{opt}}(\Delta x_1), u_1^{\text{pess}}(\Delta x_1)\right] + \min\left[u_2^{\text{opt}}(\Delta x_2), u_2^{\text{pess}}(\Delta x_2)\right] \geq 0$$

must be an improvement for all four ways the agent can sum individual good utilities. The agent thus acts as if the utility effect of a Δx_i change in the consumption of good i is given by $u_i^B(\Delta x_i) = \min\left[u_i^{\text{opt}}(\Delta x_i), u_i^{\text{pess}}(\Delta x_i)\right]$, depicted in bold in Figure 4.6. Given our convexity, concavity, and marginal utility assumptions, u_1^B and u_2^B qualify as behavioral value functions.

Theorem 4.2 *A change in consumption is preferred by an optimism-pessimism aggregator to the status quo if and only if the change in utility that results is greater than or equal to 0 as measured by the sum of two behavioral value functions.*

The min operator in the u_i^B functions indicates that it is rational for a unanimity aggregator to delegate authority to different utility functions as the alternatives under consideration change. Kinked better-than sets, the defining feature of local incomparability, are the result.

What is at stake here? Is it just a squabble over terminology to insist that an individual who sticks to the status quo has a single though incomplete preference relation that represents the same welfare judgments at each point in time? It is not: the incompleteness theory enjoys three advantages over the behavioral alternatives that assume each moment of choice is governed by a distinct preference.

First, the incompleteness account of status quo bias rests on a single principle, that it is rational for an individual to adopt a worst-case analysis of consumption changes. That principle in turn explains why an agent's decisions are compatible with the various properties of behavioral value functions. Behavioral approaches in contrast assume these properties as primitives.

Second, incomplete preferences can identify whether an individual is better or worse off as time passes. When instead a single individual is converted into a set of agents it becomes difficult for an outsider – the government, a policymaker, an economist – to assess individual welfare: the well-beings of the entire set of agents must be aggregated.

Psychological theories of changing preferences dismiss out of court the possibility that agents are guided by an underlying rationality that knits together their actions at different dates. The very point of a choice strategy can then be lost. In the case at hand, we would miss the intertemporal advantage of status quo maintenance, its capacity to prevent self-destructive trades, which I will formalize in the next section. What appears to psychologists to be arbitrary in fact has a rationality logic.

The welfare hole that opens up when an individual becomes a set of agents helps explain why behavioral economics sometimes identifies well-being with an individual's moment-by-moment, hedonic utility.[15] This

---

[15] See Kahneman et al. (1997).

view of well-being lays out a technocrat's dream. The welfare of agents can be objectively ascertained but the agents themselves, due to their cognitive handicaps, err systematically. Social science is willing and able to nudge them onto a better path.[16] But notwithstanding their cognitive limitations and irrationalities, people do make intertemporal plans – they map out careers, they save for their children's education – and their well-being through time can be understood only with reference to those plans. Even in the mundane arena of financial assets, the efficiency of the markets that trade those assets would be impossible to evaluate without some grounding in individual preferences that persist through time.

The third advantage, closely related to the second, is that incomplete preferences provide more opportunities to test hypotheses against evidence: by linking all of an individual's decisions to a single preference relation, the theory wields greater predictive power. The behavioral economics assumption of a separate preference for every decision in contrast risks unfalsifiability: the choices an individual made yesterday might have no empirical implications for the choices the individual makes today.

Prospect theory is particularly extreme in this regard: for every status quo it posits a distinct complete and transitive preference relation, represented in our two-good examples by a pair of utility functions. Most of these preference judgments cannot be observed. For every status quo $\bar{x}$, we can see only that there are some bundles an agent will agree to switch to. When the agent turns down an alternative to $\bar{x}$, the refusal need not indicate a preference judgment; an agent with no preference between two options may well decline to exchange them, if only to avoid welfare-diminishing trades (Section 4.2). For pairs of bundles where neither is the status quo, we observe even less; we do not know which bundle the agent would choose as a default decision let alone which the agent holds to be the better option. Prospect theory and many of its behavioral followers thus abandon the founding tenet of ordinalism that preferences must be observable.

The incompleteness theory of status quo bias remains agnostic at both of these decision-making junctures. If an agent holds to a status quo $\bar{x}$ when offered x, the theory asserts only that x is not preferred to $\bar{x}$, not that $\bar{x}$ is preferred to x. And for decisions between non-status-quo options, the theory remains silent. Curiously enough, the incomplete preferences account is more faithful to the behaviorism of the modern era of preference theory.

[16] Thaler and Sunstein (2008).

These methodological differences stand out when one asks if individual preferences satisfy properties such as transitivity that must be tested intertemporally. With an incomplete preference that can be sampled at multiple dates, the raw material of a test is available: if we observe that x is actively chosen over y at one date and that y is actively chosen over z at a second date, we can then test transitivity by checking if x is actively chosen over z. But if every point of decision defines a separate preference then we cannot verify the premise $x \succsim y \succsim z$ let alone both the premise and the conclusion $x \succsim z$.

Psychological theories of choice and behavioral economics have presented a vast number of decision-making anomalies that show that agents are not governed by classically rational preferences. Among the numerous examples are hyperbolic discounting and preference reversal. Hyperbolic-discounting agents make decisions between consumption at different dates in the future that depend on when they make those decisions; agents subject to preference reversal make choices between gambles that do not align with the monetary values they assign to those gambles.[17] The behavioral research that follows up on such discoveries usually puts forward more elaborate models of deliberation that splinter the unified decision-maker of economic theory into an array of agents. Following the stunned reaction of economists to evidence of preference reversal, for instance, subsequent work has multiplied the mental vantage points that agents are said to adopt when they face nearly identical choice decisions, akin to the reference dependence of prospect theory.[18] These psychological accounts, whether correct or not, omit two important questions: do agents' seemingly contradictory decisions stem from an inability to form preference judgments and are there some preference judgments lying behind the welter of discordant behavior that agents persist in?

4.4 RATIONALITY AS AN ORDERING PRINCIPLE

Must a self-interested agent make choices that satisfy the assumptions of classical rationality? I argued in Section 4.2 that the case for "yes" should not require agents always to choose the same options from a set of alternatives: that assumption would rule out decision-making rules

---

[17] On hyperbolic discounting, see Ainslie (1992), Laibson (1997), and O'Donoghue and Rabin (1999). For the original experimental evidence of preference reversal, see Slovic and Lichtenstein (1968), Lichtenstein and Slovic (1971, 1973), and Lindman (1971).

[18] Grether and Plott (1979), Slovic and Lichtenstein (1983), and Tversky et al. (1988).

such as status quo maintenance that an agent with incomplete preferences might well adopt. The revealed preferences of status quo maintainers moreover fail to be classically rational, whether the "sometimes chosen" or the "always chosen" definition of revealed preference is used. Our earlier discussion however left open whether status quo maintenance can lead an agent to inferior outcomes. More generally, will a method of choice harm an agent if it generates a revealed preference relation that fails to be classically rational? If so, the rational pursuit of self-interest would force an agent into choices that are guided by complete and transitive preferences. Rationality would itself provide an ordering principle. The project initiated by Samuelson of using revealed preferences to provide foundations for classical rationality comes down to this possibility.

To pursue this agenda, I will lay out a model of dynamic choice that confronts an agent with the potential hazards of decisions not guided by classically rational preferences. We will see that the "sometimes chosen" definition of revealed preference, which is automatically complete, can display intransitivities without leading an agent to inferior outcomes. The alternative "always chosen" definition of revealed preference can be incomplete, again without doing an agent any harm.

Our agent will face a sequence of choice sets, as in Section 4.1, but can now let his or her selection from a choice set at one date depend on the sequence of choice sets the agent has already seen and thus on the status quo. For example, if a decision-maker faces the singleton choice set $\{x\}$ at date t and $\{x, y\}$ at $t + 1$ then x will be the status quo at $t + 1$ and the choice set $\{x, y\}$ amounts to an offer to switch to y. A status-quo maintainer facing this sequence might select x at date $t + 1$ but might select y instead if the choice set at t had been $\{y\}$.

Implicitly the agent does not know when the sequence of choice sets will come to an end. Assuming that whatever new choice opportunities the agent encounters at later dates do not depend on the agent's current selections, the agent should therefore never risk selecting a dominated option at any date. That rule of course does not guarantee that an agent cannot be led over time to an option that is worse than what the agent began with. An agent who makes a sequence of voluntary exchanges recommended by a classically rational preference will not fall victim to such scenarios: every time the agent agrees to an exchange, the agent's new holding will not only be (weakly) superior to the agent's preceding holding but, by transitivity, it will also be superior to any option the agent could have earlier chosen.

Status quo maintenance will pass the same test: it is equally effective as a defense against manipulation. And if an agent fails to arrive on the scene blessed with a classically rational preference, status quo maintenance bestows the advantage of not having to manufacture preferences solely to come up with decisions immune to manipulation. The prominence of status quo maintenance for real-world decisions is therefore no accident.

Our agent at date t must make selections from the choice set A^t and if A^t is the last choice set the agent faces then the agent's actual consumption is drawn from these selections. Since the agent's decision can depend on the entire sequence $(A^1, \ldots, A^t)$, the date-t selections are given by a function c^t defined on a family of admissible sequences of nonempty sets of options. For any $(A^1, \ldots, A^t)$ in this family, $c^t(A^1, \ldots, A^t)$ will designate a nonempty subset of A^t. The families of admissible sequences will be nonempty and together obey the following two assumptions. First, if the agent can face some admissible sequence through date t then the agent at earlier dates can face the sequences that can lead up to the sequence that runs through date t. Second, following any sequence we can always confront the agent at the next date with an arbitrary pair of options. Formally, if $(A^1, \ldots, A^t)$ is admissible and x and y are alternatives then both $(A^1, \ldots, A^{t-1})$ and $(A^1, \ldots, A^t, \{x, y\})$ must also be admissible. The agent as a whole is described by $\langle c^t \rangle$, one c^t for each $t \geq 1$, which I call a *sequential choice function*.[19]

After the agent selects $c^t(A^1, \ldots, A^t)$ from A^t, one of these selections may appear in A^{t+1}. Implicitly the agent then discovers that he or she had a right to hold one of the options in A^t into the next period, and a status quo maintainer will then view that option as the status quo at $t + 1$. The agent in such holdover cases can therefore guarantee the availability at $t + 1$ of any option in A^t by setting $c^t(A^1, \ldots, A^t)$ to equal that option only. To avoid multiple status quos, we could require each $c^t(A^1, \ldots, A^t)$ and A^{t+1} to have at most one alternative in common: some unmodeled process would then determine which option in $c^t(A^1, \ldots, A^t)$ the agent can hold.[20] Requiring $c^t(A^1, \ldots, A^t)$ to be a singleton would achieve the

---

[19] One may impose further conditions to enrich the family of admissible sequences, but they will not be needed for any explicit result below. For example, to allow the possibility that all subsets of a choice set can be passed on to the next choice set with the same alternative offers available, we could assume that if $(A^1, \ldots, A^t)$ is in the date t family of admissible sequences and $A, B \subset A^t$ then there exists A^{t+1} with $A \subset A^{t+1}$ such that $(A^1, \ldots, A^{t+1})$ and $(A^1, \ldots, (A^{t+1} \setminus A) \cup B)$ are in the date $t + 1$ family.

[20] This would require a slight tweaking of admissibility.

same goal. But as with classical choice functions, an agent may consider several alternatives in a choice set to be acceptable, for example, when the status quo is dominated by more than one available option.

Given a sequential choice function $\langle c^t \rangle$, x will be revealed preferred to y – in the "sometimes chosen" sense – if there is some occasion on which x is chosen when y is available. Formally, $x\hat{R}y$ holds if there is an admissible sequence of choice sets $(A^1, \ldots, A^t)$ such that $x \in c^t(A^1, \ldots, A^t)$ and $y \in A^t$ and I will then say that $\langle c^t \rangle$ *leads to* $\hat{R}$. A $\langle c^t \rangle$ also leads to the strict revealed preference $\hat{P}$ defined by $x\hat{P}y$ if $x\hat{R}y$ and not $y\hat{R}x$. Since $x\hat{P}y$ means that the agent never selects y when x is available, it is again legitimate to conclude (as it was in Section 4.2) that the agent believes that x delivers strictly greater welfare than y: strict revealed preferences should mirror strict welfare judgments.

A sequential choice function $\langle c^i \rangle$ is *manipulation-free* if there does not exist an admissible sequence $(A^1, \ldots, A^i, \ldots, A^t)$ and alternatives $\bar{x}, x^i, \ldots, x^t$ such that

- $\bar{x} \in A^i$ and $x^t \in c^t(A^1, \ldots, A^t)$,
- $\bar{x}\hat{P}x^t$
- $x^j \in c^j(A^1, \ldots, A^j) \cap A^{j+1}$ for $j = i, \ldots, t-1$.

When x^j is in both $c^j(A^1, \ldots, A^j)$ and A^{j+1}, the agent implicitly has the right at date $j+1$ to retain one of his or her date j choices as an available option – whatever those choices may happen to be. The agent therefore ends up being manipulated if he or she trades away an $\bar{x}$ available in A^i and then makes further unforced trades that leave the agent with an x^t at date t that the agent would never directly select over $\bar{x}$. Since in this scenario the agent could stick with $\bar{x}$ throughout, the agent should regret his or her own choices. Agents are manipulation-free if they never fall into such a trap. And traps are lurking.

Example 4.1 (manipulation) Let the domain of alternatives be $\{x, y, y'\}$ and suppose some agent has only a single welfare judgment, that y' is superior to y. For an agent that cannot judge the trade-offs between two desirable goods, we could let y' have more of both goods than y and let x have more of good 1 and less of good 2 than either y or y' (as in Figure 3.1). Since y' is preferred to y, the agent should use a $\langle c^t \rangle$ that satisfies $y'\hat{P}y$. Suppose in addition that, for any sequence where A^i does not contain $\{y, y'\}$, $c^i(A^i) = A^i$. This $\langle c^t \rangle$ fails to be manipulation-free. Consider the following choice sets and decisions:

$$c^1(A^1) = A^1 = \{x, y'\} \quad \text{and} \quad c^2(A^1, A^2) = A^2 = \{x, y\}.$$

The agent declares both x and y' acceptable at date 1 and then, after getting rights to x, declares that both x and y are acceptable at date 2. By the close of date 2, the agent can therefore end up with y rather than y' even though the agent could have guaranteed y' by sticking to y' alone at both dates. The agent's choices are also intransitive in that $y\hat{R}x$ (since $y \in c^2(A^2)$), $x\hat{R}y'$ (since $x \in c^1(A^1)$), and yet not $y\hat{R}y'$ (since $y'\hat{P}y$). Whether intransitivity per se is the cause of the agent's manipulation remains to be seen. ■

Since each alternative can specify an outcome (say an amount of money) for each state of the world, an alternative can be a lottery or even a series of lotteries. A manipulation-free agent is therefore immune to a wide variety of money pumps.

The normative appeal of manipulation-freeness depends upon the causal interpretation that if an agent chooses some option at date t and that option is also in A^{t+1} then a switch to a different choice at t would lead the new choice to be in A^{t+1}. So in the above example if the agent were to choose y' alone from $\{x, y'\}$ at date 1, then implicitly the choice set the agent faces at date 2 would be $\{y, y'\}$ rather than $\{x, y\}$.

Our goal is to show that agents do not have to imitate classically rational agents to remain free from manipulation: a $\langle c^t \rangle$ can be manipulation-free even though it leads to an intransitive $\hat{R}$. But for an agent to have a chance of being free from manipulation, Theorem 4.1 suggests that an agent's strict welfare judgments and thus $\hat{P}$ must be transitive – and I will confirm this suggestion in Theorem 4.4 below. We must therefore leave open the door to sequential choice functions that lead to both a transitive $\hat{P}$ and an intransitive $\hat{R}$. The agents that might choose in this way are precisely those whose preferences are incomplete.

To identify the strict revealed preferences compatible with incomplete preferences, we need to add implicit indifference judgments to $\hat{P}$. Define $\hat{I}$ by

$x\hat{I}y$ if and only if, for every alternative w,

$$\left(w\hat{P}x \Leftrightarrow w\hat{P}y \right) \text{ and } \left(x\hat{P}w \Leftrightarrow y\hat{P}w \right).$$

Indifference then holds between x and y when and only when $\hat{P}$ views x and y as interchangeable, that is, x and y have the same sets of $\hat{P}$-superior alternatives and the same sets of $\hat{P}$-inferior alternatives. We will explore rationales for this definition in more detail in Section 6.2. I will call $\hat{P}$ *implicitly incomplete* if the binary relation R^* equal to the union of $\hat{P}$

and $\hat{I}$ – where xR^*y if and only if ($x\hat{P}y$ or $x\hat{I}y$) – is incomplete. Some pairs of options are then neither $\hat{P}$-related nor $\hat{I}$-related.

An implicitly incomplete decision-maker will face the possibility of manipulation. In the manipulation example, where $\{x, y, y'\}$ is the domain of alternatives and $\hat{P}$ asserts only that $y'\hat{P}y$, the pair x and y is not $\hat{P}$-related or $\hat{I}$-related. (Since $y'\hat{P}y$ and not $y'\hat{P}x$, it cannot be the case that $x\hat{I}y$.) Hence the $\hat{P}$ in that example is implicitly incomplete. Implicit incompleteness can also potentially serve up intransitivities of choice. For instance, if an implicitly incomplete agent always agrees to trade options that are neither $\hat{P}$-related nor $\hat{I}$-related then an intransitive $\hat{R}$ will result, again as in the manipulation example.

A status quo maintainer chooses only undominated alternatives and, when holdovers chosen in the preceding round remain available, chooses only undominated holdovers or alternatives that dominate one of the holdovers. Formally, $\langle c^i \rangle$ is *status quo maintaining* if, for any admissible $(A^1, \ldots, A^t)$,

- $c^t(A^1, \ldots, A^t) \subset \{a \in A^t$: there does not exist $b \in A^t$ with $b\hat{P}a\}$ and
- if $A^t \cap c^{t-1}(A^1, \ldots, A^{t-1}) \neq \varnothing$ then $c^t(A^1, \ldots, A^t) \subset$
  $\{s \in A^t$: for some $r \in A^t \cap c^{t-1}(A^1, \ldots, A^{t-1})$ either $s = r$ or $s\hat{P}r\}$.

Status quo maintenance is easy to execute: you have to pay attention only to the options currently available that you also chose at the previous date.

The advantage of status quo maintenance is readily apparent in the manipulation example. Like the manipulated agent, a status quo maintainer can agree to accept both x and y' from $\{x, y'\}$ at date 1. But when offered $\{x, y\}$ at date 2, a status quo maintainer must select x alone: y is unacceptable since it is not at least as good as an option available at date 2 that was also chosen at date 1. This selective refusal to trade protects a status quo maintainer from harmful sequences of exchanges.

Our quest to show that an agent can choose intransitively while remaining manipulation-free would be best served if the evidence of intransitivity occurs along a single sequence of choice sets; otherwise the agent would be observationally indistinguishable from a classically rational agent. A sequential choice function $\langle c^i \rangle$ is *observationally intransitive* if there is a triple of alternatives (x, y, z) and a sequence of choice sets $(A^1, \ldots, A^t)$ such that

(1) for some date $i \leq t$, $x \in c^i(A^1, \ldots, A^i)$ and $y \in A^i$,
(2) for some date $j \leq t$, $y \in c^j(A^1, \ldots, A^j)$ and $z \in A^j$, and
(3) $z\hat{P}x$.

Notwithstanding (3), the sequence $(A^1, \ldots, A^t)$ might not be rich enough to include a case where z is chosen and x is available. But if say $A^{t+1} = \{x, z\}$ then an active choice of z over x would be recorded. So, when choices are observationally intransitive, a witness of some sequence of decisions will see that x was chosen when y was available, that y was chosen when z was available, that z was chosen when x was available, and that x was never chosen when z was available.

Observational intransitivity and implicit incompleteness ensure that manipulation-freeness does not hold vacuously. Manipulation-freeness refers only to choice behavior, a feature that brings some advantages but that also makes the condition a little too easy to satisfy. For example, if we set $c^t(A^1, \ldots, A^t) = A^t$ for every sequence $(A^1, \ldots, A^t)$ then $x\hat{R}y$ for every pair (x, y): $x\hat{P}y$ never obtains and $\langle c^i \rangle$ is manipulation-free by default. Both observational intransitivity and implicit incompleteness preclude this scenario (since $x\hat{I}y$ would then hold for every (x, y)).

Agents with classically rational revealed preferences will be manipulation-free but those agents will not be observationally intransitive. And although it might seem that observational intransitivity would set an agent up for manipulation, that is not the case.

Theorem 4.3 *If $\hat{P}$ is transitive then any sequential choice function that leads to $\hat{P}$ and is status-quo-maintaining is manipulation-free. If in addition $\hat{P}$ is implicitly incomplete then there exist status-quo-maintaining sequential choice functions that lead to $\hat{P}$ and are observationally intransitive.*

The proofs for the results in this section are in the Appendix.

So, not only does manipulation-freeness fail to enforce classical rationality but a rule as simple as status quo maintenance leads to choice behavior that is both manipulation-free and intransitive. That status quo maintenance offers agents an easy way to protect themselves from manipulation is one of its central appeals.

Our conclusion that self interest does not require choice behavior to be classically rational applies so far only to the sometimes-chosen definition of revealed preferences. For the always-chosen definition, the same conclusion follows more readily. Assuming again that $\hat{P}$ is implicitly incomplete, it is not hard to show that there must be a triple (x, y, z) such that $z\hat{P}x$ but where neither x and y nor z and y are $\hat{P}$-ranked. Suppose the first three choice sets to confront the agent are $A^1 = \{x, y\}$, $A^2 = \{y, z\}$, and $A^3 = \{x, y\}$. A status-quo-maintaining sequential choice function that leads to $\hat{P}$ can then choose x at date 1, z at date 2, and y at date 3. With an always-chosen definition of revealed preference relation, x and y are then not weakly ordered. Theorem 4.3 therefore shows that manipulation-free agents will also fail to be classically rational from the always-chosen point of view.

Theorem 4.3 calls for an overhaul of the concept of rationality. The effective pursuit of one's interests does not require an agent to adopt complete and transitive preferences, and it is therefore misleading to call these assumptions axioms of rationality. But labeling aside, the failure of psychologists and economists to grasp that status quo maintenance and related rules actively promote the welfare of agents has turned the understanding of decision-making on its head. Economists, suspicious that status quo maintenance does agents harm, argue that the behavior is unlikely to persist: agents will eventually see the error of their ways and obey the classical axioms. Psychologists on the other hand have severed the tie between behavior and rationality. In fact, status quo maintenance serves the rational self-interest of its practitioners.

Various extensions of Theorem 4.3 are possible. Given a pair of alternatives that implies that $\hat{P}$ is implicitly incomplete – a pair that is not R^*-related – the proof of the Theorem adds a third alternative to form a triple with respect to which a status-quo-maintaining $\langle c^t \rangle$ is observationally intransitive. We could stack up these observational intransitivities across sequences of choice sets so that $\langle c^t \rangle$ displays an intransitivity for every such triple. We could also introduce more intricate dangers of manipulation. Status quo maintenance protects an agent against welfare-diminishing chains of trades where an option that an agent chooses at a date i remains available at date $i+1$. An agent might instead confront more elaborate paths where, say, an agent's choices at t and $t+1$ jointly feed into the options available at $t+2$. There are sequential choice functions that are immune to these potential manipulations as well and they can also display intransitivities of choice (see Mandler [2005]).

For an agent to remain free from manipulation, the transitivity of the strict revealed preference relation $\hat{P}$ in Theorem 4.3 is indispensable. Since $a\hat{P}b$ means that the agent always chooses a over b (whenever one of the two is chosen), the reasoning of Theorem 4.1 applies with full force.

Theorem 4.4 *If some sequential choice function $\langle c^t \rangle$ leads to $\hat{P}$ and is manipulation-free then $\hat{P}$ is transitive.*

It follows that an agent with an intransitive $\hat{P}$ cannot make manipulation-free choices, as economists and philosophers have argued since the 1950s. When an agent consistently refuses to accept option

y when x is available, across all choice sets and decision-making dates, option x will qualify as $\hat{P}$-superior to y. We can then infer that the agent believes x delivers greater welfare than y and conclude that a choice strategy that leaves the agent with y when he or she could have guaranteed x is irrational. The Theorem 4.4 case for transitivity thus relies implicitly on a welfare interpretation of strict revealed preferences. Weak revealed preferences in contrast need not indicate welfare judgments. Agents can therefore vary their decisions according to the history of choice sets they face and the manipulation argument runs aground.

5

Safety Bias

5.1 ALTERNATE METHODS OF CHOICE

How should agents choose between alternatives when they do not have a preference judgment to guide them? The question has no all-encompassing answer. When agents lack a best alternative, their behavior may well vary according to context and the relationship between context and decision can evolve through time. There is no one true model of choice.

This indeterminacy does not by itself present a vexing problem. Classically rational agents who are indifferent between alternatives face the same difficulty, and few have found this hole troubling. We have already examined one resolution of the impasse for agents with incomplete preferences, holding to the status quo. Status quo maintenance enjoys a canonical status for both agents and social scientists: it shields agents at risk of sequential manipulation from harm and it has united various camps in decision theory, from psychological theories of loss aversion to the Bewley model of decision-makers with multiple priors. But it is not the only way to make decisions in the face of incompleteness.

One alternative is for agents to "complete" their preferences – fill in $x \succsim y$ or $y \succsim x$ when initially $\succsim$ specifies neither – and let the preference that results determine their decisions. So even when an agent cannot find an ordering principle that will rank any two options, the agent could still systematically choose one of the two. As long as these newly created preferences do not lead to any intransitivities and do not overturn the welfare judgments that the agent can make, the agent will be as immune to manipulation as an individual who starts off with classically rational preferences. But a viable completion strategy cannot impose heavy burdens of time or effort: it must be easy for an agent to fill in the blanks.

Agents have leeway about how consistent these newly created preferences will be. When choice environments are not causally linked – as they were in Section 4.4 where an agent's choice at one date affects the alternatives that are available later – agents can complete their preference in one way in one environment and in another way in a different environment. Each of these completed preference relations could be orthodox, possibly even locally decisive, but the agent's behavior across environments would still deviate from the microeconomic norm.

Among the trade-offs that agents find difficult to judge are those between different versions of the same good, say apples, that an individual can consume at different times or states of the world or locations. The reasons can be varied. Agents who cannot assess their own impatience will not know at what rate to discount future goods. When confronting uncertainty, agents might not know the probabilities of states.

When agents try to piece together the preference judgments they do not know how to make, they can be cautious or daring. In the face of uncertainty, an agent can evaluate an alternative x on the assumption that, of the probability distributions the agent deems reasonable, the worst-case distribution that leads to the smallest expected utility for x will rule. Or the agent could assume that the best-case distribution rules. While rationality considerations do not mandate either answer, the theories that have found the greatest traction assume that agents facing uncertainty fall at the cautious end of the spectrum: the worst-case distribution determines the expected utility of an alternative.

This expected utility example suggests a broader plan of attack on trade-offs that an agent does not know how to judge. An agent can turn to a set of welfare functions that express the agent's various evaluations of the trade-offs and assess an option x by the smallest of the welfare levels that these functions assign to x. When deciding between two options, the agent then chooses the option with the greater worst-case assessment.

To start with a bare-bones case, suppose that each bundle pays out consumption at a sequence of dates – alternatively states or locations – and that for each date one of the agent's welfare functions declares the welfare of a bundle to equal consumption at that date. The worst-case assessment of a bundle is then the smallest of the bundle's consumption quantities. Social conventions and individual tastes will normally dictate greater subtlety however. Agents may feel that as they age their consumption should grow and that future consumption should therefore be discounted in calculations of the welfare achieved: a future quantity of consumption that is slightly greater than present consumption may then qualify as the worst-case assessment. Using consumption at a single date to define a welfare function is also too restrictive; welfare functions that allow trade-offs of goods – as expected utility functions permit – may provide agents with a more convincing basis for choice.

An agent's worst-case assessments implicitly define a preference relation and better-than sets. Though these preferences will qualify as classically rational, they will favor the safe options that guarantee a particular level of welfare, the options to which all of the agent's welfare functions assign the same welfare level. Along each supporting price line through a safe x, the welfare function that qualifies as worst-case will generally change as the line crosses x. The set of bundles $B(x)$ that are better than (preferred to) x will therefore display a kink at x with the now familiar consequence that a set of margins or price vectors will support $B(x)$ at x. These kinks generate a bias for safety: as relative prices change, agents will tend to stick with the safe options.

Safety bias is not normally absolute. When an agent's welfare functions display trade-offs, the safety-biased preference that emerges will inherit some of those trade-offs. If for example y offers a sufficiently large consumption at some date, then a safety-biased agent may well prefer y over a safe bundle where the minimum consumption across dates is greater.

Since welfare functions can be seen as representations of candidate preferences, safety bias shares some ground with unanimity aggregation; in each account some decisions are governed by a worst-case assessment. But the welfare functions of a safety-biased agent will mete out an array of welfare assessments for any option. So, for each pair of options x and y, one of the options has a worst-case assessment at least as great as the other and is implicitly preferred. And if one of the welfare functions provides the worst-case assessment of both x and y, then the agent's other welfare functions are irrelevant to the preference between x and y. For a unanimity aggregator, on the other hand, if the agent's various welfare functions disagree on how to rank two options, then the agent ends up with no bottom-line judgment and must decide by other means. Moreover with unanimity aggregation and local incomparability more generally, multiple supporting prices occur at every option, and so there are no safe options that decision-makers can flee to.

The flight-to-safety completion strategies are the subject of this chapter. These strategies can be improvised and they may lack the conviction of firm judgments of well-being, but they enjoy a simplicity that nearly matches status quo maintenance. When agents can identify a family of welfare functions, their missing preferences are easily supplied. You might predict that the caution inherent in safety bias will promote economic stability but we will see in Chapter 7 that the opposite is the case. When even a small change in the economic environment hits a safety-biased economy, dramatic price changes can be needed to convince agents to change their consumption.

5.2 SAFETY BIAS AND MIN AGGREGATION

What matters for safety bias and the instability it generates are that kinks in better-than sets and bands of margins arise at some but not all consumption bundles. An underlying psychology of caution need not play any role, and I will therefore cast the definition of safety bias solely in terms of better-than sets.

A bias for safety occurs when there are rays of safe consumption bundles that an agent favors over off-ray bundles. For an x on one of these rays, there will be multiple price lines through x that contain only bundles not preferred to x. Since a safety-biased agent cannot specify for a safe bundle x an exact rate at which goods can be substituted without gain or loss, the agent will fail to be locally decisive: the agent's better-than set $B(x)$ will be kinked at x. See Figure 5.1 where the safe bundles lie on Λ. If for example goods vary by location, the ray might consist of the bundles with equal consumption across locations (the $45°$ line if there are two locations).

The bias for safe bundles can be severe or mild: an agent might stick with a safe bundle when facing nearly every price line through that bundle or only when facing a small interval of price lines. The individual in Figure 5.1 stands in the middle: the agent will leave Λ if a small sacrifice of one good brings a large gain of the other good but will cling to Λ at many price lines. Since the absence of exact, marginal trade-offs is limited to bundles on the safe rays, safety-biased agents can be classically rational even though they fail to be locally decisive. In fact, to avoid intertwining different sources of incomparability, I will later fold classical rationality into the definition of safety bias.

A *ray of bundles* Λ is a half-line in the positive orthant rooted at the origin: $\Lambda = \{x \in \mathbb{R}_+^L : x = \lambda a \text{ for some } \lambda \geq 0\}$ where $a = (a_1, \ldots, a_L) > 0$ is a bundle of the economy's L goods. I will use rays rather than increasing paths from the origin to specify safe bundles for the sake of concreteness and to fit the safe bundles that appear in applications.

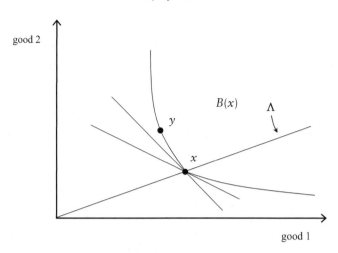

FIGURE 5.1 A better-than set $B(x)$ when x lies on a ray of safe bundles

Before proceeding to a formal definition of safety bias, we return to an agent whose ambivalence about how to trade off goods can be represented by a set of welfare functions. Welfare functions arise readily from partitions of goods into groups, for example, the goods delivered at various states or dates, with each welfare function assigning different weights to the groups. Let Λ be a *common-welfare ray* if for any bundle x on Λ all of the agent's welfare functions assign the same welfare level to x – and note that there can be more than one such ray. The rival welfare functions can of course disagree on how to compare an $x \in \Lambda$ with alternatives not on Λ.[1]

One way that an agent endowed with a set of welfare functions can decide between two bundles x and y is to mimic the unanimity aggregators of Section 3.1: choose y if and only if every welfare function judges y to be superior to x. When x is on a common-welfare ray Λ and y is off Λ, this advice cautiously evaluates the options by their worst-case welfare assessments. Since each welfare function assigns the same welfare level to

---

[1] Given a common-welfare ray Λ, the number of welfare functions must generally be no greater than the number of goods L and, for each $x \in \Lambda$, there must be an $f \colon \mathbb{R}_+ \to \mathbb{R}$ such that for each $k \geq 0$ and welfare function u, $u(kx) = f(k)u(x)$. When there are more than L welfare functions, *quasi-common* welfare rays can be defined by a subset of L of the welfare functions: a bundle is on such a ray if every function in the subset delivers the same welfare level and the remaining functions deliver at least as great a welfare level. For the min aggregation preferences below, better-than sets will remain kinked at points on these rays.

an $x \in \Lambda$, y will defeat x unanimously only if the smallest of the welfare levels assigned to y is greater than the common welfare level assigned to x, which of course is also the smallest welfare level assigned to x. The result will usually be a $B(x)$ with the kinks characteristic of unanimity aggregation: multiple price lines will support $B(x)$ for $x \in \Lambda$.[2] The agent will then consume on rather than off Λ when choosing from budget sets with a range of price lines, as in Figure 5.1.

Example 5.1 Suppose an agent is not sure how to trade off consumption today against consumption tomorrow. All of the agent's evaluations of the trade-offs do however agree on the welfare level of any consumption that is constant across dates.[3] Letting consumption today and tomorrow be goods 1 and 2, the bundles along the 45° line Λ through $a = (1, 1)$ then form a common-welfare ray. To illustrate, let the increasing function v indicate the agent's within-period utility for consumption at either date and suppose that for each bundle $z = (z_1, z_2)$ the agent has two welfare assessments given by $u^\alpha(z) = \frac{3}{4}v(z_1) + \frac{1}{4}v(z_2)$ and $u^\beta(z) = \frac{7}{8}v(z_1) + \frac{1}{8}v(z_2)$. These two functions display different evaluations of the intertemporal trade-offs but they assign the same welfare level to any $z \in \Lambda$.

If $x \in \Lambda$ and the agent decides to unanimity aggregate, then y will be weakly superior to x only if both u^α and u^β assign higher welfare to y:

$$u^\alpha(y) \geq u^\alpha(x) \text{ and } u^\beta(y) \geq u^\beta(x).$$

Multiple price lines therefore support $B(x)$ at x. Since $u^\alpha(x) = u^\beta(x) = \min[u^\alpha(x), u^\beta(x)]$ when $x \in \Lambda$, the inequalities above can be written instead as

$$\min[u^\alpha(y), u^\beta(y)] \geq \min[u^\alpha(x), u^\beta(x)]. \blacksquare$$

For pairs where one bundle is on Λ and the other is off Λ, caution coincides with unanimity aggregation. For the broader goal of safety bias – complete preferences that favor secure options – we must fill in the preference judgments that unanimity aggregation does not supply. The cautious worst-case assessments, expressed in the final inequality in Example 5.1, can provide the missing rankings. When the agent has welfare functions in hand, this guidance is easy to determine and therein lies its appeal.

To formalize these points, suppose that the welfare functions $u^1, \ldots, u^n$ define one or more common-welfare rays: if Λ is one of these

---

[2] Recall that p supports $B(x)$ at x if, for all $y \in B(x)$, $p \cdot y \geq p \cdot x$: see Figure 3.3 in Chapter 3.
[3] Similarly to Duesenberry (1949).

rays and $x \in \Lambda$ then $u^1(x) = \cdots = u^n(x)$. Each welfare function u^i represents one of the evaluations of the trade-offs among goods that the agent deems reasonable and the equalities express the welfare equivalence of bundles across these evaluations. Define the *min aggregation* preference $\succsim^{\min}$ by

$$y \succsim^{\min} x \text{ if and only if } \min [u^1(y), \ldots, u^n(y)] \geq \min [u^1(x), \ldots, u^n(x)].$$

Since $\succsim^{\min}$ is represented by a utility function, it is classically rational.

The min aggregation preference $\succsim^{\min}$ extends unanimity aggregation: it reproduces the (incomplete set of) preference judgments that unanimity aggregation endorses. Recall the definition of unanimity aggregation: given $u^1, \ldots, u^n$, $y \succsim^{\mathrm{UA}} x$ holds if and only if $u^i(y) \geq u^i(x)$ for $i = 1, \ldots, n$.

Observation. *If $y \succsim^{\mathrm{UA}} x$ then $y \succsim^{\min} x$. If $x \in \Lambda$ and $y \succsim^{\min} x$ then $y \succsim^{\mathrm{UA}} x$.*

Proof. Suppose $y \succsim^{\mathrm{UA}} x$. For some i, $\min [u^1(y), \ldots, u^n(y)] = u^i(y)$ and therefore

$$\min [u^1(y), \ldots, u^n(y)] = u^i(y) \geq u^i(x) \geq \min [u^1(x), \ldots, u^n(x)].$$

Now suppose $x \in \Lambda$ and $y \succsim^{\min} x$. Then $\min [u^1(x), \ldots, u^n(x)] = u^i(x)$ for any i and therefore

$$u^i(y) \geq \min [u^1(y), \ldots, u^n(y)] \geq \min [u^1(x), \ldots, u^n(x)] = u^i(x).$$

∎

So $\succsim^{\min}$ both replicates $\succsim^{\mathrm{UA}}$ when the worse of two options lies on Λ and extends $\succsim^{\mathrm{UA}}$ to cover the remaining pairs of options.

The Observation confirms that for $\succsim^{\min}$ multiple price vectors will normally support $B(x)$ at x when x lies on a common-welfare ray Λ. Due to the Observation, when $x \in \Lambda$ the set $B(x)$ will coincide with the set of bundles that are preferred to x under unanimity aggregation. The logic by which $\succsim^{\mathrm{UA}}$ leads to multiple supporting prices at x therefore applies to $\succsim^{\min}$ when $x \in \Lambda$: $B(x)$ will normally be kinked at x since every u^i must approve a change from x to an alternative y. See Proposition 3.1 and compare Figures 3.3 and 5.1.

While the $\succsim^{\min}$ foundation for multiple supporting prices is illuminating, a formal statement of safety bias does not need to rest on a min aggregation rationale. I will let safety-biased preferences be only weakly increasing ($x \gg y$ implies $x \succ y$) to allow for some simple examples in Section 5.3.

Definition 5.1 *A price vector p **supports** a ray Λ if, for all $x \in \Lambda$, p supports B(x) at x. A preference $\succsim$ is **safety biased** if it is complete, transitive, and weakly increasing and there exists a ray of bundles Λ such that multiple price vectors of the same length support Λ. The ray Λ then qualifies as **safe**.*

Since the multiple supporting price vectors required by safety bias have the same length, they point in different directions. Better-than sets are therefore kinked along Λ. If two price vectors p and p' both support Λ then so will any positive linear combination $\alpha p + \beta p'$, where $\alpha, \beta \geq 0$ (Section 3.1). So given any two price vectors pointing in different directions that support Λ, all of the price vectors for the directions in between will also support Λ.

Safety bias falls in a middle ground between two poles, local decisiveness where marginal rates of substitution are always well-defined and its opposite, local incomparability, where marginal rates of substitution are never well-defined. The first pole includes the early neoclassical preferences which have smooth indifference curves and can be represented by differentiable utility functions. For each x there will then be just one price line that supports $B(x)$ at x; every other price line through x will cross the indifference curve on which x lies. So the agent will select x from the budget line through x defined by this supporting price line and any other budget line through x would lead the agent to deviate from x. A safety-biased agent with a ray of safe bundles Λ, in contrast, cannot be pushed off Λ so easily.

The opposite pole consists of the locally incomparable preferences and usually the unanimity aggregations (Theorem 3.3). As with safety bias, locally incomparable preferences display a multiplicity of supporting prices and this inability to judge certain trade-offs underlies the resemblance between Figures 3.3 and 5.1. The better-than set is kinked in both cases. But for local incomparability the kinks and the multiplicity of supporting prices that results obtain at all bundles, not just at the safe bundles. In Figure 5.1, multiple price vectors support $B(x)$ at x but only a single price vector supports $B(y)$ (which coincides with $B(x)$) at y. This difference allows safety-biased but not locally-incomparable preferences to be classically rational; in Figure 5.1, the preference ranks x relative to every bundle and so every bundle not in $B(x)$ is dispreferred to x.

The min aggregation rationale for safety bias has drawbacks – which motivate the search for another path in the next section. Just as in a Rawlsian aggregation of individual preferences in social decision-making, an agent may not have an obvious way to select the u^i's to place into a min aggregation. While the ordering that a particular u^i represents is well-defined, many different functions will represent that ordering. An agent could, say, use γu^i rather than u^i where $\gamma > 0$. The choice of representation will generally affect both $\succsim^{\min}$ and which bundles form a safe ray. The contrast with the unanimity aggregation $\succsim^{\text{UA}}$ defined by the same functions $u^1, \ldots, u^n$ is sharp. Since $\succsim^{\text{UA}}$ is determined only by the candidate *preferences* that the u^i represent, $\succsim^{\text{UA}}$ will remain unchanged if we switch one of the u^i to another utility representation of the same candidate preference: the construction of $\succsim^{\text{UA}}$ is fully ordinal. The sensitivity of min aggregation to the representations employed indicates an arbitrariness of safety-biased preferences that unanimity aggregation is not guilty of. Indeed the only judgments made by $\succsim^{\min}$ that survive all possible changes of the representations for $\succsim^1, \ldots, \succsim^n$ are the judgments that $\succsim^{\text{UA}}$ makes.[4]

When $x \succsim^{\min} y$ obtains but $x \succsim^{\text{UA}} y$ does not, the agent might not view x as preferable to y. The agent might instead see x as the default decision when choosing between x and y – though one would then expect the agent to deviate on occasion and sometimes choose y over x, perhaps when y is the status quo. But if the agent does not deviate then it will do no harm to declare $\succsim^{\min}$ to be the agent's preference and indeed, since $\succsim^{\min}$ is complete, perhaps as real a preference as those imagined by the 19th century hedonists. Although agents' subjective views of their own preferences are perfectly legitimate objects of scientific inquiry, it will sow confusion to reject the nearly uniform practice in economics of declaring a preference ranking to obtain when an agent always chooses one alternative over another.[5] But keep in mind that although safety-biased preferences are complete they share with incomplete preferences an ambivalence about how to trade off goods. Curiously, the completion strategy of elevating the bundles on certain rays above other bundles, though it aligns an agent with classical rationality, will turn out to have more dramatic consequences for the operation of markets than incomplete preferences have.

---

[4] In the theory of choice under uncertainty, which I consider in the next section, Gilboa et al. (2010) and Lehrer and Teper (2014) make similar distinctions.

[5] Bewley (1986) is an exception to the rule.

5.3 SAFETY BIAS ROOTED IN PRODUCTION

A different road to safety bias, with less psychological baggage than min aggregation and more in keeping with the ordinalist tradition, simply begins with complementarities in the technology of how goods deliver consumption services.

An extreme case occurs with the Leontief preferences of textbook fame which are represented by a utility $u(x) = \min\left[\frac{1}{a_1}x_1, \ldots, \frac{1}{a_L}x_L\right]$, where $a = (a_1, \ldots, a_n) \gg 0$. A Leontief preference is safety biased with a ray Λ of safe bundles through a, and the resulting kinks in better-than sets at points on Λ will direct consumption to bundles on Λ. If, say, there are two goods and $a_1 = a_2$ then $x \succsim y$ if and only if $\min[x_1, x_2] \geq \min[y_1, y_2]$ and the 45° line forms a safe ray.

Behind the scenes of the Leontief preference, goods combine via a linear production activity to deliver a service – a comfortable walk requires one left shoe and one right shoe – and the connection to linear activities is why the preference is named after the Leontief (1951) input-output model. Unlike the thin gruel of merely positing a ray of safe bundles, the rooting of a Leontief preference in technology explains why safety bias arises.

The Leontief preference is just one example of how consumption can be based on production activities and a crude one at that. More generally an agent might combine goods together using activities, $a^1, \ldots, a^N$, where each $a^j = (a_1^j, \ldots, a_L^j) > 0$ specifies the amounts of the economy's goods needed to produce one unit of some consumption service c^j.[6] From slavery to fashion to the conformism of suburbia, consumption can require goods to be arranged in certain configurations. Since an agent can follow many prototypes and models, the array of activities can be large.

To focus on safety bias derived from the technology behind consumption rather than from an overt violation of local decisiveness, I will assume that the utility of consumption services is a differentiable, increasing, concave, and homothetic function v. The agent when handed a bundle of goods x maximizes v by solving

$$\max v(c^1, \ldots, c^N) \text{ s.t. } \sum_{j=1}^{N} a^j c^j \leq x, (c^1, \ldots, c^N) \geq 0.$$

By letting x vary, the solutions to this problem define a utility u that is a function of x and this utility represents some preference $\succsim$. When the

---

[6] This model will follow the spirit if not the details of the Lancaster (1966) theory of characteristics.

v-maximization problem above is solved at $\bar{c} = (\bar{c}^1, \ldots, \bar{c}^N)$, there will be shadow prices $\bar{p} > 0$ that for each j satisfy the first-order condition,

$$D_{c^j} v(\bar{c}^1, \ldots, \bar{c}^N) \leq \bar{p} \cdot a^j \text{ (and if } < \text{ then } \bar{c}^j = 0).$$

The prices $\bar{p}$ will then support $B_{\succsim}(x)$ at x.[7] Call the v-maximization problem *regular* at x if there is a solution $(\bar{c}, \bar{p} \gg 0)$ such that $\bar{c}^j = 0$ implies $D_{c^j} v(\bar{c}^1, \ldots, \bar{c}^N) < \bar{p} \cdot a^j$. Since a slight increase in one of the entries in a^j will allow the inequality to be satisfied when $\bar{c}^j = 0$, the implication is virtually sure to hold when the a^j are drawn from continuous distributions. The $\bar{p} \gg 0$ requirement is imposed for concreteness; without $\bar{p} \gg 0$, we would narrow attention to the goods with positive prices.

Theorem 5.1 *If the v-maximization problem is regular at some $x > 0$ and the solution $(\bar{c}, \bar{p})$ has fewer than L activities in use, then the preference that u represents is safety-biased.*

The proof is in the Appendix. Figure 5.2 illustrates the safety bias of Theorem 5.1 when $L = 2$. There are two rays of safe bundles, Λ^1 and Λ^2, where each Λ^i intersects an activity a^i. At a consumption such as x, one activity is in use and multiple prices support $B(x)$.

Since the agent's utility v for consumption services is differentiable, the multiple supporting prices that accompany safety bias and implied by Theorem 5.1 are not pre-baked in v. The multiplicity stems from the production origins of the preferences.

The two paths to safety bias we have considered – min aggregation and consumption activities – can merge. For example, we can view the Leontief preference with the utility representation $\min\left[\frac{1}{a_1}x_1, \ldots, \frac{1}{a_L}x_L\right]$ as resulting either from the consumption activity $(a_1, \ldots, a_L)$ or from the min aggregation of the L welfare functions $\frac{1}{a_1}x_1, \ldots, \frac{1}{a_L}x_L$. For the latter interpretation, the preference might arise from a pessimist who is so hesitant to agree to trade-offs that only welfare functions that weight a single good qualify as comparable to other welfare functions.

---

[7] Since the Lagrangean $v(c^1, \ldots, c^N) - \bar{p} \cdot \sum_{j=1}^N a^j c^j$ is maximized at $\bar{c}$, the budget problem $\max u(x)$ s.t. $\bar{p} \cdot x \leq \bar{p} \cdot \sum_{j=1}^N a^j \bar{c}^j$ must have a solution at $x = \sum_{j=1}^N a^j \bar{c}^j$. (If there were an x' with $u(x') > u(x)$ and $\bar{p} \cdot x' \leq \bar{p} \cdot \sum_{j=1}^N a^j \bar{c}^j$ then for the c' that solves the v-maximization problem when x' is the right-hand side, we would have $v(c') > v(\bar{c})$ and $\bar{p} \cdot \sum_{j=1}^N a^j c^{j\prime} \leq \bar{p} \cdot \sum_{j=1}^N a^j \bar{c}^j$.) So, if there were a $z \succsim x$ such that $\bar{p} \cdot (z - x) < 0$ then, for $z' = z + (\varepsilon, \ldots, \varepsilon)$ with ε sufficiently small, we would have $\bar{p} \cdot (z' - x) < 0$. Since $z' \succ z$, the budget problem then would not be solved at x.

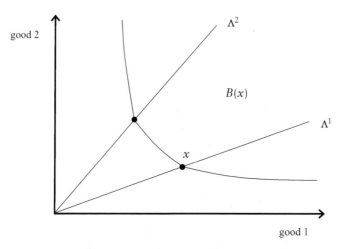

FIGURE 5.2 Two consumption goods and one activity in use

5.4 THE MAXMIN MODEL OF PREFERENCES UNDER UNCERTAINTY

An elegant example of safety bias and min aggregation holds for preferences over uncertain alternatives. Agents who are unable to settle on a single probability distribution and instead wield a set of distributions Π might unanimity aggregate, as we saw in the Bewley model of Section 3.4. Agents in the Gilboa and Schmeidler (1989) model min aggregate instead: they pessimistically evaluate an alternative x by using the worst-case distribution in Π, the distribution that leads to the lowest expected utility for x.[8]

Let the set of states be $\Omega = \{1, \ldots, S\}$ and suppose an agent is endowed with a closed set of distributions $\Pi \subset \Delta = \{\pi \in \mathbb{R}_+^S : \sum_{\omega \in \Omega} \pi_\omega = 1\}$. The agent's alternatives are bundles that specify a consumption x_ω at each state ω and the agent's utility at each state is given by the increasing, concave, and differentiable function u. As in Section 3.4, each π in Π determines a distinct expected utility function $E_\pi u$ that when evaluated at $x = (x_1, \ldots, x_S)$ equals $\sum_{\omega \in \Omega} \pi_\omega u(x_\omega)$. The agent then proceeds via min aggregation. Interpreting the expected utility functions as welfare functions, each x is associated with the smallest of the expected utility levels given by the $E_\pi u(x)$ thus defining the *maxmin utility function*

---

[8] Gilboa and Schmeidler (1989) is closely related to Schmeidler (1989). I will, sadly, neglect the most important feature of these two papers, their axiomatic development of the utility representations to be used below. Cerreia-Vioglio et al. (2015) take a similar approach to agents who act as if they were unsure about what utility function to use. For comparable results for intertemporal choice, see Chakraborty (2021).

Safety Bias

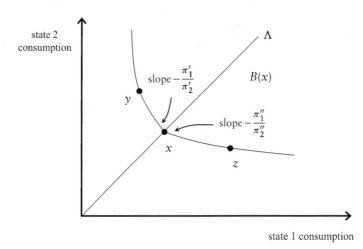

FIGURE 5.3 A maxmin utility indifference curve

$\min_{\pi \in \Pi} E_\pi u$. The utility has the appeal that the kinks in agents' better-than sets that it generates rest on a plausible psychology, the inability of agents to reduce their uncertainty about the world to a single probability distribution.

For a two-state and one-good-per-state example, suppose Π contains two distributions π' and π'' where $\pi'_1 > \pi''_1$. As depicted in Figure 5.3, the ray of safe bundles Λ is the $45°$ line and x lies on Λ. To see that the set of bundles that are better than x, $B(x)$, displays a kink at x, suppose y and z are indifferent to x and that y provides more consumption at state 2 than at state 1 compared to x while z provides less. For y, the worst-case distribution is π' since $\pi'_1 > \pi''_1$: the $\pi \in \Pi$ that minimizes $E_\pi u(y)$ is π' rather than π''. The agent will therefore judge pairs of bundles on the y side of the $45°$ line using the differentiable function $E_{\pi'} u$. For z, the worst-case distribution is π'' and bundles on its side of the $45°$ line are judged by $E_{\pi''} u$. So, except at x, the indifference curve through x – the boundary of $B(x)$ – is smooth. As for x, the slopes of the indifference curve at y and z equal $-\frac{\pi'_1 Du(y_1)}{\pi'_2 Du(y_2)}$ and $-\frac{\pi''_1 Du(z_1)}{\pi''_2 Du(z_2)}$ respectively and hence in the limit as y and z approach x these slopes equal $-\frac{\pi'_1}{\pi'_2}$ and $-\frac{\pi''_1}{\pi''_2}$. So $B(x)$ displays a kink at x.

Theorem 5.2 *If Π contains more than one probability distribution then the maxmin utility represents a safety-biased preference.*

As the proof in the Appendix shows, the set of bundles that deliver the same consumption at every state defines a ray of safe bundles Λ for the preference represented by a maxmin utility and the set of prices that support Λ consists of Π and all positive multiples of the π in Π.

But safe rays in the maxmin model do not have to be formed by constant bundles and $B(x)$ can therefore be kinked at nonconstant bundles. The constant ray is simply an easy source of examples. For instance, suppose Ω consists of three states, a, b, and c, and that an agent has a set of probabilities Π that consists of all $\pi \in \Delta$ that satisfy the equality

$$\pi_a + 2\pi_b + 3\pi_c = 2.$$

Let the agent's utility u be linear in the single consumption good that appears at each state. The agent's maxmin utility for bundle x is then

$$\min_{\pi \in \Pi} E_\pi x \equiv \min_{\pi \in \Pi} (\pi_a x_a + \pi_b x_b + \pi_c x_c).$$

Suppose x lies on the ray Λ through $(2, 3, 4)$. It is then easy to verify that the above minimization problem is solved at any $\pi' \in \Pi$. As in the second half of the Observation, for any y with $\min_{\pi \in \Pi} E_\pi y \geq \min_{\pi \in \Pi} E_\pi x$ and any $\pi' \in \Pi$,

$$E_{\pi'} y \geq \min_{\pi \in \Pi} E_\pi y \geq \min_{\pi \in \Pi} E_\pi x = E_{\pi'} x,$$

where the equality holds due to the fact that π' solves $\min_{\pi \in \Pi} E_\pi x$. Thus y is a $E_{\pi'}(\cdot)$ improvement over x for each π' in the one-dimensional family of probabilities Π. Since for any $\pi' \in \Pi$ the gradient of $E_{\pi'}(\cdot)$ at x is π' itself, $\pi' \cdot (y - x) \geq 0$: the prices π' therefore support $B(x)$ at x. Since this conclusion holds for all π' in Π, $B(x)$ displays a kink at x and the ray Λ through $(2, 3, 4)$ therefore qualifies as a ray of safe bundles.

A variety of kinked better-than sets and safe rays can thus arise across maxmin models – and in a single model. The ray through $(2, 3, 4)$ in the present example is by no means isolated: since the proof of Theorem 5.2 applies, the ray through $(1, 1, 1)$ also qualifies as safe. Indeed any convex combination of the rays through $(2, 3, 4)$ and $(1, 1, 1)$ is safe as well.

5.5 CONCLUSION

For a safety-biased preference, the safe bundles – the points at which the better-than sets are kinked – are rare: they form a set of dimension smaller than the dimension of the ambient set of possible bundles. For instance, in the maxmin model where Π consists of the probabilities that satisfy $\pi_a + 2\pi_b + 3\pi_c = 2$, the bundles where the better-than set is supported by more than one price direction form a 2-dimensional subset of the 3-dimensional set of possible bundles. This rarity might seem to imply that the kinks are unimportant. I will have more to say on this point in Chapter 7. For the moment, notice that an agent constrained by a budget set will tend to buy bundles at which better-than sets are kinked; in the extreme case of Leontief utilities, for example, agents facing positive prices will buy only bundles that lie at the kink in their indifference curves.

Local incomparability and safety bias will play important roles when we turn to classic issues of economic analysis: they provide the two main varieties of agents who do not know how to make trade-offs. But we have identified an important difference between the types. In the first, the absence of trade-offs is ubiquitous – every bundle x has a better-than set that is kinked at x and preferences consequently are incomplete. In the second, better-than sets display kinks only rarely.

6

The Myth of the Indifference Curve

In classical preference theory, an agent facing a pair of alternatives either strictly prefers one alternative to the other or holds them to be indifferent. As we have seen, there is a third possibility, that the agent makes no preference judgment. But the three possibilities do not peacefully coexist. Strict preference and incompleteness are robust outcomes. In Figure 6.1, which could stem from a unanimity aggregation of two candidate preferences, $SB(x) = \{w : w \succ x\}$ is the set of options strictly better than (preferred to) x and $SW(x) = \{w : x \succ w\}$ is the set of options strictly worse than x. Both $SB(x)$ and $SW(x)$ and the bundles such as y or z where there is no preference judgment vis-à-vis x are all nonnegligible: the sets have positive area and contain nonempty open sets. In contrast we have not yet in this book run across any pair of indifferent bundles when the underlying preference $\succsim$ is incomplete. For a unanimity aggregator to be indifferent between two options, all of the agent's candidate preferences must judge the options to be indifferent. So if the boundary of $SB(x)$ in Figure 6.1 is formed by the indifference curves of two candidate preferences, then the only point on that boundary that can be indifferent to x is x itself. The sets $SB(x)$ and $B(x)$ in Figure 6.1 thus nearly coincide.

Beyond unanimity aggregation, the boundaries of better-than sets will not consist of indifferent options when the boundaries of $SB(x)$ and $SW(x)$ intersect only at x and $\succsim$ is transitive and increasing: if v in Figure 6.1 were indifferent to x then $x \succsim v \succ y$ and hence $x \succ y$, which contradicts $y \notin SW(x)$. The classical indifference curve has vanished. So when agents face options they cannot strictly rank – a common occurrence in decision-making – they cannot convincingly plead indifference: the agents

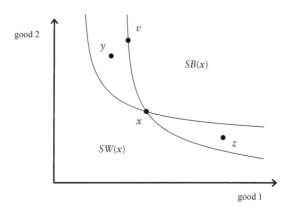

FIGURE 6.1 The absence of indifference with incomplete preferences

must concede that they are unable to form even weak judgments among their options.

The distinction above between indifference and incompleteness is extracted from a weak preference relation $\succsim$: when $x \succsim y$ and $y \succsim x$ the options are indifferent, while if neither $x \succsim y$ nor $y \succsim x$ incompleteness holds (the options are not $\succsim$-ranked). But can we assemble a $\succsim$ that can make these distinctions from observations of an agent's behavior? The most common view is that we cannot. Though weak preference judgments are the normal primitive of economic analysis, when it comes to identifying indifference and incompleteness economists typically assume that only strict preferences are observable. In this view, when an agent faces a choice between x and y we can witness only a strict preference judgment or the absence of a strict preference. Indifference and incompleteness between x and y therefore lead to the same behavior and so any distinction between the concepts is said to be unscientific. The dominant terminology in economic theory accordingly places all absences of strict preference under one heading – indifference of course.[1]

This chapter investigates the relative prevalence of indifference and incompleteness and will confirm the pictorial argument above that incompleteness dominates the scene. To do so, we will need to distinguish between indifference and incompleteness and we must therefore cast aside the received wisdom that such a distinction is invalid. A classification of indifference and incompleteness will prove more broadly useful. On the

[1] See, for example, Fishburn (1970b) or Kreps (1988). Exceptions, such as Cettolin and Riedl (2019), Costa-Gomes et al. (2022), and Eliaz and Ok (2006), are becoming more common.

rare occasions when incomplete preferences appear in economic theory, they come disguised as cases of "intransitive indifference." To sort out whether this form of intransitivity exposes an agent to the manipulations considered in Chapter 4, we must sift through the options classified as indifferent to see when the agent's underlying preferences are transitive and hence manipulation-free.

The claim that the only observational possibilities are strict preference and its absence is hardly indisputable. To infer a strict preference reliably, an observer would need to witness an agent's decisions from a variety of choice sets, distinguished by the status quo that prevails, and would declare x to be strictly preferred to y only if the agent sometimes selects x when y is available and never selects y when x is available. An absence of strict preference would be declared if x is selected from some choice set that contains y and y is selected from some choice set that contains x. In the latter case, the pattern of these selections might well reveal something about the agent's state of mind. For example, if x and y are always both selected whenever one is selected and both are available, then the agent would appear to regard the options as interchangeable in every respect; on every occasion, the agent displays an active judgment that x is as good as y and vice versa.

But to avoid getting bogged down in this squishy terrain and to satisfy, for the sake of argument, the strictest demands of behaviorism, I will adopt the orthodox view that our only information about an agent is a strict preference relation $\succ$. Limiting our information to $\succ$ will avoid the impression that the observational distinction between indifference and incompleteness that I will introduce has been smuggled into the starting point. The epistemology of which preference judgments are knowable will in any event turn out to be a red herring; indifference can be distinguished from an absence of preference no matter how that issue is resolved.

Since in this chapter $\succ$ rather than a weak preference relation $\succsim$ will be our primitive, I will place assumptions on $\succ$ rather than $\succsim$. A defining feature of a strict preference is its asymmetry: $x \succ y$ and $y \succ x$ cannot hold simultaneously. When neither holds, I will for brevity write $x \sim^* y$ which in the orthodox vocabulary means that x and y are indifferent. This convention defines the binary relation $\sim^*$ and I will say that $\succ$ *leads to* $\sim^*$.

Though a wide gulf separates the assumption that only the strict preference $\succ$ is observable from the conclusion that $\succ$ cannot be used to distinguish between indifference and incompleteness, the mainstream of preference theory routinely makes this leap without remark. It is true that

$x \sim^* y$ cannot by itself tell us whether x and y are indifferent or unranked. But, as we will see, the entirety of $\succ$ can make this distinction. Since incompleteness will be inferred from $\succ$ alone, no principle of behaviorist methodology will be breached.

Once we have pinned down an operational distinction between indifference and incompleteness, I will return to the question of which relationship is more likely.

6.1 INTRANSITIVE INDIFFERENCE

There are hints in the classical literature on preferences of the 1950s and 1960s that a strict preference $\succ$ might be used to distinguish indifference from incompleteness. The suggestion is easy to miss, however, since it was camouflaged as the intransitivity of indifference, or the intransitivity of $\sim^*$ in our terminology.[2]

One reason routinely given for why $\sim^*$ might be intransitive is that transitivity would require implausible powers of discrimination. For example, an agent who prefers more sugar to less but cannot detect small differences might make the ranking $x \succ y$ between two different quantities of sugar only when the difference in the number of grains is greater than, say, 5. Since then $108 \sim^* 105 \sim^* 102$ but not $108 \sim^* 102$, $\sim^*$ is intransitive. This model, which originated with Luce (1956), achieved wide recognition but its standing did not rise beyond an amendment to classical rationality, a friction to be acknowledged when a magnifying glass focuses intently on alternatives that are nearly identical.

The more significant cases of an intransitive $\sim^*$ occur with the incomplete and transitive weak preferences $\succsim$ of Chapters 3 and 4 where agents do not know how to compare disparate alternatives. Suppose we extract the strict preference $\succ$ that is defined by $\succsim$, that is, we retain only the pairs where $x \succsim y$ and not $y \succsim x$ hold and ignore the indifferences that $\succsim$ specifies. The incompleteness of $\succsim$ will then reappear as the intransitivity of $\sim^*$. In Figure 4.1, a bundle x slightly to the northeast of s is neither strictly preferred nor strictly dispreferred to s'. Consequently $\sim^*$ is intransitive: $s \sim^* s'$, $s' \sim^* x$, and yet $x \succ s$.

The incomplete preferences considered in Chapters 3 and 4 therefore lead to an intransitive $\sim^*$ when we switch to representing agents by their

---

[2] Armstrong (1948, 1950) and Luce (1956) were key early proponents of intransitive indifference. Fishburn (1970a) surveys comprehensively.

strict preferences. Indeed, with some perseverance, each case of incompleteness in this book could be reread as an intransitive $\sim^*$. But had we begun with intransitive indifference, the possibility that an agent does not have a complete set of preference judgments would be easy to miss – as it often has been. The presentation of incompleteness would be convoluted at best.

An intransitive $\sim^*$ moreover raises the specter of the dangers of intransitive choice considered in Chapter 4. As we saw, agents who freely trade options they cannot rank can be manipulated (Example 4.1) but they will be protected if they stick to the status quo and their strict preferences are transitive. A partition of the pairs that are $\sim^*$-related into indifference and incompleteness relations, in addition to letting us see whether indifference or incompleteness is more common, will also let us examine if and when intransitive indifference exposes agents to harm. Our conclusions will fit with our earlier status quo advice: you can potentially fall prey to manipulation if your $\sim^*$ is intransitive but only if you agree to trade the options we will classify as unranked.

A further drawback of the merging of indifference and incompleteness in $\sim^*$ appears when we try to build a weak preference from $\succ$ and $\sim^*$. No matter which $\sim^*$-related pairs we label as indifferent, if $\sim^*$ is intransitive the weak preference that results will fail to be classically rational. But that failure does not tell us which axiom of classical rationality is violated.

Formally, let $\succ$ and thus $\sim^*$ be defined on some domain of alternatives. A candidate indifference relation $\sim$ drawn from $\sim^*$ defines the weak preference $\succsim$ that equals the union of $\succ$ and $\sim$ (the $\succsim$ where $x \succsim y$ if and only if $x \succ y$ or $x \sim y$).[3] The following result, proved in the Appendix, shows that intransitive indifference implies that any such $\succsim$ fails to be classically rational and supplies a converse as well. I assume that a binary relation $\sim$ must be symmetric ($x \sim y$ implies $y \sim x$) to qualify as an indifference relation.

Theorem 6.1 *Let the strict preference $\succ$ lead to $\sim^*$ and suppose the indifference relation $\sim$ satisfies $x \sim y$ only if $x \sim^* y$. If $\sim^*$ or $\succ$ is intransitive then the union of $\succ$ and $\sim$ cannot be classically rational. If both $\succ$ and $\sim^*$ are transitive then the union of $\succ$ and $\sim^*$ is classically rational.*

---

[3] Each binary relation R under discussion – whether $\succsim$, $\succ$, $\sim$, or $\sim^*$ – is defined as a set of ordered pairs of alternatives and xRy means that (x, y) is an element of R. The union of $\succ$ and $\sim$ is therefore the binary relation that contains (x, y) if and only if (x, y) is an element of either $\succ$ or $\sim$.

So a transitive strict preference $\succ$ is compatible with classical rationality if and only if $\sim^*$ is transitive. But the merging of indifference and incompleteness in $\sim^*$ stops us from diagnosing any breakdown of classical rationality. Indeed, in nominating an indifference relation drawn from an intransitive $\sim^*$ we can pick our poison. If the indifference relation is all of $\sim^*$ then the resulting weak preference $\succsim$ will be complete but intransitive. Any other symmetric indifference relation will leave $\succsim$ incomplete but $\succsim$ can at least be transitive if $\succ$ is transitive, for example, if we label no pairs with $x \sim^* y$ as indifferent.

As I have remarked, orthodoxy holds that it is impossible and pointless to single out some pairs of $\sim^*$-related items as indifferent and to label the remainder as unranked. These claims will not survive minimal scrutiny. While $x \sim^* y$ does not dictate whether indifference or incompleteness holds between x and y, no methodological principle, behaviorist or otherwise, decrees that pairs of alternatives must be examined in isolation. As we will see, the information in an agent's strict preference relation $\succ$ taken as a whole can distinguish with precision between indifferent and unranked options. An agent's weak preferences can then be identified and the intransitivity of $\sim^*$ will imply that these weak preferences are incomplete.

Moreover the distinction between indifference and incompleteness that I will lay out in the next section does make predictions about behavior: it lays down which trades can lead an agent to inferior outcomes and thus are less likely to occur and which trades are risk-free. This connection is tight enough that we could instead use the risky and risk-free trades to define indifference and incompleteness relations. An agent that freely trades alternatives classified as unranked will be exposed to manipulation and a refusal to make such trades will protect an agent from harm, as with the status quo maintainers of Chapter 4. But the emphasis here will be different. For the alternatives classified as indifferent, agents do not need to refuse trades in order to remain free from manipulation, they can trade these items at will. Once an intransitive $\sim^*$ is partitioned into indifferent and incompleteness relations, the underlying weak preference that emerges will be transitive when $\succ$ is transitive, thus reestablishing the connection between transitivity and being free from manipulation.

After pinning down a dividing line between indifference and incompleteness, we will return to the main theme, an empirical test that shows that when agents cannot declare a strict preference, incompleteness is more likely than indifference to be the cause.

6.2 INDIFFERENCE VERSUS INCOMPLETENESS

The naive way to figure out if an agent is indifferent between two alternatives is to ask. Consider an agent with impeccably rational strict preferences, those that generate a Cobb-Douglas utility. Letting bundles $z = (z_1, z_2)$ consist of two goods, $x \succ y$ holds if and only if $x_1^{\delta_1} x_2^{\delta_2} > y_1^{\delta_1} y_2^{\delta_2}$. The agent might be cooperative enough to fill in indifference judgments that match standard Cobb-Douglas weak preferences by declaring $x \sim y$ whenever $x \sim^* y$ or equivalently $x_1^{\delta_1} x_2^{\delta_2} = y_1^{\delta_1} y_2^{\delta_2}$. The classically rational $\succsim$ that results is then defined by $x \succsim y$ if and only if $x_1^{\delta_1} x_2^{\delta_2} \geq y_1^{\delta_1} y_2^{\delta_2}$. The agent could alternatively declare the same $\sim$ except for one pair of bundles a and b with $a_1^{\delta_1} a_2^{\delta_2} = b_1^{\delta_1} b_2^{\delta_2}$ that the agent decides is not preference ranked after all: instead of $a \sim b$, the agent reports that neither $a \succsim b$ nor $b \succsim a$ obtains. The $\succsim$ that results then will not be transitive since for any $c \neq a, b$ with $c_1^{\delta_1} c_2^{\delta_2} = a_1^{\delta_1} a_2^{\delta_2} = b_1^{\delta_1} b_2^{\delta_2}$, we have $a \succsim c \succsim b$ but not $a \succsim b$. Another possibility is that the agent declares for every pair with $x \sim^* y$ that neither $x \succsim y$ nor $y \succsim x$ obtains. Then $\succsim$ will equal $\succ$ and will be transitive.

These declarations might correspond to different patterns of choice behavior. It could be that with the first declaration the agent is willing to trade a for b and vice versa, whereas with the second and third declarations the agent refuses such trades, as a status quo maintainer might. Or perhaps with the second and third declarations the agent does remain willing to swap a and b. It will come as no surprise that none of these trading rules can lead the agent to harm.

Nothing turns on trades of Cobb-Douglas utility ties and certainly not on whether Mr. Cobb-Douglas declares a and b to be indifferent or unranked. Even if the agent asserts that a and b are unranked, the options remain functionally equivalent: the bundles strictly preferred to a coincide with the bundles strictly preferred to b and the bundles strictly dispreferred to a coincide with the bundles strictly dispreferred to b. Bundles a and b provide an example of the implicitly indifferent pairs that I used to define implicitly incomplete strict preferences in Section 4.4. We can harness this definition of equivalence to fence off indifference from incompleteness. Keep in mind that an asymmetric strict preference relation $\succ$ and the $\sim^*$ to which $\succ$ leads provide the primitive description of an agent.[4]

---

[4] The definitions to come roughly follow the lead of Mandler (2009) though the present definitions do not presume that $\succ$ is transitive. The binary relation $\approx$ below is long-standing, see Fishburn (1970b) for example.

Definition 6.1 *Alternatives x and y are **behaviorally indifferent**, or $x \approx y$, if, for all alternatives w, $(w \succ x \Leftrightarrow w \succ y)$ and $(x \succ w \Leftrightarrow y \succ w)$ and **behaviorally incomplete**, or $x \perp y$, if $x \sim^* y$ and not $x \approx y$.*

As promised, the definitions above of indifference and incompleteness (and Definition 6.2 to come) draw solely on the information in an agent's strict preference $\succ$.

The first fruit of Definition 6.1 is an answer to the question "which axiom of classical rationality is violated when $\sim^*$ is intransitive?" When $\succ$ is transitive, the verdict of Definition 6.1 is clear: $\sim^*$ is intransitive if and only if the weak preference that results from Definition 6.1 is incomplete. Let $\succ \cup \approx$ be the weak preference that preserves $\succ$ and declares any pair of $\approx$-related alternatives to be indifferent: $\succ \cup \approx$ labels x as weakly preferred to y if and only if either $x \succ y$ or $x \approx y$.[5] It is straightforward to show that if $\succ$ is transitive then $\succ \cup \approx$ is also transitive. Moreover, due to Theorem 6.1, we know that $\succ \cup \approx$ cannot be classically rational when $\sim^*$ is intransitive. Hence $\succ \cup \approx$ must be incomplete.

Theorem 6.2 *If $\succ$ is transitive and $\sim^*$ is intransitive, then $\succ \cup \approx$ is transitive and incomplete.*

So if $\approx$ is the appropriate definition of indifference, an intransitive $\sim^*$ is not a sign of intransitive weak preferences when $\succ$ is transitive: an intransitive $\sim^*$ instead offers an alternative representation of incomplete weak preferences. This path to incompleteness is circuitous but it leads ultimately to the same destination.

When $a \approx b$ holds, an exchange of a and b will not change an agent's position relative to alternative possibilities. If the agent prefers c to a then $a \approx b$ implies that the agent also prefers c to b. So the agent would give up a to acquire c or, if the agent first switches from a to b, would give up b to acquire c. And any trade the agent would agree to following a switch from a to b will not leave the agent worse off relative to a. We saw in Section 4.4 that agents who do not know how to rank some pairs of alternatives can protect themselves from harmful sequences of trades by sticking to the status quo. But trading a for b or b for a when $a \approx b$ poses no such risks. Even if as a matter of psychological fact the agent cannot assess whether a or b delivers greater welfare, the agent can act "as if" a and b are indifferent and freely exchange them without any exposure to manipulation.

[5] See footnote 3.

This observation suggests a substitute definition of behavioral incompleteness that declares incompleteness to hold between two $\sim$*-related options when a trade of the options *does* risk lowering an agent's welfare. Under this proposal, incompleteness obtains between alternatives x and y when neither $x \succ y$ nor $y \succ x$ obtains but where a trade of x and y in conjunction with further seemingly safe trades will harm the agent, the very danger that status quo maintenance aims to protect an agent from. The new definition characterizes behavioral incompleteness: the two definitions turn out to be equivalent.

A willingness to trade a single pair of $\sim$*-related alternatives will not expose an agent to danger. If $\succ$ is transitive and $x \sim^* y$ then the extended preference $\succsim^*$ that adds indifference between x and y to $\succ$ cannot lead an agent by a chain of $\succsim$*-improvements to an inferior alternative. Formally, for any pair a and b, let $a \succsim^* b$ hold if and only if either $a \succ b$ or $\{a, b\} = \{x, y\}$. The agent would then be led by $\succsim^*$ to an inferior alternative if there is a chain $w_1 \succsim^* \cdots \succsim^* w_n$ such that $w_n \succ w_1$. If there were such a chain then there would also be a chain such that x and y are neighbors and do not appear elsewhere in the chain. If say $w_i = x$ and $w_{i+1} = y$ then

$$y \succ w_{i+2} \succ \cdots \succ w_n \succ w_1 \succ \cdots \succ w_{i-1} \succ x$$

which by the transitivity of $\succ$ would lead to the contradiction $y \succ x$. Similarly, $w_i = y$ and $w_{i+1} = x$ would lead to the contradiction $x \succ y$.

The danger of trading unranked alternatives instead comes when an agent agrees to trade more than one $\sim$*-related pair. Define $x \dashrightarrow y$ to mean that either $y \succ x$ or $y \sim^* x$. If the agent is willing to give up alternative x for alternative y whenever x is not strictly preferred to y then $\dashrightarrow$ indicates the trades the agent will agree to.

Definition 6.2 *Alternatives x and y form a **dangerous trade** if $x \sim^* y$ and there is an alternative z such that either (i) $z \succ x$ and $z \dashrightarrow y \dashrightarrow x$ or (ii) $x \succ z$ and $x \dashrightarrow y \dashrightarrow z$ or (i) or (ii) hold when x and y are interchanged.*

The two definitions of incompleteness coincide, which suggests that they identify a well-founded distinction.[6]

---

[6] A third definition of incompleteness that follows the philosophical theory of incomparability defines two alternatives to be *incomparable* if they are unranked by $\succ$ and an improvement or diminishment in one of the alternatives does not necessarily lead it to be strictly ranked relative to the other alternative (Raz [1986, chapter 13]). It would be inappropriate to label such alternatives indifferent: if initially the welfare levels they

Theorem 6.3 *Two alternatives are behaviorally incomplete if and only if they form a dangerous trade.*

Proof. Suppose first that $x \perp y$. Then, exchanging the labels x and y if necessary, there is a z such that either $(z \succ x$ and not $z \succ y)$ or $(x \succ z$ and not $y \succ z)$. In the first case $z \dashrightarrow y \dashrightarrow x$ and in the second $x \dashrightarrow y \dashrightarrow z$. So in both cases x and y form a dangerous trade. Conversely, suppose x and y form a dangerous trade. Again exchanging labels as needed, there is a z such that either $(z \succ x$ and $z \dashrightarrow y \dashrightarrow x)$ or $(x \succ z$ and $x \dashrightarrow y \dashrightarrow z)$. In the first case, $z \dashrightarrow y$ implies not $z \succ y$. Since $x \sim^* y$ due to x and y forming a dangerous trade, we have $x \perp y$. In the second, $y \dashrightarrow z$ implies not $y \succ z$ and once again $x \perp y$. ∎

For an application of this common definition of incompleteness, let's return to the sugar example but suppose now that there are two colors of sugar, white and brown. Assuming the colors have the same taste, a bundle of white and brown grains $x = (x_w, x_b)$ will be strictly preferred to $y = (y_w, y_b)$ if and only if $(x_w + x_b) - (y_w + y_b) > 5$. With this definition of $\succ$ we have $x \approx y$ if and only if $x_w + x_b = y_w + y_b$. If $x \perp y$ and assuming that $x_w + x_b > y_w + y_b$ for concreteness then

$$0 < (x_w + x_b) - (y_w + y_b) \leq 5.$$

Bundles x and y then form a dangerous trade: just one further agreement to trade bundles not ranked by $\succ$ will lead to a welfare-diminishing sequence of trades. For example, if the agent agrees to trade x and any $z = (z_w, z_b)$ such that $z_w + z_b = x_w + x_b + 5$ then the sequence $z \dashrightarrow x \dashrightarrow y$ leaves the agent worse off.

Theorem 6.3 complements the Theorem 4.3 conclusion that status quo maintenance, though it displays intransitivities of choice, protects an agent with incomplete preferences from welfare-diminishing trades.[7] Theorem 6.3 adds the converse that if an agent throws caution to the wind and freely trades a pair of alternatives that are behaviorally incomplete, then the agent will be courting danger: a willingness to exchange

---

deliver were tied then the improvement or diminishment should lead to a strict preference. Incomparability is equivalent to the two definitions of incompleteness in this chapter (Mandler [2009]).

[7] Theorem 4.3's demonstration of intransitive but rational choice behavior notably did not rely on agents selectively choosing whether to trade $\approx$-equivalent options. The status quo maintainers in the Theorem never switch to $\approx$-equivalent options when the status quo remains available.

just one more pair of unranked alternatives will lead the agent to trade away welfare.

6.3 INCOMPLETENESS CROWDS OUT INDIFFERENCE

You may recall Jamie and Pat from the Introduction, the couple trying to settle on a movie who both pled indifference – apparently unaware that for orthodox preferences over bundles of goods indifference is a vanishingly unlikely event. One empirical benefit of consumer theory with incompleteness is that it is no longer so unusual for an agent to fail to strictly rank a chance pair of alternatives. When for example the strict preference $\succ$ arises from unanimity aggregation, pairs of alternatives that are $\sim^*$-related (not $\succ$-ranked) arise robustly. Figure 6.1, which is consistent with unanimity aggregation, illustrated this fact when there are two goods. More generally, if each candidate preference is continuous and all strictly rank some pair x and y but do not agree on which option is better, then $x \sim^* y$ and any small adjustment of x and y will leave the candidate rankings unchanged; the adjusted versions of x and y will therefore also be $\sim^*$-related.[8]

This reasoning casts some doubt on the veracity – or at least the self-understanding – of Jamie and Pat. The definitions of indifference and incompleteness from Section 6.2 will allow us pose the contest between indifference and incompleteness formally. Letting $\succ$ be a strict preference relation, we ask: which is more likely for a pair x and y, that indifference holds, $x \approx y$, or that there is no preference, $x \perp y$? Since incompleteness is the cause of the abundance of $\sim^*$-related pairs, the $\perp$-related pairs should presumably outnumber the $\approx$-related pairs. But the contest turns out to be more lopsided: the $\approx$-related bundles nearly vanish altogether. Incompleteness crushes the textbook indifference curve.

Suppose due to unanimity aggregation or some other source of incompleteness that we can add increments to a bundle y with $y \sim^* x$ to yield a new bundle z that is also $\sim^*$-related to x. See Figure 6.2, where again $SB(x)$ is the set of bundles strictly preferred to x and $SW(x)$ is the set of bundles that x is strictly preferred to. Under mild assumptions, that $\succ$ is weakly increasing and transitive, x will then be $\perp$-related to both y and z and to each bundle in the interior of the box in Figure 6.2 formed by y and z. Incompleteness thus holds when alternatives are drawn from sets

---

[8] The preference $\succsim$ is *continuous* if $\{y \in X : y \succ x\}$ and $\{y \in X : x \succ y\}$ are open sets, where $\succ$ is the strict preference derived from $\succsim$.

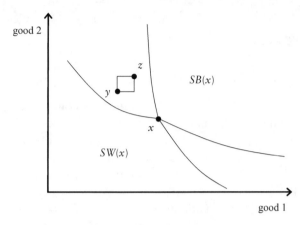

FIGURE 6.2 Robust incompleteness

of positive area, a contrast to textbook indifference curves which with L goods are $L-1$ dimensional sets.

Theorem 6.4 *Suppose the strict preference $\succ$ is weakly increasing and transitive and that $y \sim^* x$ and $z \sim^* x$ for some $z \gg y$. Then $y \perp x$, $z \perp x$, and $w \perp x$ for any w such that $z \gg w \gg y$.*

Proof. Since $\succ$ is weakly increasing, $z \succ y$. Given that $z \sim^* x$, this implies that it is not the case that $y \approx x$. And given that $x \sim^* y$, $z \succ y$ implies that it is not the case that $z \approx x$. Therefore $y \perp x$ and $z \perp x$.

For any w such that $z \gg w \gg y$, the increasingness of $\succ$ implies $z \succ w \succ y$. Suppose that $w \succ x$. Then the transitivity of $\succ$ would imply $z \succ x$, contradicting the assumption that $z \sim^* x$. Similarly, $x \succ w$ would imply $x \succ y$, contradicting $y \sim^* x$. Thus $w \sim^* x$ and hence, as in the previous paragraph, $w \perp x$. Theorem 3.2 relied on similar reasoning. ∎

The bundle z in Theorem 6.4 could lie on the boundary of $SB(x)$ and y could lie on the boundary of $SW(x)$. So, unlike $SB(x)$ and $SW(x)$ as they pictured on classroom blackboards, where the boundaries of these sets form an indifference curve, the boundaries can now consist of $\perp$-related bundles. A path can therefore travel from bundles strictly preferred or dispreferred to x to a bundle that is $\perp$-related to x without passing through indifference. In fact, if the assumptions of Theorem 6.4 hold then as Figure 6.2 is drawn the proof of the Theorem implies that every bundle that is not in $SB(x)$ or $SW(x)$ (except for x itself) is $\perp$-related to x. Every point on the boundary of $SB(x)$ or $SW(x)$ besides x is therefore either $\succ$- or

⊥-related to x: the indifference curve in Figure 6.2 is a singleton. This extreme conclusion is however an artifact of Figure 6.2; the boundaries of $SB(x)$ and $SW(x)$ can intersect at multiple points, not just at x. And if there were a further intersection v then adding or subtracting increments from v will result in a bundle that is $\succ$-related to x. Theorem 6.4 therefore does not imply that $v \perp x$ in such a case: v can be indifferent to x.

But under mild conditions, the boundaries of $SB(x)$ and $SW(x)$ can intersect only at isolated points. Indifference therefore comes close to disappearing. So, if we let preferences be incomplete to accommodate the failure of agents to strictly rank so many options, Jamie and Pat's claims of indifference become even more unconvincing. The incomparability we must add to give their claims a fighting chance chases away even the limited scope for indifference that classical preferences permit.

To establish the unlikeliness of indifference, I will go a little further than the local incomparability requirement that an agent's better-than sets are supported by multiple price or normal vectors (Chapter 3); I will assume that the supporting sets always have at least a minimum size.

The set of normal vectors of common length that support $SB(x)$ at x is given by

$$N(x) = \{p \in \mathbb{R}_+^L : p \cdot (x' - x) \geq 0 \text{ for all } x' \in SB(x) \text{ and } \|p\| = 1\}.$$

Let the *radius* $r(x)$ of $N(x)$ equal the maximum r such that, for some $p \in N(x)$, all p' that lie within distance r of p are also in $N(x)$. Formally,

$$r(x) = \sup\{r \in \mathbb{R} : \exists p \in N(x) \text{ such that }$$
$$(\|p - p'\| \leq r \text{ and } \|p'\| = 1) \Rightarrow p' \in N(x)\}.$$

To define when the agent's better-than sets display kinks of at least some minimum size, suppose that as x varies $r(x)$ is bounded away from 0: there is a $\varepsilon > 0$ such that $r(x) \geq \varepsilon$ for all x. When this condition holds, I will say that $\succ$ is *nontrivially kinked*.

In addition to $\succ$ being nontrivially kinked, which is the heart of Theorem 6.5 below, I will also restrict the agent's consumption to a compact $X \subset \mathbb{R}_+^L$, and assume that $\succ$ is convex, which here will mean that the set $SB(x)$ is convex for each $x \in X$, and weakly increasing.

The test for concluding that indifference is rare will be that each bundle indifferent to an arbitrary x is isolated. Since X is compact, isolation in turn means that the set of bundles indifferent to x is finite. If this test is

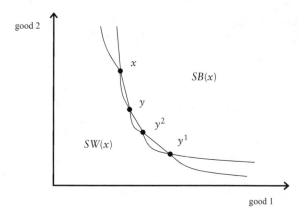

FIGURE 6.3 Four indifferent bundles and the linearity of $SB(x)$ as $y^n \to y$

met, indifference will be exceptionally rare compared to the uncountably many pairs in X that a classical preference would deem to be indifferent.

In Figure 6.3, for any $z \approx x$ the increasingness assumption implies that any bundle to the southwest of z must be in $SW(x)$ and any bundle to the northeast of z must be in $SB(x)$: the $\approx$-equivalent (indifferent) bundles can arise only where $SB(x)$ and $SW(x)$ touch, that is, where their closures intersect. So, in Figure 6.3, only the four identified points are $\approx$-equivalent to x. Suppose, contrary to Figure 6.3, that infinitely many bundles are $\approx$-equivalent. Then there will be a sequence $\langle y^n \rangle$, with each $y^n \approx x$, that accumulates at some point y. Narrowing our focus to a subsequence of $\langle y^n \rangle$, we may assume that the y^n quantities of good 1 are either all greater than or all less than the y quantity of good 1, either $y_1^n > y_1$ or $y_1^n < y_1$ for all n. Letting the first possibility hold for concreteness, Figure 6.3 illustrates with points y^1 and y^2. For each y^n, the radius of the set of normal vectors of common length that supports $SB(x)$ at y^n will be greater than some minimum size (since $SB(x) = SB(y^n)$). Equivalently, in this two-good case, there is a positive minimum width for the intervals formed by the slopes of the price lines that support $SB(x)$ at the y^n. But since $SB(x)$ is convex, any sequence of slopes for the price lines that support $SB(x)$ – one price line for each y^n – must converge to the most horizontal price line that supports $SB(x)$ at y. So as we proceed along the sequence of indifferent bundles, $y^1, y^2, \ldots$, the surface of $SB(x)$ would become progressively more linear as it approaches y. The radius of $N(y^n)$ would therefore converge to 0. But that would violate the assumption that $\succ$ is nontrivially kinked.

Theorem 6.5 *If ≻ is convex, weakly increasing, and nontrivially kinked then for any x ∈ X only finitely many y ∈ X can satisfy y ≈ x. If in addition ≻ is transitive then infinitely many y ∈ X will satisfy y ⊥ x.*

The second half of Theorem 6.5 shows that omnipresent kinks (of non-negligible size) by themselves imply incompleteness, as I mentioned in the Introduction and Section 3.2. Local incomparability, which is cast solely in terms of kinked better-than sets, is therefore aptly named.

Theorem 6.5 indicates that indifference – where an agent feels that two alternatives are truly interchangeable – is one of the great fictions of economics. Though the indifference curve is ubiquitous in textbooks, a small dose of local incomparability, a nod to realism, will lead the construction to all but disappear.[9] When agents cannot declare a strict preference between alternatives, it is far more likely that they cannot come to any judgment at all. The indecisive vacillator – Buridan's ass – has the better claim to the title of Homo Economicus.

---

[9] This conclusion aligns with Tversky (1972).

PART II

ECONOMIC ANALYSIS AND POLICY
WITHOUT PREFERENCES

7

Marginal Utility and the Volatility of Prices

7.1 THE CLASSICAL PURPOSE OF MARGINAL UTILITY

Consumers in the everyday models of economics are locally decisive: they smoothly substitute one good for another. While the marginal utilities that lay behind substitutability were a point of pride for the neoclassical pioneers, economic theory by the mid-20th century could no longer see what the smooth indifference curve was designed to do. The marginal utility parables of early neoclassical economics did in fact serve a purpose: the willingness of agents to make substitutions in consumption buffers a society from shocks and modulates the reaction of market prices. Economies that display little or no substitutability will be volatile; small changes in supplies or other parameters will lead to a dramatic response in prices whether in the markets for necessities or luxuries. An unprecedented cold spell can send the price of access to the power grid soaring; the shifting fads of social conventions can lead to inelastic consumer demand and boom-and-bust prices. Marshall's insistence that nature does not jump downplayed these scenarios: the reaction of marginal utilities and equilibrium prices to shocks in this view should be muted.

In early neoclassical orthodoxy, the equilibrium price ratio of a two-good exchange economy equals the ratio of marginal utilities of any agent who consumes both goods. Let each consumer i have a differentiable, concave, and increasing utility function u^i and let $D_k u^i(x^i)$ be the marginal utility of good k when i consumes bundle x^i. If p_1 and p_2 are the equilibrium prices of the goods and $x^i \gg 0$ is i's equilibrium consumption then

$$\frac{D_1 u^i(x^i)}{D_2 u^i(x^i)} = \frac{p_1}{p_2}.$$

Now let the environment change slightly, say by an increase in the aggregate endowment of good 1. Each agent's equilibrium consumption will then normally change slightly in response. Since u^i is concave, $D_1 u^i(x^i)$ and $D_2 u^i(x^i)$ are continuous functions of x^i and a small shift in x^i will therefore lead to a small change in $\frac{D_1 u^i(x^i)}{D_2 u^i(x^i)}$ and thus in the equilibrium price ratio as well. The local decisiveness of early neoclassical utilities should therefore eliminate or at least dampen price volatility, even for necessities.

If instead, contrary to the early neoclassical vision, marginal utilities fail to be well-defined at an equilibrium then the addition of a quantity of good 1, no matter how small, can lead to a discrete change in prices. Suppose for each consumer i that u^i represents a safety-biased preference and that Λ^i is one of i's rays of safe bundles (Section 5.2). Let the u^i remain concave and increasing. Due to safety bias, u^i will fail to be differentiable at points on Λ^i and an interval of normalized prices will support i's better-than set at each x^i on Λ^i. Beginning from an equilibrium where agents consume on these safe rays, a small increase in the endowment of good 1 may force some or all agents off their safe rays. The new equilibrium prices that result, which must support these agents' better-than sets at their new consumptions, will then have to fall outside their initial intervals of supporting prices. So, as long as prices begin in the interior of some of these intervals, prices must jump discretely in response to the endowment change. See Figure 7.1 where the price line that supports j's better-than set at a point $\tilde{x}^j$ that is off Λ^j lies outside of the interval of price lines that support Λ^j.

Life is complicated however. In addition to the case at hand where an endowment shock forces some consumers off their safe rays, there are other cases where consumers can remain on their safe rays; a rearrangement across individuals of the scale of their consumption can sometimes adapt aggregate demand to an endowment change. And when some consumers are forced off their safe rays, the safety-bias price response to an endowment change will be discontinuous but it does not have to be large. If at the initial equilibrium consumers' better-than sets are supported by only a narrow band of relative prices – because consumers display only a minimal failure of substitutability – then the price volatility that results may well be small. So although an absence of smooth substitution in consumption undercuts one source of price stability, there may be other lines of defense to fall back on. An economy's capacity to deal with disruptions

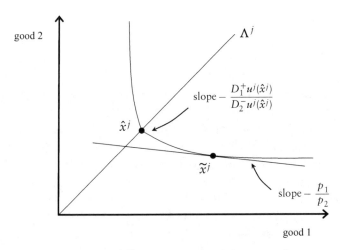

good 2

Λ^j

slope $-\dfrac{D_1^+ u^j(\hat{x}^j)}{D_2^- u^j(\hat{x}^j)}$

$\hat{x}^j$

$\tilde{x}^j$

slope $-\dfrac{p_1}{p_2}$

good 1

FIGURE 7.1 Indifference curve restrictions on prices

in supply is not cut and dried; the buffer of substitutability depends on the content of preferences, not as postwar economic theory would have it on necessary features of competitive equilibria.

To fill in some details for the volatile case, the concavity of the utilities implies that each u^i, although it fails to be differentiable on its safe rays, will still have well-defined left- and right-hand derivatives at these points. Let the economy begin at an equilibrium where each i consumes some x^i on some safe ray Λ^i and the equilibrium price ratio lies in the interior of an interval of price ratios that support Λ^i and hence strictly between

$$\frac{D_1^+ u^i(\hat{x}^i)}{D_2^- u^i(\hat{x}^i)} \quad \text{and} \quad \frac{D_1^- u^i(\hat{x}^i)}{D_2^+ u^i(\hat{x}^i)}$$

for each i and $\hat{x}^i$ on Λ^i. Following an increase in the endowment of good 1, there may not be any allocations where each i consumes on Λ^i. A simple case occurs when each Λ^i is the 45° line, the ray through $(1, 1)$. Since each x^i initially lies on Λ^i, the ex ante aggregate consumption of the goods must be equal, and hence after the increment of good 1 arrives the supply of good 1 will outstrip the supply of good 2. Some agent j's new consumption $\tilde{x}^j$ must then satisfy $\tilde{x}_1^j > \tilde{x}_2^j$ and hence the new equilibrium price ratio $\frac{p_1}{p_2}$ can no longer lie in the interval of price ratios that support Λ^i. See Figure 7.1.

Prices can thus become volatile when agents lack well-defined marginal utilities. An increment to the endowment, no matter how small, can lead to a discrete price change. This conclusion redeems the early neoclassical focus on margins though not the presumption that each agent at every consumption bundle has a single, well-defined marginal rate of substitution that responds nicely to changes in the environment. Had the early neoclassicals only separated the valid claim that margins govern equilibrium prices from the shakier assumption that agents have unique marginal rates of substitution, they could have acknowledged that individual valuations and market prices can be turbulent.

The volatility of prices that can accompany safety bias rests on individual consumptions that cluster to some extent – as in the case above where each agent consumes on the 45° line. For goods that vary by the state or date, the full-insurance and intertemporally-constant bundles (multigood versions of a 45° line) may well qualify as safe for each agent. Extreme clustering, where all agents consume on the same ray, is then possible. The locally decisive utilities of neoclassical orthodoxy lie at the opposite extreme: agents never stick to any ray and volatility does not arise. In between lies the messy real world, where agents often stick to specific patterns of consumption but those patterns may or may not be diverse enough to prevent volatility. In the rare cases when economic theory has peered into the world of nonconvex or nonsmooth preferences, it has presumed that diversity is substantial, a questionable judgment that rests on the prejudice that individuals are driven by independent desires rather than molded by common origins.

Production will play midwife to the volatility of prices that stems from safety bias: it ensures that an economy's aggregate endowments occur at just the points where volatility obtains. But production can also engineer the movement of resources across time that can cure or ameliorate volatility. It is the first exhibit of several to come in the remainder of the book where production rather than preferences drives equilibrium and alleviates economic disorder.

7.2 THE GENERAL EQUILIBRIUM REBUTTAL

That well-behaved marginal utilities help explain why equilibrium prices respond smoothly to changes in the economic environment would once have been a routine observation: the willingness of agents to substitute one good for another helps moderate the scarcities and other surprises of economic life. Postwar general equilibrium theory has since muddied the waters. The theory of regular economies, initiated by Debreu (1970), has argued that equilibria where relative prices jump discontinuously in reaction to small changes in the endowments of goods are exceedingly unlikely to arise when the parameters of a model are drawn randomly.[1] The regularity literature can allow agents to be safety-biased. So among the equilibria claimed to be unlikely are those where safety-biased agents at first consume along rays of safe bundles but where small endowment changes can force some of them to shift their consumption off these rays. While the absence of marginal utilities along the safe rays implies that prices would have to jump discontinuously in response, the regularity literature argues in rebuttal that the parameters where this scenario unfolds will nearly never occur.

Depending on how the regularity literature is interpreted, the conclusion that the volatile scenarios are unlikely is either false or misleading: safety bias can lead to price volatility. General equilibrium theory has been blinded by its focus on exchange rather than production. Among the parameters that this literature deems to be random variables are an economy's stocks of goods, an unobjectionable assumption in a world of pure exchange. But when the stocks of goods are the outcome of production decisions, those decisions can be precisely geared to land agents along their rays of safe bundles. A focus on exchange also hides the possibility that production can sometimes cushion the disruptive effect of discontinuities in agents' marginal valuations: production can shift the distribution of consumption across time to stop agents from being forced off their safe rays.

To lay out the general equilibrium position, let there be $L \geq 2$ goods with prices $p = (p_1, \ldots, p_L)$ and let each consumer i have a safety-biased preference with finitely many rays of safe bundles that can be represented by an increasing and concave utility u^i that fails to be differentiable only at points on these rays. Individuals will often display considerable commonality in their rays of safe bundles. One of the canonical cases of safety bias, the maxmin model of preferences under uncertainty (Section 5.4), can generate complete commonality.

Example 7.1 (maxmin) Each of the L goods is a single commodity delivered contingently at one of $L > 1$ states. Each agent i has a closed and strictly convex set of distributions Π^i with more than one element and a von-Neumann-Morgenstern utility v^i for consumption at each state that is concave, differentiable, and increasing.[2] Agent i then has the

---

[1] See Mas-Colell (1985) for an overview and Pascoa and Werlang (1999) and Rigotti and Shannon (2012) for more specific results pertinent to the models in this chapter.

[2] The set Π^i is *strictly convex* if, for all pairs of distinct distributions π and π' in Π^i and all $0 < \alpha < 1$, $\alpha\pi + (1-\alpha)\pi'$ is in the interior of Π^i (relative to the simplex Δ).

maxmin objective function $\min_{\pi \in \Pi^i} E_\pi v^i$ which when evaluated at the random variable $x^i = (x_1^i, \ldots, x_L^i)$ equals $\min_{\pi \in \Pi^i} \sum_{\omega \in \Omega} \pi_\omega v^i(x_\omega)$. We know from Theorem 5.2 that the preferences this objective function represents are safety-biased and that the ray Λ through the full-insurance bundle $(1, \ldots, 1)$ is safe. So if each individual satisfies the assumptions above Λ will serve as a common ray of safe bundles.

Each agent's maxmin utility will also be differentiable off Λ. To see this, observe first that when x^i is not on Λ there will be a unique probability in Π^i that solves $\min_{\pi \in \Pi^i} E_\pi v^i(x^i)$. Suppose to the contrary there are distinct solutions π and π'. Then $\tilde{\pi} = \frac{1}{2}\pi + \frac{1}{2}\pi'$ would also be a solution and, since the strict convexity of Π^i implies that $\tilde{\pi}$ is interior, we could construct an improvement by decreasing $\tilde{\pi}_k$ for some k where $x_k^i = \max [x_1^i, \ldots, x_L^i]$ and increasing $\tilde{\pi}_l$ for some l where $x_l^i = \min [x_1^i, \ldots, x_L^i]$. The uniqueness of the solution to $\min_{\pi \in \Pi^i} E_\pi v^i(x^i)$ in turn implies that the solution to $\min_{\pi \in \Pi^i} E_\pi v$ is a differentiable function of the L-vector v at $(v^i(x_1^i), \ldots, v^i(x_L^i))$: this is the content of what is sometimes called the duality theorem (Rockafellar [1970, ch. 25]). Since v^i is a differentiable function, $\min_{\pi \in \Pi^i} E_\pi v^i$ is a composition of differentiable functions and therefore is itself differentiable at any x^i off Λ. Thus with multiple maxmin agents of the type described, every individual i shares the common ray of safe bundles Λ and has an objective function that is differentiable off Λ. ■

In intertemporal choice each agent might view the constant consumption streams as the safe choices, as in Example 5.1. Each agent's utility will then fail to be differentiable on the common ray of safe bundles through $(1, \ldots, 1)$, just as in Example 7.1. As these cases illustrate, the rationale for why some individual consumes on a particular ray of safe bundles can apply to many individuals at once, though volatility does not require such an extreme commonality.

For the general model, $\{\Lambda^1, \ldots, \Lambda^N\}$ will qualify as a *family of safe rays* if each agent i in the economy has a safe ray that belongs to the family. Each Λ^h is parameterized by some bundle $a^h > 0$ that Λ^h that intersects. Let e^i be individual i's initial endowment of goods.

The regularity literature that followed in the wake of Debreu (1970) has argued that if the e^i and the a^h parameters are drawn from continuous distributions, then it is virtually certain that for any competitive equilibrium that results any small change in endowments will lead to a small change in the equilibrium. Specifically if ex ante each i consumes on a safe ray then any small change in endowments will lead to a new equilibrium where each i will continue to consume on the same ray and at nearly the same scale. Equilibrium prices will also change only slightly from their original values rather than shifting discretely. Volatility is therefore an unusual event.

To assess this argument, suppose that an equilibrium *assigns* each agent to consume on some ray in the family $\{\Lambda^1, \ldots, \Lambda^N\}$ and that the first order conditions for each agent hold strictly. That is, for an agent i assigned to Λ^h there is a Lagrange multiplier $\lambda^i \geq 0$ for i's utility maximization problem and a scale $\gamma^i \geq 0$ of i's consumption on Λ^h such that

$$D^+ u^i(\gamma^i a^h) < \lambda^i p < D^- u^i(\gamma^i a^h). \qquad \text{(FOC)}$$

For $\gamma^i a^h$ to be affordable when i's endowment is e^i, the budget constraint

$$p \cdot \gamma^i a^h = p \cdot e^i \qquad \text{(BC)}$$

must be satisfied. Finally, letting I be the number of individuals, market clearing – demand equals supply – requires that

$$\sum_{h=1}^N a^h \left(\sum_{i \in \Gamma^h} \gamma^i \right) = \sum_{i=1}^I e^i, \qquad \text{(MC)}$$

where Γ^h is the set of agents assigned to Λ^h.

Given an assignment of agents to the family $\{\Lambda^1, \ldots, \Lambda^N\}$, a p and $\gamma = (\gamma^1, \ldots, \gamma^I)$ is a *safe equilibrium* for this assignment if MC holds, $\sum_{i \in \Gamma^h} \gamma^i > 0$ for each h, and for each i BC holds and there is a $\lambda^i \geq 0$ such that (γ^i, λ^i) satisfies FOC. This definition rules out some borderline cases. First, in what amounts to an accounting convention, rays with 0 consumption are excluded from the family of safe rays, and second the first-order conditions that hold along safe rays are not permitted to hold with equality.[3] Since a safe equilibrium is defined relative to an assignment of agents to safe rays, an economy can have multiple safe equilibria associated with different assignments; and of course there can be equilibria where one or more agents do not consume on a safe ray.

The safe equilibria fall into two types. A safe equilibrium is *regular* if any small change in the economy's endowments $e = (e^1, \ldots, e^I)$ is compatible with a new equilibrium for the same assignments of agents to rays and the scale of each i's equilibrium consumption is a continuous function of e. Equilibrium price volatility then does not arise. A safe equilibrium is *critical* if there is a small endowment change that either moves some agent i off his or her ex ante safe ray or causes the scale of some i's

---

[3] Put differently, the second feature requires that, for each consumer i, p lies in the relative interior of the set of prices that support i's better-than set at $\gamma^i a^h$.

equilibrium consumption to respond discontinuously. Prices are then volatile. The prevailing view in general equilibrium theory is that the regular cases predominate.

Example 7.2 In the examples of volatility in Section 7.1, small endowment changes disrupt a safe equilibrium and lead equilibrium prices to jump. That conclusion might suggest, contrary to the regularity literature, that safe equilibria are always critical. That is not the case. A redistribution of buying power across agents can sometimes adjust demand to supply; the different proportions of goods consumed by different agents may be able to play the same role as substitution within individual consumption bundles. Suppose $L = N = I = 2$, where Λ^1 and Λ^2 are parameterized by the bundles a^1 and a^2, and that each individual i has a concave utility u^i that is differentiable off the ray Λ^i. Since $\Lambda^1 \neq \Lambda^2$, a^1 and a^2 cannot be proportional. Using γ^i to indicate the scale of i's consumption on Λ^i, let u^1 and u^2, endowments $\bar{e} = (\bar{e}^1, \bar{e}^2)$, and $(\bar{p}, \bar{\gamma}, (\bar{\lambda}^1, \bar{\lambda}^2)) \gg 0$ satisfy for $i = 1, 2$,

$$D^+ u^i(\bar{\gamma}^i a^i) < \bar{\lambda}^i \bar{p} < D^- u^i(\bar{\gamma}^i a^i), \qquad \text{(FOC}_{\text{Ex}}\text{)}$$

$$\bar{p} \cdot \bar{\gamma}^i a^i = \bar{p} \cdot \bar{e}^i, \qquad \text{(BC}_{\text{Ex}}\text{)}$$

$$\bar{\gamma}^1 a^1 + \bar{\gamma}^2 a^2 = \bar{e}^1 + \bar{e}^2. \qquad \text{(MC}_{\text{Ex}}\text{)}$$

So $(\bar{p}, \bar{\gamma})$ forms a safe equilibrium when agents 1 and 2 are assigned to Λ^1 and Λ^2 respectively and the endowments equal $\bar{e}$. Following a small exogenous change in e, small adjustments in the scales of consumption γ^1 and γ^2 can clear markets (MC$_{\text{Ex}}$) which in turn will require a redistribution of buying power (BC$_{\text{Ex}}$). As is standard in general equilibrium theory, one of the four equations in BC$_{\text{Ex}}$ and MC$_{\text{Ex}}$ is redundant and the above conditions do not pin down the price level (if you multiply $\bar{p}$ by $\alpha > 0$ and the $\bar{\lambda}^i$ by $\frac{1}{\alpha}$ the conditions will remain satisfied). Suppose that $\bar{\gamma}^1 a^1 \neq \bar{e}^1$. There is then a continuous function f from e to (p, γ) such that $f(e)$ will satisfy the price normalization $p_1 + p_2 = 1$ and BC$_{\text{Ex}}$ and MC$_{\text{Ex}}$ when the endowments equal e.[4] The function f can be found in two steps. First, for any given e, solve the linear equations MC$_{\text{Ex}}$ for γ, thus adjusting aggregate demand to e. Then solve one of the budget constraints and the normalization, which are linear once γ is fixed, for p, thus adjusting the distribution of buying power. It follows that f is continuous and that $f(\bar{e}) = (\bar{p}, \bar{\gamma})$. Consequently if e is near $\bar{e}$ then $f(e)$ will be near $(\bar{p}, \bar{\gamma})$ and hence $f(e)$ and $(\bar{\lambda}^1, \bar{\lambda}^2)$ will jointly satisfy FOC$_{\text{Ex}}$.

---

[4] Agent 1 does not have special status: if $\bar{\gamma}^1 a^1 \neq \bar{e}^1$ then MC$_{\text{Ex}}$ implies $\bar{\gamma}^2 a^2 \neq \bar{e}^2$.

So $f(e)$ forms a safe equilibrium – in fact the only safe equilibrium near $(\bar{p}, \bar{\gamma})$ when endowments equal e. The equilibrium $(\bar{p}, \bar{\gamma})$ we began with is consequently regular: small endowment changes lead to small equilibrium responses. ∎

There is nothing pathological about the regular equilibrium in Example 7.2. In some cases, therefore, agents can consume along safe rays and stick to those rays when endowments shift or the economy is buffeted by some other shock. But the regularity literature goes further: it argues that with high likelihood all of the safe equilibria will be regular. Although this conclusion will crumple under inspection, it will be helpful to lay out an explicit regularity analysis of safe equilibria; although safety bias is hardly a common modeling choice, it is easily tackled by regularity tools.

Fixing the utility functions for the agents, let an *array of parameters* be the endowments $e = (e^1, \ldots, e^I)$ and the bundles $a = (a^1, \ldots, a^N)$ that define a family of safe rays through these bundles. When a property holds for a full (Lebesgue) measure set of arrays, then it holds *almost always*.

Theorem 7.1 *Fix an assignment of agents to a family of safe rays. For almost every array of parameters, every safe equilibrium for the assignment will be regular. Moreover given a regular safe equilibrium $(\bar{p}, \bar{\gamma})$ for one of these arrays $(\bar{a}, \bar{e})$, there is a continuous function f of the endowments e such that (1) for each e near $\bar{e}$, $f(e)$ is the only safe equilibrium for the assignment near $(\bar{p}, \bar{\gamma})$ when endowments equal e and (2) $f(\bar{e}) = (\bar{p}, \bar{\gamma})$.*

Theorem 7.1 reiterates Example 7.2: if the economy begins at a regular safe equilibrium then small shocks will lead to small price responses. The theorem focuses on the safe equilibria solely to concentrate on the likeliest candidates for volatility. Similar conclusions hold for the equilibria where some or all agents consume off their safe rays.

Theorem 7.1 suggests that the critical safe equilibria that lead to volatility can be dismissed as highly unlikely. A full reply to this claim will have to wait until the next two sections. For now, we will take a preliminary look at the specifics of the critical equilibria and see why under a superficial view they might appear unlikely.

Letting the economy-wide level of consumption on ray Λ^h be represented by $y^h = \sum_{i \in \Gamma^h} \gamma^i$ and the profile across rays by $y = (y^1, \ldots, y^N)$, we can rewrite the market-clearing condition MC as

$$\sum_{h=1}^{N} a^h y^h = \sum_{i=1}^{I} e^i, \qquad (\text{MC}^*)$$

or, defining the matrix $A = \begin{bmatrix} a^1 \cdots a^N \end{bmatrix}$, as

$$Ay = \sum_i e^i.$$

Consider a safe equilibrium where the number of safe rays on which individuals consume is less than the number of goods: individual consumption thus clusters to some degree. Then MC* will have more equations than unknowns – the y^h – or equivalently A will have more rows than columns. As a consequence, when endowments change there are not enough y^h variables that scale aggregate consumption to clear all of the goods markets. In fact, MC* will have no solution for almost every value of e. Most changes in endowments will therefore push some agent i off the ray on which i originally consumed. Price volatility then results for the reasons given in Section 7.1: to satisfy the first-order conditions of the agents that depart from their safe rays, the economy's relative prices must respond discontinuously to an endowment change. The safe equilibrium at hand is therefore critical.

The preferences in Example 7.1 illustrate. If in an initial safe equilibrium each agent consumes on the ray of full-insurance bundles then MC* will consist of $L > 1$ equations (the number of goods and states) and one variable. The clustering of individual consumption is extreme in this case but with the benefit that the volatility is easy to grasp. Any change in the endowment that is not itself constant across states will force at least one agent to consume a bundle that varies by state; volatility therefore ensues. At the initial safe equilibrium, FOC implies that the prices p must be proportional to a probability π that is interior to each Π^i. For instance, if there are two states and agent i holds the set of probabilities $[\underline{\pi}_1^i, \overline{\pi}_1^i]$ for state 1 and consumes z at each state, then the equilibrium price ratio will lie initially in the interior of

$$\left[\frac{\underline{\pi}_1^i Dv^i(z)}{(1-\underline{\pi}_1^i)Dv^i(z)}, \frac{\overline{\pi}_1^i Dv^i(z)}{(1-\overline{\pi}_1^i)Dv^i(z)} \right] = \left[\frac{\underline{\pi}_1^i}{(1-\underline{\pi}_1^i)}, \frac{\overline{\pi}_1^i}{(1-\overline{\pi}_1^i)} \right].$$

Once an endowment change has moved some j off the ray of full-insurance bundles to a state-dependent consumption (x_1^j, x_2^j), agent j will calculate his or her expected utility using one of the extreme probabilities $\underline{\pi}_1^j$ or $\overline{\pi}_1^j$ for state 1. Agent j's ratio of marginal utilities $\frac{\pi_1^j Dv^j(x_1^j)}{(1-\pi_1^j)Dv^j(x_2^j)}$ and hence the equilibrium price ratio must therefore fall outside of the interval above. For instance, if $x_1^j > x_2^j$ following the endowment change then j will use the ratio of probabilities $\frac{\underline{\pi}_1^j}{(1-\underline{\pi}_1^j)}$ and, since v^j is concave,

$\frac{Dv^j(x_1^j)}{Dv^j(x_2^j)}$ can be no greater than 1. The endowment change thus leads the

equilibrium price ratio to drop to a value less than or equal to $\frac{\pi_1^j}{(1-\pi_1^j)}$.

The volatility above occurs when the goods outnumber the safe rays on which individuals consume. A more general precondition for volatility is that, given a family of safe rays that defines a matrix A, the rows of A are linearly dependent. A safe equilibrium defined for this family must satisfy the market-clearing requirement $Ay = \sum_i e^i$ but, due to linear dependence, this equality cannot continue to hold following most changes in e. Endowment changes will again force some agents off their safe rays and relative prices will shift discontinuously in response. The linear dependence of the rows of A provides a weaker condition for volatility since one route, but not the only route, to an A with linearly dependent rows occurs when there are more goods than safe rays on which agents consume: with $L > N$, the matrix A will have more rows than columns. A matrix A with $L > N$ in fact provides the generic case of linear dependence: for most choices of its entries, a matrix will have linearly dependent rows if and only if it has more rows than columns.

Theorem 7.1 is the general equilibrium camp's seemingly devastating response to the volatility scenarios we have considered. The very possibility of a solution y to MC* when the rows of A are linearly dependent can apparently be dismissed. Only for unusual endowments can there be an equilibrium where the rays on which individuals consume are defined by $a^1, \ldots, a^N$ that form a matrix A with linearly dependent rows.

In this general equilibrium perspective, there is nothing inherently problematic about agents who consume along rays of safe bundles and therefore fail to have well-defined marginal utilities. For the safe equilibria that are then likely to arise, each agent's consumption will continue to lie along the same ray when endowments or other parameters change slightly. The troublesome chain of events occurs when a small perturbation of endowments leads to a regime change that moves consumers from safe rays onto differentiable portions of their utility functions: prices must then jump in response. But it would seem that these scenarios are so unlikely that we can safely ignore them.

7.3 ENDOGENOUS VOLATILITY

The case for discarding the critical or regime-change equilibria where prices are volatile will not withstand closer examination. So far we have taken endowments to be given exogenously, a feature that holds for static models of pure exchange. When an economy proceeds through time, however, each period's endowment will be determined in part by past production decisions. The possibility then arises that firms will be forced by the requirements of equilibrium into producing exactly those outputs that lead to the endowments that generate volatility.

While this possibility might seem remote, it is not. Suppose agents can invest consumption today to earn an increase in some consumption good tomorrow. When agents' preferences for tomorrow's goods are safety-biased, the kinks in their better-than sets can cause the future utility return of such an investment to drop discontinuously at the point where the bundles of tomorrow's consumption achieved lie on agents' safe rays. This discontinuity will ensure that equilibrium investment can occur robustly at exactly the level at which the discontinuity occurs: the economy can systematically end up at the endowments where agents consume on their safe rays – the site of volatility. Since there are also plausible cases where firms do not produce these special endowment levels and the prices of tomorrow's goods therefore adjust smoothly to changes in tomorrow's environment, we cannot lay down general results that apply to all equilibria of all market economies. The only recourse is to lay down robust examples of both cases.

The economy will for simplicity have just two periods. At the initial date, labor can be used either to produce a single output at date 0 or can be invested to produce $L_1 \geq 2$ outputs at date 1. Each consumer i is endowed with labor and has an intertemporal utility function u^i that equals the sum of two increasing and concave per-period utilities u_0^i and u_1^i that are functions of date-0 consumption x_0^i and date-1 consumption $(x_1^i, \ldots, x_{L_1}^i)$ respectively. The single date-0 good can be viewed as a stand-in for a larger set of goods – though keep in mind that the goal is only to build robust examples.

Each agent's date-1 utility will represent a safety-biased preference and, throughout this section, these date-1 preferences will share a common ray of safe bundles Λ that passes through some bundle a, which will be a parameter of the model. A common Λ provides the quickest path to the matrix A of Section 7.2 having linearly dependent rows: since every agent at date 1 will consume on the ray through a, the A that arises at date 1 will be the column vector a with $L_1 \geq 2$ entries. Any other family of safe rays that leads to an A with linearly dependent rows would do just as well. We also need some technical assumptions on the utilities: each u_0^i will be differentiable while each u_1^i will be differentiable off of ray Λ and differentiable on Λ in the direction where date-1 consumption is constrained to lie on Λ.

The leading example of date-1 utilities that meet these conditions is the maxmin model of Example 7.1 where agents consume one good at each state of the world and a is proportional to $(1, \ldots, 1)$. The full-insurance bundles then lie on Λ, each agent's better-than set at these points is supported by a continuum of price vectors, and the differentiability of each i's von-Neumann-Morgenstern utility and the strict convexity of i's set of probabilities ensure that the differentiability assumptions above are satisfied.

Each good will be produced by a linear activity that uses only date-0 labor: the unit labor requirements will be $c_0 > 0$ for the date-0 output and $(c_1, \ldots, c_{L_1}) \gg 0$ for the date-1 outputs. I will assume through the remainder of this chapter that some small sacrifice of date-0 consumption can increase any agent's utility if to begin the agent does not consume any of the date-1 goods: for each i, $u_1^i \left(\varepsilon \frac{c_0}{c_1}, \ldots, \varepsilon \frac{c_0}{c_{L_1}} \right) > u_0^i(\varepsilon)$ for all $\varepsilon > 0$ sufficiently small. Pareto efficiency will then require that any agent that consumes anything at all must consume some of the date-1 outputs.

The budget constraint of a consumer i is

$$p_0 x_0^i + p_1 x_1^i + \cdots + p_{L_1} x_{L_1}^i \le w e_i^i,$$

where $e_i^i > 0$ is i's endowment of labor, p_0 is the price of date-0 output, and $(p_1, \ldots, p_{L_1})$ are the prices of the date-1 outputs. Since competitive equilibria are Pareto efficient, equilibrium demand for any good must exactly equal rather than fall short of supply. An *intertemporal equilibrium* therefore consists of prices for outputs $p = (p_0, p_1, \ldots, p_{L_1})$, a wage rate w, and consumption demands $x^i = (x_0^i, x_1^i, \ldots, x_{L_1}^i) \ge 0$ for each consumer i such that each x^i is utility-maximizing among bundles that satisfy i's budget constraint, the demand for labor equals supply,

$$c_0 \sum_i x_0^i + \sum_{k=1}^{L_1} c_k \sum_i x_k^i = \sum_i e_i^i,$$

the production activity for any good k that is produced breaks even, $p_k = w c_k$, and no activity makes positive profits.

Now consider an allocation where some agent i's date-1 consumption $(x_1^i, \ldots, x_{L_1}^i)$ does not lie on Λ. Let k and j be the date-1 goods that i consumes the least and most of respectively: x_k^i is the minimum and x_j^i is the maximum from $\{x_1^i, \ldots, x_{L_1}^i\}$. If the ratio

$$\frac{D_k u_1^i(x_1^i, \ldots, x_{L_1}^i)}{D_j u_1^i(x_1^i, \ldots, x_{L_1}^i)}$$

is sufficiently large then it will be efficient to reallocate at least some labor from good j to good k: a small reduction in x_j^i in favor of x_k^i will increase i's utility and harm no one. I will say that Λ-*efficiency* holds if, beginning from any allocation where some agent i does *not* consume on Λ, such a utility-increasing reallocation of labor exists or, equivalently, given a quantity of labor available for i's consumption u_1^i is maximized only if a bundle on Λ is produced. Since equilibria are Pareto efficient, Λ-efficiency implies that in any intertemporal equilibrium each agent i must consume on Λ at date 1. In the maxmin case, Example 7.1, Λ-efficiency will be satisfied if each Π^i is sufficiently near to the entire set of distributions.

If Λ-efficiency holds and agents in an intertemporal equilibrium therefore consume on Λ, the economy's endowments will end up at precisely a point where prices are potentially volatile. Any deviation in the date-1 outputs from what is produced in equilibrium that is not proportional to a will push some consumers off Λ and compel a discrete change in prices. In the maxmin example, agents in equilibrium will consume the same quantity at every state – and a small change in the aggregate endowment that is not itself constant across states will force some agents into consumptions that vary by state. In this and any other case where the matrix A that rules at date 1 has linearly dependent rows, volatility will normally result when the date-1 outputs are disrupted. To incorporate potential volatility as an equilibrium event, I will presently add these output disruptions to the model.

If on the other hand Λ-efficiency fails to hold then in intertemporal equilibrium agents can consume off Λ at date 1. When for instance agents have a sufficiently small marginal utility for good k an allocation where $\frac{x_k^i}{x_j^i} < \frac{a_k}{a_j}$ for each i can be efficient: it will not be worthwhile to switch production from good j to k. Small deviations in date-1 outputs then need not cause relative prices to jump discontinuously: consumers can remain on the same differentiable portions of their indifference curves and the price response can therefore be modest. Both the scenarios for potential price volatility and stability are robust possibilities.

Deviations in the date-1 outputs can be placed into the model by letting production be stochastic. Suppose that when a unit of labor is used to produce some date-1 good k its productivity is clustered around $\frac{1}{c_k}$ but rarely if ever equals $\frac{1}{c_k}$ exactly. The difference between the realization of good-k's labor productivity and $\frac{1}{c_k}$ will be given by a mean-0 random variable ε_k with finite support and a unimodal distribution whose mode is interior.[5] A state ω will indicate the independent realizations of these perturbations, one for each date-1 good. The state is revealed when the date-1 outputs appear.[6] When Λ-efficiency holds and the distributions assign sufficiently large probability to a sufficiently small interval, it will be efficient to choose labor inputs that lead to a distribution of date-1 outputs that is concentrated in a small neighborhood of Λ.

An intertemporal equilibrium must now introduce a price $p_k(\omega)$ for each date-1 good k at each state ω. The production of a date-1 good k will then break even if its revenue across states matches its cost, $\sum_{\omega} p_k(\omega) = wc_k$. Each consumer i maximizes the expectation of $u_0^i(x_0^i) + u_1^i(x_1^i, \ldots, x_{L_1}^i)$, where $x_1^i, \ldots, x_{L_1}^i$ are now random variables, subject to a budget constraint.[7] In equilibrium, prices – p_0, a $p_k(\omega)$ for each k and ω, and w – must clear the date-0 output market, the date-1 output market for each good k and state ω, and the labor market.

The intertemporal equilibria of the extended model remain Pareto efficient. Consequently, when Λ-efficiency holds and the uncertainty of the labor productivity perturbations (the ε_k) is small, the equilibrium distribution of date-1 outputs will lie in a small neighborhood of Λ. Since the perturbations have independent distributions and interior modes, a broad range of relative prices for the date-1 outputs will occur as the various date-1 outputs are realized. If moreover for each date-1 output the support of the perturbations lies in a sufficiently small interval then arbitrarily small changes in the realizations of the date-1 outputs can lead to a discrete price jump.

These volatility conclusions are robust to small changes in the parameters of the model – in the utility functions, the distributions of the productivity perturbations, and the bundle a that defines the safe ray Λ. Our assumptions of Λ-efficiency and that some investment in date-1 goods is utility-enhancing will also persist after a small change in parameters. So if ex ante the equilibrium realizations of the date-1 outputs lie

---

[5] That is, there exist $\underline{\varepsilon}_k$ and $\bar{\varepsilon}_k$ in the support of ε_k such that the mode $\hat{\varepsilon}_k$ of ε_k satisfies $\underline{\varepsilon}_k < \hat{\varepsilon}_k < \bar{\varepsilon}_k$.

[6] If output disruptions are added to the maxmin model then a state would specify both a realization of ε_k for each date-1 good k and one of the states given in the original non-disrupted model.

[7] Consumer i's budget constraint is now:

$$p_0 x_0^i + \sum_{\omega} \left(p_1(\omega) x_1^i(\omega) + \cdots + p_{L_1}(\omega) x_{L_1}^i(\omega) \right) \le we_i^i.$$

near the common Λ then they will continue to do so after a small change in parameters.

Just as when there is no uncertainty about output realizations, Λ-efficiency might not hold and agents might not consume in a neighborhood of Λ. Small changes in realized outputs then need not lead to pronounced volatility.

To sum up, let an *intertemporal model* specify utilities, labor endowments, and unit labor requirements that satisfy our stated assumptions. Fix a sequence of increasingly smaller productivity perturbations by letting the nth perturbation be the random variable $\frac{1}{n}\varepsilon_k$.[8] As n increases, all of the possible labor requirements will be near $(c_1, \ldots, c_{L_1})$. But for any n the realizations of the quantities of date-1 outputs produced will not always be proportional to a. Indeed the realized values of the output of any date-1 good k will sometimes lead to an oversupply relative to other goods and sometimes to an undersupply. A nonnegligible variance in the relative price of good k results.

Theorem 7.2 *There are intertemporal models such that, for all pairs of date-1 goods k and j, and all sufficiently small productivity perturbations, the equilibrium relative price $\frac{p_k}{p_j}$ will display a variance across states that exceeds a strictly positive lower bound. There are other intertemporal models where for each pair of date-1 goods k and j the variance of $\frac{p_k}{p_j}$ converges to 0 as the size of the perturbations converges to 0. Both conclusions are robust to small changes in the endowments and labor requirements and to small changes in the utilities that preserve a common safe ray.*[9]

The ill-defined marginal utilities brought by safety bias can therefore endogenously lead to price volatility. As any economist of the early 20th century would have taken for granted, the smooth trade-offs of the neoclassical consumer do serve an important purpose. Conversely, the early neoclassical confidence in local decisiveness led to a neglect of volatility and of related pathologies that the remainder of this chapter will explore.

The link between safety bias and price volatility identifies a divergence between the pursuit of individual welfare and its social consequences. As we saw in Chapter 5, agents are liable to seek out safe options when

---

[8] The probability of $\frac{1}{n}\hat{\varepsilon}_k$ for the nth perturbation will equal the probability of $\hat{\varepsilon}_k$ given by the original distribution.

[9] A changes in the utilities must have a small impact on the a that each Λ^i intersects and, for each i and $\gamma^i > 0$, on the vectors of one-sided partial derivatives $D^+u_1^i(\gamma^i a)$ and $D^-u_1^i(\gamma^i a)$ and on the directional derivative $D_a u_1^i(\gamma^i a)$.

they cannot figure out how to resolve a trade-off. Yet if all agents follow the same escape path the result for society as a whole can magnify the variability of equilibrium relative prices. Since individuals will usually be net buyers or sellers of some goods, the greater variability of prices will lead to greater variability in their welfare. Individual safety-seeking thus has the unintended collective consequence of making economic life riskier.

The conclusion that price volatility cannot be dismissed as a fluke event may seem to clash with the regularity literature of general equilibrium theory. At a formal level there is no clash and I intentionally have begun with a model where the volatility and regularity conclusions are easy to reconcile. Both classes of equilibria in the intertemporal models above – those with outputs on or near to Λ which lead to volatility and those distant from Λ – will typically qualify as regular and determinate: the equilibria are isolated from one another. When the quantities of date-1 goods produced are deterministic rather than random, the intertemporal equilibrium price of each date-1 good k must equal its cost of production: $p_k = wc_k$. Profit maximization therefore pins down the relative prices of outputs. When the results of production are random, typical models will continue to have determinate equilibria: if for each state, the realization of the labor productivity for the good produced at that state is treated as a parameter then for almost every array of parameters the aggregate date-1 outputs will not lie on Λ and consumers' ratios of marginal utilities will therefore pin down relative prices. It so happens that the equilibrium relative prices of goods will differ markedly across states but that fact is formally consistent with determinacy.

That generic, regular models are compatible with price volatility has gone virtually unnoticed in general equilibrium theory. From the general equilibrium point of view, the goods that appear at different states of the world are as distinct as different goods that appear at the same state. Just as the equilibrium price of apples need bear no particular relationship to the equilibrium price of oranges, the equilibrium price of tomatoes at one state is not tied to the equilibrium price of tomatoes at other states. Since in this view the realizations of the labor productivities across states are exogenous parameters and the set of states is fixed, the entire state-by-state vector of equilibrium prices typically will not respond discontinuously to small changes in the labor productivities or in other parameters. By modeling the randomness of output as a vector that lists the labor productivities at every state rather than as an exogenous shift of the model's parameters, the discontinuity of prices appears as a sizable difference in the price of output between nearly identical states rather than as a sizable response to a parameter change. As long as it remains clear that equilibrium prices will vary substantially in response to arbitrarily small output changes, this terminological sleight of hand will do little harm.

7.4 KNIFE-EDGE INDETERMINACY

Intertemporal equilibria are typically regular and isolated from one another; a continuum of equilibria will arise only in unusual models. But when production is certain, an intertemporal equilibrium can bring about date-1 outputs that define a *date-1 economy* where equilibria are critical and indeterminate: these equilibria are buried within an intertemporal equilibrium and will emerge only if markets reopen at date 1. To unearth this indeterminacy, we must depart from the Arrow-Debreu tradition where agents trade once at the beginning of economic time for delivery of goods at all dates. Agents will instead trade every period, using assets to transfers resources across time and spot markets to deliver their consumption at each date. Critical, indeterminate economies will then routinely appear as an intertemporal equilibrium unfolds through time. As in Section 7.3, we will consider models with only two time periods; in a longer time horizon trade would occur at every period and indeterminacy could arise systematically at any date except the initial time period.

The main model of Section 7.3 – where Λ-efficiency holds for a common safe ray Λ and productivity perturbations are absent – illustrates the principles at work. Each agent in an intertemporal equilibrium of this model consumes on Λ at date 1 and aggregate date-1 outputs therefore also lie on Λ. Now suppose that, instead of trading once, agents at date 0 exchange date-0 assets and consumption, in part influenced by the prices they expect to rule at date 1, and then trade again at date 1 for final consumption. Once markets open at date 1, relative prices can vary within a continuum without disturbing the equality of demand and supply at date 1: due to their safety bias, agents will continue to consume on Λ following the change in relative prices. These price variations will affect the scale of individual demands and utility levels and change how the date-1 stocks of output are divided among the agents, but markets will continue to clear. Although agents may well regret their date-0 decisions after the fact – once they see that the prices that rule at date 1 have diverged from the prices they anticipated – those regrets have no bearing on their trades at date 1.

The critical equilibria that lead to indeterminacy arise only at knife-edge configurations of the date-1 outputs, but as we have seen these special production levels can arise systematically in the later periods of an intertemporal equilibrium. The combination of indeterminacy that occurs only at a priori unlikely endowments and a dynamic process of production that generates exactly those endowments explains why safety bias can endogenously generate volatility when production levels are stochastic. Indeterminacy is the counterpart for nonrandom economies of the volatility that accompanies stochastic production.

If instead of safety bias, consumers obey the more radical model of local incomparability, where preferences are incomplete (Section 3.3), then the economy would not display indeterminacy only at knife-edge endowments. Locally incomparable consumers need not display the sudden jumps in marginal valuations that accompany safety bias; they instead have sets of margins that can respond continuously to changes in consumption. Volatility therefore does not arise as easily. Knife-edge indeterminacy also leads to further abnormalities: agents can reap substantial gains from manipulating market prices and therefore will not behave as the price-takers imagined in theories of perfect competition.

To show how an intertemporal equilibrium generates an economy that operates only at date 1, I will adapt the no-perturbation version of the model of Section 7.3. Each firm will produce some subset of the economy's goods with its purchase of date-0 labor for date-1 production funded by issuing shares. A consumer who at date 0 buys shares of firm j receives at date 1 a fraction of j's assets – the date-1 outputs that j produces – equal to i's ownership share of j. The consumers therefore have access to assets that allow them to carry wealth between the time periods. A consumer in the initial period will sell date-0 labor to acquire date-0 output and shares in firms, and then in the latter period trade for date-1 consumption by selling the date-1 outputs that his or her share holdings pay out.[10] Each good can be produced by at least one firm.

Each consumer i will again have a utility u^i that is a sum of date-0 and date-1 utilities u_0^i and u_1^i. Consumers are not required to share a common safe ray at date 1. We retain our earlier notation where applicable and let [1] indicate a vector of date-1 quantities, prices, or labor requirements. For example, $p[1] = (p_1, \ldots, p_{L_1})$. Let r denote the interest rate, θ^{ij} the share of firm j purchased by consumer i, and l^j the labor bought by firm j.

---

[10] The use of sequential budget constraints to model intertemporal equilibria was pioneered by Arrow (1964) and Radner (1972).

When prices are $(p[1], r)$ and firm j purchases labor that will produce $q^j[1]$, the firm's date-0 present value is $\frac{1}{1+r}(p[1] \cdot q^j[1])$.

Consumer i chooses $x^i = (x_0^i, x^i[1]) \geq 0$ and a $\theta^i = (\ldots, \theta^{ij}, \ldots)$ to maximize $u^i(x^i)$ subject to a date-0 and a date-1 budget constraint:

$$p_0 x_0^i + \sum_j \theta^{ij} \frac{1}{1+r}(p[1] \cdot q^j[1]) \leq we_i^j \text{ and}$$

$$p[1] \cdot x^i[1] \leq \sum_j \theta^{ij}\left(p[1] \cdot q^j[1]\right). \quad \text{(BC}_\text{seq})$$

Firm j chooses a vector of outputs $q^j = (q_0^j, q^j[1]) \geq 0$ and a $l^j \geq 0$ to maximize its present-value profits

$$p_0 q_0^j + \frac{1}{1+r}(p[1] \cdot q^j[1]) - wl^j$$

subject to

$$l^j \geq c_0 q_0^j + c[1] \cdot q^j[1],$$

where q_0^j or a coordinate of $q^j[1]$ must equal 0 if j cannot produce that good.

A *sequential-trading equilibrium* consists of prices (p, w, r), a (x^i, θ^i) for each consumer i, and a (q^j, l^j) for each firm j such that (1) each agent's action is optimizing given (p, w, r), (2) markets for labor, the date-0 good, and date-1 goods clear, and (3) $\sum_i \theta^{ij} = 1$ for each firm j.

The standard interpretation of a sequential-trading equilibrium imagines that agents at date 0 observe p_0, w, and the present value (market price) of each firm j and unanimously anticipate that $p[1]$ will rule at date 1. On this basis, each consumer i selects (x^i, θ^i) and each firm j selects and executes (q^j, l^j). Then at date 1 consumer i exchanges the goods i owns due to his or her share purchases, $\sum_j \theta^{ij} q^j[1]$, for date-1 consumption $x^i[1]$.

While sequential-trading equilibria let agents trade at each date, they are little more than a rewrite of the intertemporal equilibria à la Arrow-Debreu of Section 7.3: p_0, $p[1]$, r, w, and the x^i will form part of a sequential-trading equilibrium if and only if p_0, $\frac{1}{1+r}p[1]$, w, and the x^i form an intertemporal equilibrium. This equivalence follows from the fact that a consumption bundle is affordable for a consumer in the sequential-trading model when prices are p_0, $p[1]$, r, and w if and only if it is affordable in the intertemporal model when the prices are p_0, $\frac{1}{1+r}p[1]$, and w. Using the same transformation of prices, a (q^j, l^j) will

earn the same level of profits in the sequential-trading and intertemporal models. Perfect foresight implicitly underlies the equivalence of these
equilibrium concepts: the date-1 prices that agents anticipate at date
0 in a sequential-trading equilibrium must govern the prices of date-1
goods.

The surprises that sequential-trading equilibria can bring occur as
the equilibria play out. Following the date-0 trades and production
that a sequential-trading equilibrium prescribes, agents will arrive at
the markets for date-1 goods equipped with the standard prerequi-
sites of Walrasian trading: endowments and preferences. If, given some
sequential-trading equilibrium, a typical firm j initiates the production of
$q^j[1]$ at date 0 then consumer i will appear at date 1 with the endowment
$\sum_j \theta^{ij} q^j[1]$. The underlying sequential-trading equilibrium thus generates
a date-1 economy. A *date-1 equilibrium* of that economy is a $p[1]$ and
a $x^i[1]$ for each i that maximizes $u_1^i(\cdot)$ subject to the second budget
constraint in BC_{seq} such that demand equals supply, $\sum_i x^i[1] = \sum_j q^j[1]$.

If each consumer at date 1 chooses the bundle identified by the
underlying sequential-trading equilibrium, then the prices $p[1]$ previously
anticipated will clear markets at date 1: the $p[1]$ and $x^i[1]$ for each i specified by the sequential-trading equilibrium qualify as a date-1 equilibrium.
But since a date-1 equilibrium needs to satisfy no more and no less than
the standard requirements of Walrasian market clearing, the expectations
that agents held at date-0 of the underlying sequential-trading equilibrium are no longer relevant for the market behavior of agents once they
arrive at date 1. Why should a date-1 trader care whether or not the price
of good k covers the labor costs incurred at the previous date? Bygones
are bygones. Other candidates for date-1 equilibria are therefore equally
legitimate.

The date-1 equilibria moreover are ripe for indeterminacy. If consumers have a common safe ray Λ and Λ-efficiency holds, then the
aggregate date-1 outputs will lie on Λ and the prices $p[1]$ that rule in
the sequential-trading equilibrium will support each consumer i's better-
than set at $x^i[1]$. As long as FOC from Section 7.2 is satisfied for each
consumer when Λ is the consumer's safe ray, the date-1 equilibria will
display indeterminacy: small deviations in the relative prices defined by
$p[1]$ will leave each agent content to consume on Λ and will not disturb
market clearing.

To move beyond a common Λ to more general varieties of date-1
indeterminacy, we return to consumers that at date 1 have safety-biased

preferences that satisfy the assumptions of Section 7.2.[11] Suppose at some safe intertemporal or sequential-trading equilibrium that the number of date-1 goods L_1 is greater than the number of rays N in the minimal family of safe rays that contains each agent i's equilibrium date-1 consumption $x^i[1]$. The safe equilibria of Section 7.3 qualify as examples since there are at least two date-1 goods ($L_1 \geq 2$) and all of the date-1 consumptions lie on a single ray ($N = 1$). For any case with $L_1 > N$, the matrix A whose columns are the N bundles $a^1, \ldots, a^N$ that the rays intersect will have more rows than columns and hence its rows will be linearly dependent, the prerequisite of volatility. Let $q[1] = \sum_j q^j[1]$ be the equilibrium value of aggregate date-1 production, which equals equilibrium aggregate date-1 consumption $\sum_i x^i[1]$. Mimicking our terminology from Section 7.2, let Γ^h be the set of agents that consume on the ray through a^h at date 1 and let y^h be the scale of their date-1 consumption. The date-1 endowment of the consumers in Γ^h, acquired via date-0 share purchases, is given by $e^h = \sum_{i \in \Gamma^h} \sum_j \theta^{ij} q^j[1]$.

Suppose that $\bar{p}[1]$, $\bar{q}[1]$, and $(\bar{y}^h, \bar{e}^h)$ for $h = 1, \ldots, N$ rule in some intertemporal or sequential-trading equilibrium and that FOC (from Section 7.2) is satisfied. For a $p[1]$ near $\bar{p}[1]$ to qualify as a date-1 equilibrium price vector, the markets that open at date 1 must clear at $p[1]$. To pass this test, it is sufficient for the supply of date-1 goods to equal the date-1 consumption that occurs when, for each a^h, the consumption of the agents in Γ^h is determined by the value of their date-1 endowments. In short, $p[1]$ and the y^h must satisfy:

$$\sum_h a^h_k y^h = \bar{q}_k[1], \qquad \text{for } k = 1, \ldots, L_1,$$
$$p[1] \cdot y^h a^h = p[1] \cdot \bar{e}^h, \quad \text{for } h = 1, \ldots, N.$$

These two conditions imply that all requirements of a date-1 equilibrium are met. The inequalities in FOC, since they are strict to begin with, will remain satisfied when prices and the scale of consumption change slightly. And if for some h the second condition above is satisfied – all of the agents that consume on the ray through a^h can collectively afford their consumption – then each such agent can afford his or her individual consumption as well.

As usual, one of the equilibrium conditions is redundant and we can therefore ignore one of the final N equalities. To see that indeterminacy

---

[11] That is, each consumer i's date-1 safety-biased preference has finitely many rays of safe bundles and can be represented by an increasing and concave utility u^i_1 that fails to be differentiable at a point $x^i[1]$ if and only if $x^i[1]$ lies on one of these rays.

obtains, fix the y^h at their equilibrium values $\bar{y}^h$. The first condition above evidently remains satisfied as $p[1]$ varies. Since the remaining $N-1$ equalities are linear in p, the set of p's that solve these equalities has a dimension of at least $L_1 - (N-1)$. One of these dimensions is due to the fact that the price level is not pinned down. Adding the price normalization $\sum_{k=1}^{L_1} p_k[1] = 1$, the set of equilibrium relative prices contains a set of dimension $L_1 - N$ which by assumption is positive: there is at least one dimension of indeterminacy of relative prices. The volatility of prices if we were to let production be stochastic thus translates into the indeterminacy of date-1 equilibria when production is certain.

Theorem 7.3 *If an intertemporal equilibrium generates a date-1 economy that has a safe equilibrium such that $L_1 \geq N$ then there exists a set of date-1 equilibrium relative prices of dimension $L_1 - N$.*

Although not relevant for indeterminacy per se, the individual utility levels will typically vary as the equilibrium $p[1]$ changes. The aggregate consumption of the individuals that consume on one of the safe rays is fixed in the indeterminacy argument above, but the scale of consumption of the individuals that consume on this ray will usually change as $p[1]$ varies. As the qualifications typically and usually indicate, there are exceptions. For example, if each individual i's date-1 endowment coincides with his or her date-1 consumption, then small price changes will not affect any agent's utility. But if we introduce initial endowments of date-1 goods then the restrictions on which goods each firm produces will imply that consumers generally will not be able to make share purchases that exactly align their total date-1 endowments with their date-1 consumptions.

Although the date-1 markets may well be indeterminate, the intertemporal equilibrium that creates a date-1 economy will typically remain regular and determinate whether the equilibrium is given its original Arrow-Debreu definition or its sequential reinterpretation. In both versions, any change in date-1 prices must be compatible with market clearing at date 0 as well: equilibrium prices and quantities at both dates are determined simultaneously. In the sequential-trading interpretation, the prices that rule at date 1 are nailed to the expectations of those prices that agents form at date 0 and that requirement by itself delivers determinacy. To confirm this, observe that the equilibrium condition that governs the production of some date-1 good k at date 1 requires $\frac{1}{1+r}p_k = c_k w$ (or $p_k = c_k w$ in an intertemporal equilibrium). The relative prices of date-1 goods are therefore pinned down.

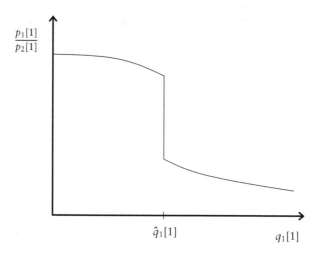

FIGURE 7.2 An indeterminate point of the equilibrium correspondence

The combination of indeterminacy when production is certain and determinate prices when production is subject to even the smallest amount of randomness underlies the volatility that accompanies safety bias. The map from date-1 supplies of goods to date-1 equilibrium relative prices – the equilibrium correspondence – will then display a continuum of values at one level of supplies but disparate single values at nearby supplies. For an economy with two goods at date 1, Figure 7.2 shows the date-1 equilibrium price of good 1 relative to good 2 as a function of the aggregate supply $q_1[1]$ of good 1, doled out to consumers according to some continuous formula, say, an equal gift to every consumer. All other parameters remain fixed. Indeterminacy obtains at a single value of the date-1 aggregate supply of good 1, labeled $\hat{q}_1[1]$ in the Figure. If for instance each consumer's safe ray for date-1 goods intersects $(1, 1)$, as in Example 7.1, then $\hat{q}_1[1]$ will equal the date-1 aggregate supply of good 2. A small increase in $q_1[1]$ relative to $\hat{q}_1[1]$ will force at least some agents to consume more of good 1 and drive its relative price to fall discretely while a small decrease in $q_1[1]$ will drive the relative price of good 1 up. Volatility is therefore a normal outcome when safety bias and the passage of time endogenously drive aggregate date-1 supplies near to the knife-edge values that lead to indeterminacy.

The power of knife-edge indeterminacy comes into relief when we compare it to cases where indeterminacy obtains at every level of aggregate supply and the entire set of equilibrium relative prices changes

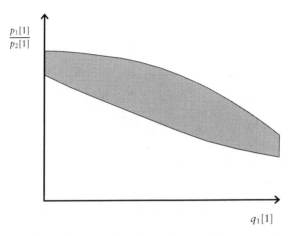

FIGURE 7.3 Indeterminacy at all points of the equilibrium correspondence

smoothly as a function of supplies. Local incomparability and the Bewley model of Section 3.4 in particular provide characteristic examples if consumers are willing to select as their market demands all preference-undominated affordable bundles.[12] There can then be a continuum of equilibrium relative prices that persists as $q_1[1]$ varies, as in Figure 7.3. Suppose for some equilibrium that prices lie in the interior of the set of prices that support each consumer i's better-than set (at the equilibrium value of $x^i[1]$) and, as in the Bewley model, each i's set of supporting price vectors changes continuously as a function of i's consumption. Then if $q_1[1]$ changes a small amount no agent i will be forced off the consumptions at which i's better-than set is kinked: the better-than set is kinked at every $x^i[1]$. Since the posited equilibrium prices lie in the interior of consumers' sets of supporting prices, agents will be content to consume the increments of date-1 goods they receive as $q_1[1]$ changes. This model therefore does not compel price volatility – indeed since indeterminacy is omnipresent, it is hard to come to any definitive conclusion about how prices will respond to endowment changes.

The curiosity of this comparison is that although local incomparability stakes out a more radical rejection of smooth indifference curves than safety bias, it is local incomparability that comes to the gentler conclusions. Agents under local incomparability are so pervasively agnostic about how to trade off goods that prices need not respond to fluctuations

[12] See Rigotti and Shannon (2005).

in supply: increments to endowments can simply change consumption without prodding agents into a market response. But if the absence of marginal utilities is embedded in complete preferences then agents can be so determined to secure a safe bundle that prices must respond sharply following an endowment change to induce them to give up the attempt.

7.5 VOLATILITY AND MANIPULATION

The volatility of relative prices induced by small changes in outputs undermines the foundation of competition, that each agent takes prices as given. Consider one of the indeterminate equilibria, possibly a date-1 equilibrium from Section 7.4, where each agent consumes along some safe ray Λ^h and the number of rays in the relevant safe family is greater than the number of goods. Since prices will then respond discontinuously to endowment changes, an agent by disposing of an arbitrarily small portion of his or her endowment can induce a discrete change in relative prices. The endowment reductions can usually be designed to lead to an advantageous price change. Suppose that a negligibly small endowment reduction can lead prices to change from p to $\hat{p}$. As long as there is some consumer j whose ex ante trades z^j satisfy $\hat{p} \cdot z^j \neq 0$, there must be a consumer i with $\hat{p} \cdot z^i < 0$ (since the ex ante trades clear the market, $\sum_i z^i = 0$). This consumer will gain from the price change since he or she can make the same trades at a lower cost and use the profits to consume more.

This argument rests on the discontinuity of the price response to an endowment change; otherwise the endowment loss needed to induce the price change might outweigh the fall in the cost of a would-be manipulator's ex ante trades. But as we saw in Section 7.2, when the number of safe rays outstrips the number of goods – or for some other reason the rows of A are linearly dependent – most arbitrarily small endowment changes will force some consumers off their safe rays and compel relative prices to respond discontinuously. Since the discontinuity will persist as the population size increases, agents will have an incentive to manipulate prices even in large anonymous markets.

Classical general equilibrium models are commonly said to behave differently. The incentive to act strategically is supposed to shrink as the number of agents increases; competitive price-taking behavior should therefore become rational in the limit. These arguments however presuppose that a small adjustment in a model's parameters, such as the economy's endowments, will lead to a continuous change in equilibrium prices and quantities.[13] The models we have considered – where indeterminacy obtains when production is certain and small endowment changes lead to discrete price responses – violate this continuity assumption. While such violations occur only at unusual endowments, the intertemporal model of Sections 7.3 and 7.4 shows that equilibrium production decisions at date 0 lead those endowments to arise routinely at date 1. So at the date-1 equilibria that result, price-taking need not be approximately rational even when the number of agents is large.

To avoid the game-theoretic details of a model of strategic behavior, I will show in a safety-bias example that the incentive for manipulation does not fade away as an economy grows in size.[14] Consider again one of the simplest cases of safety bias: the maxmin model of Example 7.1 with two states 1 and 2 and hence two goods, a nontrivial interval of probabilities common to all consumers,

$$\bigcap_i \Pi^i = \{(\pi_1, \pi_2) : \underline{\pi}_1^i \leq \pi_1 \leq \bar{\pi}_1^i \text{ for all } i \text{ and } \pi_1 + \pi_2 = 1\},$$

and equal aggregate endowments of goods $(\sum_i e_1^i = \sum_i e_2^i)$. I call this model an *equal-endowment maxmin economy*. As we have seen, equal aggregate endowments arise robustly at date 1 when this model is embedded in a two-period intertemporal production economy.

Prices $p = (p_1, p_2)$ that satisfy the normalization $p_1 + p_2 = 1$ can serve as equilibrium prices for an equal-endowment maxmin economy if and only if $p \in \bigcap_i \Pi^i$. For a consumer i with the maxmin preference $\succsim^i$, any p in Π^i will support the better-than set $B_{\succsim^i}(x^i)$ when x^i is constant across states (see Section 5.4). Hence if p lies in $\bigcap_i \Pi^i$ then each consumer i's first-order condition will be satisfied at the state-invariant consumption level γ^i defined by the budget constraint $(p_1 + p_2)\gamma^i = p_1 e_1^i + p_2 e_2^i$. It follows that $\sum_i \gamma^i = \sum_i e_1^i = \sum_i e_2^i$. Conversely any normalized p outside of $\bigcap_i \Pi^i$ will lead to a mismatch between demand and supply. One good k will become cheap relative to $-k$ in the sense that

$$\frac{p_k}{p_{-k}} < \min\left\{\frac{\pi_k}{\pi_{-k}} : \pi \in \bigcap_i \Pi^i\right\}$$

which will lead consumers to demand more of k than $-k$.

---

[13] See Mas-Colell (1983) for an overview of the literature on the limit behavior of general equilibrium models as the number of agents increases.

[14] For formal games of endowment manipulation, see Aumann and Peleg (1974), Postlewaite (1979), and implicitly Hurwicz (1979).

Definition 7.1 *An equilibrium of a maxmin economy with a normalized price vector* (p_1, p_2) *is* **manipulable** *if there exist a price increment* $\phi > 0$ *and a good* k *such that if any agent* j's *endowment of* k *is reduced by any* $\varepsilon > 0$ *and no other endowment is changed then the normalized equilibrium price for good* k *that results is greater than* $p_k + \phi$.

Agents wield considerable market power at a manipulable equilibrium: an arbitrarily small endowment reduction of either of the goods can increase that good's price discretely. In one exceptional case, where each agent has the same endowments of goods 1 and 2, no one will have an incentive to use that power: the rise in the value of the good that becomes scarcer will be fully counterbalanced by the fall in the value of the good that is disposed of. (This is the case mentioned earlier where the value of every agent j's ex ante trades z^j is 0 when evaluated at the prices $\hat{p}$ the endowment reduction leads to.) But state-invariant individual endowments would be unusual: typically any individual agent will have endowments of the two goods that differ. When embedded in a two-date model, production can adjust aggregate supplies to equalize the total stocks of the two goods at the latter date but production will typically not be able to equalize each individual's holdings. If agents can transfer wealth between time periods only by buying or selling shares in firms (which produce goods in specific proportions) then the sum of an agent's initial endowment and the outputs delivered by his or her shares will usually vary by state.

Beginning with I consumers, a *replication* is a model with nI consumers, where n is a positive integer, such that each $j \in \{1, \ldots, nI\}$ has the same utility function, endowment, and set of probabilities as the consumer in the original model whose index equals the remainder of j after division by I.[15]

Any equilibrium of an equal-endowment maxmin economy will be manipulable, regardless of how many times the model is replicated. A normalized equilibrium price vector p cannot be equal to both boundary points of $\bigcap_i \Pi^i$: either

$$p_1 < \max\{\pi_1 : \pi \in \bigcap_i \Pi^i\} \text{ or } p_1 > \min\{\pi_1 : \pi \in \bigcap_i \Pi^i\}$$

or both. Suppose for concreteness that the first condition holds. Then there is a discrete increase in the price of good 1 that any agent can engineer by disposing of an arbitrarily small quantity of that good. After

---

[15] That is, the consumer in the original model with index $j - I \left\lceil \frac{j}{I} \right\rceil + I$.

the disposal, some agent j must consume more of good 2 than good 1 in the equilibrium that results and consequently the ratio of the marginal utilities of good 1 to good 2 for this agent must be at least as great as

$$\frac{\max\{\pi_1 : \pi \in \Pi^j\}}{\min\{\pi_2 : \pi \in \Pi^j\}}.$$

This ratio will equal the limit of the ratio of j's marginal utilities that holds for a sequence of bundles with $x_2^j > x_1^j$ that converges to the $45°$ line (see Section 7.2 and Figure 5.3). The normalized price p_1 must therefore rise to at least $\max\{\pi_1 : \pi \in \Pi^j\}$. This argument applies without alteration no matter how many times the economy is replicated.

Theorem 7.4 *Any equilibrium of an equal-endowment maxmin economy or one of its replications is manipulable.*

Since self-interest would drive agents facing a manipulable equilibrium to exploit their influence over prices, classical models of competition will no longer give a plausible account of how markets function. The price-taking assumption of competitive equilibrium theory must therefore be dropped or at least reconceived. This conclusion moreover cannot be blamed on the usual suspects – agents who derive market power from their size. It is the absence of well-defined marginal utilities, due to safety bias, that undermines price-taking.

The potential for manipulation and the corrosion of price-taking are more complicated when the aggregate supplies of the two goods are random and the event where $\sum_i e_1^i = \sum_i e_2^i$ holds precisely is unlikely. Depending on how we model increases in the size of the economy, it could be that as the number of agents increases the likelihood that $\sum_i e_1^i$ and $\sum_i e_2^i$ are within any given distance will shrink to 0. In that case, no individual agent in a large economy will be able via an endowment disposal to switch which good has the greater supply; the incentive to manipulate prices will then disappear as the number of agents increases. But if for some small $\varepsilon > 0$ there is a positive floor to the probability that $\sum_i e_1^i$ and $\sum_i e_2^i$ are within distance ε, no matter how many times the economy is replicated, then the incentive to manipulate will not fade away. The economics in any event is clear. If the supply of goods is distributed tightly near points where the aggregate supplies are constant across states, then endowment manipulations will earn a substantial reward. If nearly equal aggregate supplies are a rare event – and the size of the economy may sometimes lead to that conclusion – then manipulation becomes a minor issue.

7.6 PRODUCTION AND VOLATILITY

The manipulability of prices that stems from safety bias suggests why the prices of produced goods are usually managed by their suppliers: auction markets do not offer a viable institutional arrangement. Suppliers can insure their customers against the volatility brought by safety bias by smoothing out extreme price variations or by bundling together goods for which consumers display safety bias.

Production can also alleviate price volatility by counteracting the output fluctuations that induce acute price changes. When for example the output of some good enjoys a windfall at date t, a transfer of some of the windfall to date $t + 1$ (and reduced production of the good at $t + 1$) may be able to return consumers to their safe rays or reduce the number of goods where consumption quantities deviate from their safe levels. The extent of relative price volatility then recedes. These dampening intertemporal movements of output can be accomplished in some cases by storage, which formally qualifies as a type of production. The ongoing nature of production thus explains both why volatility arises and how it is mitigated.[16] The intertemporal transfer of resources that raises the possibility of volatility gives firms the capacity to temper that volatility.

The upshot of safety bias is not therefore that, as an empirical matter, volatility and price manipulation are pervasive. Safety bias instead sets a theoretical agenda. Have institutions developed that curtail volatility and manipulation? Can production ease price volatility?

Although the active management of prices by firms is usually explained as an outgrowth of market power, safety bias implies that even goods that are produced for a competitive market will be subject to price setting. Since the special configurations of endowments that lead to volatility and manipulation can arise only when goods are produced, this analysis predicts that produced goods will be more likely to have managed prices, as is in fact the case.

7.7 THE SCOPE OF PRICE VOLATILITY

Despite the clear causal chain running from safety bias to price volatility, there is no firm dividing line that separates equilibria that display volatility from those that do not. Compare on the one hand equilibria where

---

[16] Chambers (2014) makes a somewhat similar argument about the capacity of production to eliminate the indeterminacy of equilibria in Bewley models.

agents consume on safe rays and the number of goods consumed is greater than the number of rays and on the other hand equilibria of a nearly-identical model where a few of the consumers instead have differentiable utility functions. As we have seen, in the former case a displacement of the aggregate supply of one good, no matter how small, will lead to a discrete change in relative prices. In the latter case, adjustments in the consumption of the differentiable agents will usually prevent a discrete price change when the endowment shock is sufficiently small. But there is a limit to the shock absorption that the differentiable consumers can accomplish: if they have to absorb the whole of a supply shock and they are few in number, the price response can be substantial. So although the safe equilibria with more goods than active safe rays deliver the mathematical simplicity that price responses are discontinuous, without that discontinuity price volatility can still appear.

Even an entire economy of differentiable consumers can lead to volatility. Suppose that we approximate a safety-biased preference with a ray of safe bundles Λ by a differentiable utility with marginal rates of substitution that change rapidly in a neighborhood of Λ. In an economy of consumers with this preference, a small change in endowments will once again lead to a large price response. Appropriate qualifications must be laid down of course: for a large price response, the endowment change cannot be small relative to the rate at which the ratios of marginal utilities change. Both of these approximations of a pure safety-bias model – where a few of the agents consume at points of differentiability or where marginal rates of substitution change rapidly – smooth the map from endowments to equilibrium prices. For example Figure 7.4, which can be viewed as a general equilibrium demand function, smooths Figure 7.2. Once these tweaks are introduced, there might not be equilibria that display a formal indeterminacy of equilibrium prices or where small supply shocks trigger a discontinuous price response. Instead equilibrium prices will change continuously but rapidly, since demand curves will be steep.

These mathematical variations do not change the fundamentals of price volatility. The heart of the classical explanation of the stability of relative prices is that there is a large pool of agents for whom small adjustments in consumption do not lead to dramatic changes in their marginal valuations. So, as long as the consumption impact of a supply disturbance is widely dispersed, the effect on consumers' ratios of marginal utilities and hence on relative prices will be modest. When agents' valuations instead respond precipitously to consumption changes, redistributions of buying power across individuals may come to rescue by helping to adjust

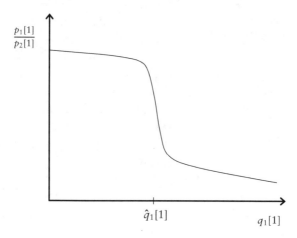

FIGURE 7.4 A smooth approximation of isolated indeterminacy

demand to supply, as we saw in Example 7.2. But one line of defense for price stability will be missing.

Viewed more abstractly, three conceptual ingredients must be in place for volatility to arise: the marginal valuations of goods must change rapidly as the consumption of goods shifts, time must pass to let agents accumulate goods in volatility-inducing configurations, and trading must be recurrent rather than once-and-for-all. The final item blocks the Arrow-Debreu idiosyncrasy of supposing that trade occurs only once when the economic clock takes its first tick, a trick that converts a dynamic into a static model and neuters the passage of time. In every temporal theory of markets besides the Arrow-Debreu general equilibrium model, agents trade repeatedly as time passes.

The starkest models of volatility arise when the valuation of goods is given by a nondifferentiable function; and these cases highlight the link to indeterminate equilibria. But utility functions do not have to be the source of the differentiability failure. When production functions display kinks, as in the linear activity analysis model, agents will over time accumulate factors of production in combinations that lead to indeterminate factor prices, thus setting the stage for volatility when factor endowments undergo a small further change.[17]

The early neoclassical economists did not understand with precision the exact conditions that drive indeterminacy and volatility. But their

---

[17] Mandler (1995, 1999a chapter 2).

founding visions were prescient. The paramount importance of well-defined marginal utilities in blocking price volatility needs no further emphasis. What is more surprising is that the social philosophy implicit in neoclassical economics – that agents' traits are determined independently of social interaction – should identify so precisely one of the key mathematical assumptions that can ensure determinacy and price stability. In a static model with randomly chosen parameters, traders meet with no advance planning, as if they had just stumbled across one another at an oasis in the desert. Determinacy and price stability are then secure. But when traders accumulate goods with an eye to market, as they will in a dynamic model, indeterminacy and volatility can arise.

A necessary link between safety bias and price volatility, that agents in their consumption decisions will flock to a small number of safe rays, also jars with the neoclassical presumption that individual preferences flow from separate springs. When economic theory has explored the demand functions that arise from unorthodox (e.g., nonconvex) preferences, it has gravitated to models where the diversity of individuals ensures that aggregate or mean demand is nicely behaved.[18] In the alternative laid out in this chapter, individuals shaped by common forces cluster and herd.

---

[18] See Sondermann (1975), Hildenbrand (1980), and Dierker et al. (1984).

8

The Trouble with Welfare Economics

When preferences are incomplete, the scope for government action narrows. If for instance agents are unable to pin down the trade-offs between the goods and services governments provide and their own private consumption then policymakers can find their hands tied; they will have no leeway to revise the arbitrary policies inherited from the past, even policies economists are loath to accept.

To take a simple case, consider a government that must decide whether to undertake a public works project, say a project that will help clean up the environment. Eager to lend a hand, a well-intentioned economist recommends that the decision be made by comparing the sum of agents' dollar valuations of the project to its cost. Suppose that due to incomplete preferences one or more agents have better-than (preferred) sets supported by multiple price lines and hence intervals of dollar valuations. Such an agent can fail to have a preference between undertaking the project (and paying his or her share of the cost) versus abandoning the project. The agent will be better off when the project is undertaken only if the cost the agent will have to pay is less than his or her minimum valuation and the agent will be better off when the project is canceled only if the payment averted is greater than the agent's maximum valuation. When the agent's payment falls between the minimum and maximum valuation, the agent cannot judge which decision is better.

As long as some individuals have intervals of valuations, the possible sums across agents of valuations will also range over an interval. With some luck, all of the sums will be greater than the project's cost or all of the sums will be less than the cost: economics can then give clear-cut advice. But the interval of possible sums might well be substantial.

152

For environmental quality, agents report sizable gaps between their maximum and minimum valuations: agents require hefty compensations to agree to a cutback in quality but will pay little for improvements.[1] And even if each individual band of valuations is thin, their sum can still be thick. Projects with costs that land inside the interval of summed individual valuations will therefore arise routinely. Individuals in such cases are unwilling to pay for a public good but they also would not want to lose the public good if it were the status quo, a common political predicament. Our economic adviser will then have nothing to say: both backing and rejecting the project will qualify as optimal.

So when agents lapse from the early neoclassical ideal by failing to pin down valuations of the goods that governments provide, a glut of optimal decisions can appear. The path from incompleteness to policy paralysis is straightforward, as the above sketch suggests, and Section 8.2 will provide detailed examples. Policy paralysis will arise in any allocative decision, not just a yes-or-no decision on one project, and in any classical version of welfare analysis, from sums of dollar valuations to utilitarian aggregations of individual satisfaction to Pareto efficiency. It can nevertheless be challenging to detect the paralysis amid the characterizations of efficiency that theoretical welfare economics focuses on and to see how as a practical matter applied economists continue to hand out precise policy recommendations.

In the early neoclassical era, the policy advice of economists was decisive and far-reaching. As long as agents had smooth utilities with diminishing marginal utility, any allocation would yield to the machinery of utilitarian maximization and that machinery would spit out a single solution. Edgeworth showed that a single distribution of income maximized the sum of utilities; Pigou argued that when a good generates an externality, only one tax rate will maximize national income which in turn he linked to the sum of utilities.[2] When the decades of utilitarian dominance fell to the Paretian assault of the 1930s and 1940s, welfare economics turned to Pareto efficiency to judge markets and other economic institutions. Since many policy decisions will qualify as optimal by that test, economists could no longer offer the crisp advice they used to provide. The profession could live with the portion of the indeterminacy that stemmed from a retreat from distributional value judgments. But the

---

[1] See Section 4.3 for the link between incomplete preferences and the willingness-to-accept willingness-to-pay disparity.

[2] Edgeworth (1897), Pigou (1932).

problem went deeper: economic theory had to face the possibility that Paretian welfare economics could not go beyond the vacuity that, since any change in policy harms someone, every policy is optimal. In the drive to address this worry, hope briefly rested on the Hicks-Kaldor compensation criteria, which recommended policy changes that led to allocations that could be redistributed to achieve a Pareto improvement. But following the rapid discovery that compensation criteria will not lead to a coherent ordering of policies, welfare economics found itself in limbo.[3]

As economic theory faced this impasse, the new sheriffs arrived in town. In 1951 Arrow and Debreu independently proved the first and second welfare theorems: if markets are complete and no externalities are present then competitive equilibrium allocations will be Pareto efficient and, with convexity assumptions in place, any Pareto-efficient allocation can be achieved through the decentralized operation of markets if agents receive suitable lump-sum transfers. These two results have stood as the pillars of welfare economics ever since and still mark the peak to which the teaching of price theory ascends.

The welfare theorems unified the scattered connections between markets and efficiency that earlier generations of economists had laid down and without the marginal-utility foundations that those economists thought indispensable. But amid the gains, something was lost. Pareto efficiency had previously been intertwined with local decisiveness: efficiency in this older view obtains when agents' ratios of marginal utilities or marginal rates of substitution are aligned and a misalignment will show how to achieve both utilitarian and Pareto improvements. If for example the ratio of the marginal utilities of good 1 to good 2 is greater for agent a than for agent b, then some transfer of good 1 from b to a and of good 2 from a to b will make both agents better off. Modern formulations of the welfare theorems in contrast do not require either smooth utilities or marginal rates of substitutions. As a consequence, the allocations that arise when markets are distorted – for example when different agents face different prices – can be efficient: no Pareto improvements may be available. The welfare theorems thus do not show how discriminating the Pareto criterion is: they show only a correspondence between Pareto-efficient allocations of goods and the allocations that perfectly competitive markets can deliver. The question of whether there is workable Paretian distinction between efficient and inefficient economic policies was discreetly finessed.

---

[3] See Hicks (1939b, 1940), Kaldor (1939), Samuelson (1950), and Scitovsky (1941).

This conclusion clashes with classroom renditions of the welfare theorems where the advice offered appears to be sweeping and unequivocal. For example, an economy with restrictions on trade and relative prices distorted by taxation can achieve a Pareto improvement according to the textbooks if the restrictions and taxes are eliminated and suitable lump-sum transfers among agents arranged. Even putting aside that the welfare theorems do not imply the availability of Pareto improvements when preferences fail to be smooth, this program requires policymakers to know inaccessible details about agents' preferences. Once policymakers' ignorance is taken into account, the door left ajar by the welfare theorems opens wide: policies that *seem* obviously distorted can qualify as efficient. The Pareto criterion has become mute.

Similar difficulties appear when preferences are incomplete. If preferences are locally incomparable, the marginal rates of substitution that drove pre-Arrow-Debreu welfare analysis will be missing. Agents will instead have ranges of margins, which will again let a vast set of policies qualify as efficient: the multiplicity of margins for an agent in effect reproduces the uncertainty of policymakers about what preferences that agent has.

The authority of postwar general equilibrium theory has been so entrenched that the inability of the Pareto criterion to discriminate among policy choices now rarely receives notice.[4] The orthodox question to ask has been: "What type of institutions will achieve efficiency?"[5] From this point of view, the incompleteness of preferences has seemed irrelevant: completeness is not needed to prove that competitive allocations are Pareto efficient. The trouble brought by incompleteness is the possibility that no policy option will be inefficient – just as a government with limited information cannot rule out as inefficient policies that economists have long deemed to be distortionary.

The practical side of the profession has never taken the Pareto criterion very seriously. The advice sought by governments requires a welfare calculus that can crank out decisions, and so applied economists in the wake of the Paretian revolution had little choice but to return to their grandparents' dollar measures of economic costs and benefits. The updates

---

[4] The goal of decisiveness does sometimes emerge implicitly. See Arrow (1977) for example.

[5] In the wake of Arrow (1951) and Debreu (1951), research accordingly focused on how to weaken the convexity assumption of the second welfare theorem (the only substantive assumption that arises in either welfare theorem). See Guesnerie (1975) and Khan and Vohra (1987).

of 1950s – Marshallian consumer surplus analysis reemerged as compensating and equivalent variations and as cost-benefit analysis – did little to mask the backsliding and, despite great effort, could draw little justification from Paretian theory.[6]

For present purposes the drawback of dollar measures of economic welfare is not their shaky rationale: the larger problem is that when agents due to their incompleteness cannot pin down smooth trade-offs between goods, these welfare measures will also fail to discriminate effectively among policy options. As in theoretical welfare economics, the discrimination shortfall can be hard to detect. Applied economics never abandoned the early neoclassical view that the marginal benefits of policies to agents are always well-defined. Given that starting assumption, a policy will pass a cost-benefit or monetary test of efficiency if and only if agents' maximum willingness to pay for the policy exceeds the policy's dollar cost. When that assumption does not hold – because preferences are incomplete – there will be an additional and distinct path to efficiency: a policy will qualify as efficient if the harm done by refraining from the policy, measured in dollars, exceeds the costs saved. So when agents have ranges of valuations for a public good and consequently will pay less to gain access to the good than they must be compensated for its loss, as in the earlier environment example, the result will often be that both approving and rejecting the public good is optimal. The clean dividing line between winning and losing policies is smudged.

Applied welfare economics has largely been unwilling to concede its undercount of efficient policies or to use the harm done to agents when a policy is not undertaken to measure the value of a policy. The result has been a bias in cost-benefit analysis against government action. As we will see in one of the money-linear models designed to rationalize cost-benefit analysis, the presumption of complete preferences lowballs the value of public goods.

The possibility that the dollar benefit of a public good can take on multiple values has been sidestepped in subtle ways. Sometimes benefits are measured by the market prices of the items individuals buy in order to enjoy the public good more extensively: the greater price of the apartment overlooking Central Park quantifies the value of the view. Such methods owe their popularity to the dogma that market prices reveal the marginal

---

[6] One can build coherent policy orderings based on money measures of agents' utilities (see Hicks [1939a, 1956], McKenzie [1957], Samuelson [1974], Chipman and Moore [1980], and Khan and Schlee [2022]), but they have little connection to applied work or to the Pareto program.

values of individuals. But if the smooth indifference curve is a fiction then those marginal values will not be there to be found.

Is it necessary to add that there are policy decisions to which classical efficiency advice is perfectly suited? When for example regulators set safety standards for cars, they may aim to equalize the expected lives saved from the marginal dollar spent on different safety features; this goal will discriminate effectively between efficient and inefficient standards. When however it comes to the trade-off between the cost of producing cars and expected lives saved, individual preferences are likely to be locally incomparable; a technocratic solution may then be impossible. The difference between the two cases turns on the presence of an ordering principle. If citizens and government agree that it is better to save more lives, all else being equal, then an efficiency analysis can allocate a fixed sum of money to different safety features. But efficiency criteria will have little bite when deciding how much money to devote to greater safety: that would require a resolution of the trade-off between money and expected lives. With its presumption that agents can always form preferences, no matter what decision they face, welfare economics intertwines legitimate means-ends calculations with the pricing of ends that agents do not know how to value.

8.1 PARETO EFFICIENCY

The welfare theorems, the opening move and greatest success of postwar general equilibrium theory, completed the victory of Paretian welfare economics over utilitarian orthodoxy. In the new consensus, the task of economics was to identify the Pareto-efficient allocations – those allocations where any improvement for one agent harms some other agent. In their capacity as scientists, economists should remain silent about which individuals and preferences should be given greater weight in policymaking; harm to the rich, in this view, has the same standing as harm to the poor. Decisions about which efficient allocation a government ought to choose should be left for politicians and philosophers to argue about.

Whereas individuals in neoclassical economics can judge every trade-off among competing goods and pleasures, the Paretian consensus adopts the opposite view of trade-offs across individuals: none of them can be judged. This agnosticism about distribution has been subject to steady attack. Both the utilitarian bitter enders of the 1950s and the social choice theorists of the 1970s onward were unwilling to abandon the priority assigned to the poor or to join the broader retreat from interpersonal welfare comparisons.

Paretian welfare economics prevailed over these philosophical misgivings, but it could not have done so had Paretianism not appeared to provide decisive policy advice. The preexisting orthodoxy of smooth indifference curves propped up this endeavor. With smooth indifference curves, a converse to the first welfare theorem will hold: distortions of competition, such as taxes and subsidies, will lead to inefficiency. Suppose that the poor and only the poor enjoy a subsidy on bread. With smooth indifference curves, marginal rates of substitution will be well-defined and due to the subsidy they will differ across agents. Pareto improvements will then be available and any of these improvements that is also Pareto efficient can be reached by removing the distortion and paying appropriate lump-sum compensations.

Orthodox preferences will also ensure that the Pareto criterion is decisive at the more fundamental level of allocations. In an exchange economy with I consumers and L goods and a given aggregate endowment, there will be a large set of possible allocations: since for each good we can independently pick consumption levels for $I - 1$ individuals, the set has dimension $L(I - 1)$. Only a low-dimensional subset and hence a 0 proportion or measure of the allocations will qualify as Pareto efficient. If consumers have increasing and convex preferences that can be represented by continuous utility functions, the utility possibility frontier will have dimension $I - 1$. If in addition preferences are strictly convex then each point on the utility frontier can be delivered by only one allocation of goods; the dimension of the Pareto-efficient allocations will therefore also be $I - 1$. The Pareto criterion when applied to classical preferences thus narrows the large $L(I - 1)$ dimensionality of the entire set of allocations to a manageable dimension of $I - 1$. The Edgeworth box provides the iconic illustration: out of a two-dimensional set of possible allocations (since $L = I = 2$ in the box), the Pareto-efficient allocations form a one-dimensional subset. Almost every allocation is therefore ruled out as inefficient.

These Paretian parables will break down when preferences are incomplete, as we will see in Section 8.3. To lay the groundwork, I will begin in this section with the problems faced by the Pareto criterion when preferences meet every test of orthodoxy. A Paretian failure to discriminate arises here as well and points to the difficulties to come.

The welfare theorems have long been viewed skeptically by economists outside of theoretical circles. There have been many complaints. To guarantee that competitive markets achieve Pareto efficiency, externalities must be absent and every source of economic benefit to agents must be packaged as a privately tradable good. So public goods cannot be accommodated and markets must be open for every good and insurance contract, even those that apply to the distant future. And since transfers must be lump-sum, they cannot reward or penalize specific economic decisions. The government therefore cannot target redistributions to agents whose own decisions lead them to poverty.

Although these objections undermine the clean laissez-faire conclusions of the welfare theorems, they do not threaten the broader Paretian agenda. If we relax the dubious assumptions that underlie the welfare theorems and acknowledge the practical constraints on government policy tools, the arbitrary policies passed down by tradition or chosen by bureaucrats unschooled in economic analysis will normally still call for reform. Miracles aside, the initial specifications of policy instruments will leave room for Pareto improvements and thus qualify as suboptimal. Even when taxes and subsidies on particular goods cannot be entirely eliminated or transfers must be undertaken repeatedly or public goods must be provided collectively, Pareto improvements will still be available and the government's policy instruments must be fine-tuned to capture them. The second-best policies that result will often retain much of the original flavor of the welfare theorems.

If for example farmers ex ante receive crop subsidies, the first-best Paretian recommendation would be to replace the subsidies with one-time lump-sum compensation payments. But if that option is infeasible, policymakers can turn to a roughly comparable back-up plan: annual payments to farmers who remain minimally active that approximate their original subsidy receipts and that are mostly unaffected by the farmers' crop decisions. Real-world reforms have mirrored this evolution of policy advice. For instance, the European Union's Common Agricultural Policy in 2003 replaced crop-specific subsidies with "single farm payments" though the payments are not independent of all decisions farmers can make.[7] A notable feature of real-world compensation payments, including this example, is that they aim to replicate the value of the trades that agents made prior to a policy change and do not try to guarantee agents their unobservable ex ante utility levels, a point that I will return to in Chapter 9.

The practical limitations of the welfare theorems have therefore not led economists to retreat from the broader Pareto program. In the majority

---

[7] See Cunha and Swinbank (2011) and Roederer-Rynning (2014).

view, the distinction between optimal and suboptimal policies stands unthreatened – and the next section will illustrate the discriminatory power that welfare economics can achieve in models where well-defined margins remain embedded in the foundations. So while the ideological tidiness of welfare economics becomes blurred when the welfare theorems are adapted to the demands of governance, the bedrock message that economics offers a decisive science of policymaking soldiers on.

But this consensus is deceptive. Arguments about the exact accuracy of the assumptions underlying the welfare theorems are a distraction from the deeper problem of the Pareto program, its informational presuppositions. Consider a government that has in the past subsidized the fine arts (theater, opera, classical music) and taxed the low arts (television, video games) or has taxed these goods at different rates. Assume, for the sake of argument, that all of the preconditions of the welfare theorems are met: markets are complete and no externalities are present. To achieve a Pareto improvement and Pareto efficiency as well, the theorems recommend eliminating the differential taxes and replacing them with lump-sum transfers. A policymaker however will typically not know agents' preferences and therefore will not know whom to compensate or by how much.[8] In the absence of this information, each possible change in policies might harm some agent. In what sense then are the status quo taxes inefficient? In this example it so happens that eliminating the tax will lead to an allocation that is Pareto efficient relative to the set of all feasible allocations delivered with certainty. But, given the government's limited information, the same policy need not lead to an allocation that is Pareto efficient relative to the set of allocations that policymakers must choose from: the government faces uncertainty about agents' characteristics and thus implicitly chooses policies that deliver uncertain allocations. And even Pareto efficiency relative to the certain allocations would collapse if we drop the textbook trick of considering one distortion at a time; with say a slight externality added to the model, the no-tax allocations will not be Pareto efficient relative to the set of certain allocations. The Pareto criterion therefore does not recommend unrestricted competition or indeed any change from the status quo.

Policymakers can of course try to estimate which preferences an individual might potentially have and use those estimates to make payments that will in expectation compensate the individual for any change in taxes

---

[8] I do not mean to suggest that economic theory is unaware of this informational shortfall: it has been understood at least since Mirrlees (1971).

or subsidies. Among the potential agents that an individual could be are extreme consumers of the high-arts goods and these agents will not be left whole if high-art subsidies are withdrawn: their compensation payments will not allow them to buy their ex ante consumption bundles and, unless they are rescued by a large elasticity of substitution, their utility will fall. To conclude that a policy change leaves an individual who receives an expected compensation payment better or worse off will thus depend on how a policymaker weights the utilities of the potential agents the individual might be.[9] The Paretian project of freeing welfare economics from the value-laden task of weighing one utility function against another therefore cannot succeed by this path.

To avoid the taint of interpersonal comparisons of utility, Paretian policymakers have little choice but to endorse only policy changes that do not harm any of the *potential* agents that each individual could be. This expansion of the number of agents – from the original *I* individuals to the vast number of potential agents the *I* individuals could be – will usually lead the Pareto criterion to supply only hollow advice. No pair of policies will end up being Pareto-ranked and hence every policy will qualify as Pareto efficient. A common lament of welfare economics, that every policy change harms some agent, comes close to capturing the problem. But the adage needs to be refined: the difficulty is that every policy change harms some potential agent.

To return to the concrete, suppose again that the government subsidizes some item in the fine arts. If policymakers know the characteristics of all relevant individuals – both those who consume the good and those affected by any policy-induced price changes – then the subsidy can be replaced with lump-sum transfers and a Pareto improvement can be achieved. In the absence of that knowledge the subsidy appears in a different light. While economists tend to view subsidies as an overweening government's attempt to dictate what individuals consume, they can instead serve as tools to prioritize certain classes of preferences: the government would ideally send out lump-sum payments to the individuals with these preferences but if it cannot identify these agents then policymakers must bend relative prices to approximate that goal.[10] Subsidies for particular goods are thus not only consistent with Pareto efficiency, they maximize social welfare functions that policymakers might plausibly

---

[9] Mandler (2007).
[10] Mandler (2007), Dworczak et al. (2021).

embrace, given the informational constraints they face. But if a government loyal to the Paretian cause aims to remain neutral about which social welfare function to maximize, then it will end up declaring any status quo policy to be acceptable.

Examples in this vein are manifold. When a government confronts different agents with different prices for goods – as when the poor but not the rich can rent housing at below-market prices – economists see the opportunity for a Pareto improvement. But if the government cannot access agents' preferences and trades, then it will not be able to determine the compensations that the implementation of a Pareto improvement would require. An arbitrary initial policy that misaligns marginal rates of substitution can therefore efficiently serve one of the social welfare goals economics deems legitimate.

Economists are hardly slaves to the status quo. Since Adam Smith, economists have vigorously opposed the distortions – in the tax code for example – that result when the rich and powerful win government favors. But however just and well-intentioned these views are, their rationale remains vague. Calls to eliminate distortions are draped in the language of Pareto efficiency and yet such reforms rarely if ever aim for Pareto improvements. Governments do however come closer to the Paretian ideal when they use information about agents' trades to design compensations and we will push this strategy further in Chapter 9.

From the Groves mechanisms of the 1970s through several iterations of implementation theory, economists have worked tirelessly to construct mechanisms that will induce agents to use their private preference information to institute Pareto-efficient social decisions. Even a casual summary of this massive effort would dwarf this book. Game-theoretic mechanisms for social decision-making remain a largely normative exercise however. In contrast to the support provided by the welfare theorems for laissez-faire competition and Paretian compensation payments, mechanism design and implementation theory have had little dialogue with government decision-making; this work therefore does not help adjudicate any policy debate. The one substantial exception, the design of government auctions, notably harnesses the private information of firms rather than the preference information of consumers. The remainder of the book will explain why this asymmetry is no accident: the preferences that game-theoretic welfare economics postulates often do not exist, while firms do have well-defined objectives. In any event, even if games that induce agents to reveal information could usher in a revolution of Pareto improvements, they will not be relevant to the analysis to come;

none of our conclusions will turn on the availability or unavailability of private information.

8.2 POLICY INDECISIVENESS AND INCOMPLETE PREFERENCES

The multiple preferences that an individual believes it is reasonable to adopt closely parallel the multiple preferences that a policymaker could think an individual might have. The damage done to the usefulness of any preference-based definition of economic efficiency – from utilitarianism to the Pareto criterion – is comparable.

The unanimity aggregators of Chapter 3 provide a case in point: they are stymied about how to prioritize their candidate preferences and will therefore frequently fail to come up with a preference judgment. A policy change must then pass a debilitatingly large set of tests. A cost-benefit evaluation of a public good, for example, can approve a change only if the change raises all of the sums of agents' welfare, as measured in money, that can arise from the agents' candidate utility functions. So, if many individuals are torn between utilities that place large and small weights on the value of a public good then both a decision to approve the public good and a decision to reject it can pass muster. An aggregation of the welfare of individuals cannot somehow evade the inability of the agents themselves to come to judgment.

Local incomparability will lead to policy indecisiveness on the margins. When preferences are locally incomparable and the quantity of a public good is chosen efficiently, society's marginal valuation (in terms of private consumption) of the public good will occupy a band of values that contains the public good's marginal cost. A small deviation to a new quantity will then usually also qualify as efficient: the marginal cost of the public good will still fall within that band.

I will begin with two benchmarks of the conclusive policy advice that complete preferences and well-defined marginal valuations deliver. The *cost-benefit model* will lay out a prototypical 0–1 policy decision, say to build a public good or rectify an externality. The agents in this model will have the special money-linear utility functions under which Paretian and dollar measures of economic welfare will coincide. The *continuous public goods model*, where utilities will take a more general form, analyzes how the extent or intensity of policies should vary. In both cases, the well-defined valuations of individuals will ensure that a government can discriminate effectively among its policy options. Accidents aside, policymakers in the cost-benefit setting will not have to shrug their shoulders;

one of the policy options will lead to efficiency and the other will not. In the continuous setting, an arbitrary initial policy will almost always lead to inefficiency and call for an intervention. These analyses do not preach the laissez-faire advice of the welfare theorems – public goods and externalities defy pure-competition remedies – but they do prescribe determinate policy solutions.

In the cost-benefit model, a society of I individuals must decide whether to undertake a public works project, perhaps a new art museum. Each individual i has a utility function $x^i + v^i(h)$, where x^i is i's private consumption and h equals 1 or 0 depending on whether the museum is built or not. We normalize utility levels by setting $v^i(0) = 0$. The $h = 1$ decision can also be read as a government program to eliminate a negative externality, such as pollution, that can affect every individual's utility. The program could for example lower carbon emissions and global warming.

Let the museum cost a quantity c of private consumption to construct (or let the externality cost c to remove) which must be raised in taxes. Letting e be the aggregate initial endowment of private consumption and x be the profile of private consumption $(x^1, \ldots, x^I)$, the allocation (h, x) is feasible if either $(\sum_i x^i = e$ and $h = 0)$ or $(c + \sum_i x^i = e$ and $h = 1)$.[11]

Since each agent holds an unambiguous evaluation of the museum in terms of private consumption, the efficient building decision is readily identified. With the utilitarian or cost-benefit goal of maximizing $\sum_i (x^i + v^i(h))$, the gain from building the museum will strictly exceed the aggregate loss in private consumption if and only if $\sum_i v^i(1) > c$ and the gain will be strictly less than the loss if and only if $\sum_i v^i(1) < c$. Only in the unlikely event that $\sum_i v^i(1) = c$ holds exactly will a utilitarian planner be indecisive.

The Pareto criterion leads to the same decisiveness. An allocation (h, x) is Pareto efficient if it is feasible and no other feasible $(\hat{x}, \hat{h})$ has $\hat{x}^i + v^i(\hat{h}) \geq x^i + v^i(h)$ for each agent i and with strict inequality for some i. When $\sum_i v^i(1) > c$, building the museum is efficient: the c saved by not building cannot fund a compensation payment of $v^i(1)$ to each agent i. And not building is inefficient: a tax on each i of less than $v^i(1)$ can cover the cost c. Similarly, when $\sum_i v^i(1) < c$ not building is efficient since a tax of $v^i(1)$ on each i, the maximum consistent with a Pareto improvement, will not cover c and building is inefficient since not building will pay for

---

[11] Beware of a change in notation relative to Chapter 7 where e denoted the profile of all individual endowments.

a tax reduction for each i of more than $v^i(1)$. It is only when $\sum_i v^i(1) = c$ that Pareto efficiency fails to identify a unique optimal decision.

The second model offers a variation where the policy variable is continuous rather than discrete. Let the quantity h of the public good now be a positive number, let each individual i have the utility function $u^i(x^i) + v^i(h)$, let e again be the aggregate endowment of private consumption, and let $c(h)$ be the private-consumption cost of h. I assume that each u^i and v^i is strictly concave, increasing, and differentiable on $[0, e]$ and that c is convex and differentiable. To fund h, the sum of the individuals' private consumption must fall by $c(h)$ which can again be raised by taxation. So allocation $(h, x) \geq 0$ is feasible if $c(h) + \sum_i x^i = e$.

The smooth preferences of this model make it easy to identify when Pareto improvements are available. A marginal increase Δh in the public good will have a cost well-approximated by $Dc(h)\Delta h$ and a benefit to agent i well-approximated by $Dv^i(h)\Delta h$. Since the maximum private consumption Δx^i that i would sacrifice to obtain this benefit is defined by $Du^i(x^i)\Delta x^i = Dv^i(h)\Delta h$, there is an increase in h that will lead to a Pareto improvement when $\sum_i \frac{Dv^i(h)}{Du^i(x^i)} > Dc(h)$. Similarly there is a decrease in h that will lead to a Pareto improvement when $\sum_i \frac{Dv^i(h)}{Du^i(x^i)} < Dc(h)$. Pareto improvements are unavailable only when neither inequality holds. A $(h, x) \gg 0$ is therefore Pareto efficient if and only if it is feasible and the *Samuelson optimality condition* for a public good,

$$\sum_i \frac{Dv^i(h)}{Du^i(x^i)} = Dc(h),$$

is satisfied.[12]

Since society's resources e can be allocated among the $I + 1$ uses h, x^1, ..., x^I and must satisfy the constraint $c(h) + \sum_i x^i = e$, the feasible allocations form a I-dimensional set. The Pareto-efficient allocations must in addition satisfy the Samuelson optimality condition and will therefore form a $I - 1$ dimensional set. It would therefore be a fluke if an arbitrary choice of h and of the taxes (consumption reductions) that pay the cost $c(h)$ led to a Pareto optimum. Policymakers therefore have a nontrivial job to do. Moreover as the parameters of the model change, the policymakers' selection of an allocation will change in response. If for example

---

[12] This sum-of-marginal-rates-of-substitution characterization of Pareto optimality for economies with public goods originates with Samuelson (1954).

the marginal cost of the public good $Dc(h)$ increases for each h the previously optimal allocation will no longer be; policymakers need to respond accordingly.

A utilitarian planner that maximizes the sum $\sum_i \left(u^i(x^i) + v^i(h) \right)$ subject to feasibility can pin down a unique optimal allocation. In addition to the Samuelson optimality condition, which a utilitarian must also satisfy, the marginal utilities of private consumption across agents must be set equal: $Du^i(x^i) = Du^{i+1}(x^{i+1})$ for $i = 1, \ldots, I-1$. So, along with the feasibility constraint, $I+1$ conditions will determine the $I+1$ variables (h, x). As with Paretian policymakers, utilitarian planners have a job to do: as the model's parameters shift, the optimal (h, x) will change.

The above two models illustrate the technocratic nature of classical economic policy analysis. The world begins with a jumble of arbitrary and poorly thought out policy decisions that call for correction. As long as agents have well-defined objectives – complete preferences – and an efficiency criterion can aggregate these objectives, economists can play the role of Mr. Fixit and rectify the initial disorder. Policymakers may have some leeway to choose from a variety of improvements, but an arbitrary status quo is highly likely to stand in need of reform.

We now add in the incompleteness that arises when agents do not know what preferences to adopt. For the cost-benefit decision of whether to build a museum, suppose each individual i is torn between two candidate utility functions of the form $x^i + \alpha^i v^i(h)$ where $v^i(1) > v^i(0) = 0$: a connoisseur candidate utility where α^i equals a high value $\bar{\alpha}^i$ and a philistine candidate where α^i equals a low value $\underline{\alpha}^i$. Given the agent's mixed feelings, i's welfare will be given by the unanimity aggregation of the two utilities, that is, by the preference $\succsim^i$ defined by $(x^i, h) \succsim^i (\hat{x}^i, \hat{h})$ if and only if the following inequalities hold,

$$x^i + \underline{\alpha}^i v^i(h) \geq \hat{x}^i + \underline{\alpha}^i v^i(\hat{h}),$$
$$x^i + \bar{\alpha}^i v^i(h) \geq \hat{x}^i + \bar{\alpha}^i v^i(\hat{h}).$$

The preference $\succsim^i$ is incomplete and, were it not for h being a 0–1 variable, it would qualify as locally incomparable. It would be more realistic to allow more values for the α^i, but all that will matter for policy indecisiveness are the smallest and the largest values.

The interpretation of $h = 1$ as a carbon reduction policy that lessens global warming is particularly conducive to incomplete preferences. Both agents and the government do not know how to assign precise likelihoods to the small-probability possibility that modest carbon reduction will lead to an extreme difference in global warming outcomes (see Section 2.3). Even a small diversity in the probability distributions induced by carbon reduction will therefore lead to a large gap between $\bar{\alpha}^i$, the largest estimate of the expected future utility gain of carbon reduction today and $\underline{\alpha}^i$, the smallest estimate (see Section 3.4).[13] But for brevity's sake I will as before stick to a more prosaic "build" or "not build" interpretation of h.

A utilitarian planner will consider any sum of candidate utility functions, one for each agent, to furnish a valid objective function for society. A build or not build decision is therefore *utilitarian optimal* if the alternative decision cannot increase all of these objective functions and strictly increase at least one of them. As with individuals, we need only look at the extremes, $\sum_i (x^i + \underline{\alpha}^i v^i(h))$ and $\sum_i (x^i + \bar{\alpha}^i v^i(h))$. Building is optimal when $c < \sum_i \bar{\alpha}^i v^i(1)$ (since a switch to not building would lower $\sum_i (x^i + \bar{\alpha}^i v^i(h))$) and not building is optimal when $c > \sum_i \underline{\alpha}^i v^i(1)$ (since then a switch to building would lower $\sum_i (x^i + \underline{\alpha}^i v^i(h))$).

When c lands between the aggregate pessimistic valuation $\sum_i \underline{\alpha}^i v^i(1)$ of the public good and the aggregate optimistic valuation $\sum_i \bar{\alpha}^i v^i(1)$, there is no unique best decision: both building and not building are optimal. Economic advice then brings nothing to the policymaking table; Mr. Fixit will need a new job.

The same conclusions hold for a Paretian. If $c < \sum_i \bar{\alpha}^i v^i(1)$ then building is Pareto efficient: a Pareto-improving switch to not building would require a boost in private consumption of at least $\sum_i \bar{\alpha}^i v^i(1)$, which would outstrip the savings of c from not building. If $c > \sum_i \underline{\alpha}^i v^i(1)$ then not building is Pareto efficient: a Pareto-improving switch to building would require a fall in private consumption no greater than $\sum_i \underline{\alpha}^i v^i(1)$, and so the cost of building would not be covered. Once again both decisions will gain approval if $\sum_i \underline{\alpha}^i v^i(1) < c < \sum_i \bar{\alpha}^i v^i(1)$.

Proposition 8.1 *In the cost-benefit model, if c lies strictly between $\sum_i \underline{\alpha}^i v^i(1)$ and $\sum_i \bar{\alpha}^i v^i(1)$ then both "build" and "not build" are utilitarian-optimal and Pareto-efficient policy choices. In all other cases, there is a unique utilitarian-optimal and Pareto-efficient decision.*

Policy indecisiveness in the cost-benefit model will nevertheless be hard to detect if one presumes that agents have precise valuations of the public good. Starting from a "not build" status quo, a cost-benefit technician would simply check whether agents' maximum aggregate willingness to

---

[13] See Mandler (2023).

pay for the public good, $\sum_i \underline{\alpha}^i v^i(1)$, exceeds its cost c. If the public good fails this test then the executive summary will report that the public good is a bad idea. But it is entirely possible that if building were instead the status quo then a switch to not building would also be rejected. With the conceptual vice of complete preferences clamped in place, this possibility rarely enters the orbit of analysis. Yet, when agents have a range of valuations, this conclusion is very much a live possibility. Agents can both be unwilling to pay the cost of a public good and judge the loss of the public good to lead to a dollar harm, $\sum_i \bar{\alpha}^i v^i(1)$, that exceeds the good's cost. By ignoring the latter possibility, a bias against public goods slips in unnoticed.

The difference between agents' high and low valuations of the public good, $\sum_i \left(\bar{\alpha}^i - \underline{\alpha}^i \right) v^i(1)$, measures the extent of policy indecisiveness. So even if many or most agents i have little or no gap in their valuations, there can still be a sizable gap between the aggregate valuations, $\sum_i \underline{\alpha}^i v^i(1)$ and $\sum_i \bar{\alpha}^i v^i(1)$, and policy indecisiveness will occur when c lands in this interval. The extent of policy indecisiveness moreover will increase as the number of individuals grows.

The complete-preferences version of the model, in contrast, stakes out the extreme claim that $\underline{\alpha}^i = \bar{\alpha}^i$ for *every* agent i: only then will policy indecisiveness arise at just one value of c. Since it takes only a single agent with a valuation gap to overturn this claim, policy indecisiveness should be considered the norm; and the burden of proof falls on the position that the value of a public good must be a single number. But the extent of policy indecisiveness is at least bounded: if $c > \sum_i \bar{\alpha}^i v^i(1)$ or $c < \sum_i \underline{\alpha}^i v^i(1)$ a single optimal decision rules. And if the aggregate gap $\sum_i \left(\bar{\alpha}^i - \underline{\alpha}^i \right) v^i(1)$ is small – there is only a little incompleteness economy-wide – then the incompleteness does not matter much: only a narrow band of values for c will lead both build and not build to be optimal.

For public goods that agents find too difficult to assess – for example how clean the environment should be – the aggregate gap is likely to be large. Agents systematically judge the value of a marginally cleaner environment to be much smaller than the harm of a marginally despoiled environment and that difference persists regardless of agents' initial wealth and the environment's initial condition.[14] This gap in evaluations is well-documented and many theorists and applied welfare economists realize that the gap undermines cost-benefit evaluation (though, perhaps

---

[14] See the references in Section 4.3 and Hammack and Brown (1974).

inevitably, economists at the practical end of spectrum back the smaller valuations for policy decisions).[15] But the gap has not been integrated into the practice of welfare economics: for goods less emotive than the environment, the default assumption that agents carry well-defined marginal valuations remains largely unquestioned.

Similar policy paralysis conclusions hold for the continuous public goods model. Letting the preference $\succsim^i$ for each individual i again be formed by unanimity aggregation, a candidate utility for i will now be a function $u^i(x^i) + \alpha^i v^i(h)$ where α^i equals either $\bar{\alpha}^i$ or $\underline{\alpha}^i$ and our previous assumptions on u^i and v^i are satisfied. So $(x^i, h) \succsim^i (\hat{x}^i, \hat{h})$ holds if and only if both utility functions weakly recommend (x^i, h) over $(\hat{x}^i, \hat{h})$. Since h is now a continuous variable, each $\succsim^i$ fully qualifies as locally incomparable. To ensure that agents find the public good sufficiently desirable when it is not consumed but can become sated with it, I will impose a *range assumption* à la Inada that $\lim_{h \to 0} Dv^i(h) = \infty$ and $Dv^i(e) = 0$ for all i and $Dc(h) > 0$ for all $h \geq 0$. When the range assumption is satisfied and there is an individual i with $\bar{\alpha}^i > \underline{\alpha}^i$, I will call the setting a *continuous public goods model with incomplete preferences*.

Given a feasible $(h, x) \gg 0$, an increase of h to a larger value $\hat{h}$ will leave an individual i weakly better off with his new private consumption $\hat{x}^i$ if and only if the utility that gives the worst-case (more pessimistic) evaluation of an increase in h approves the change,

$$u^i(\hat{x}^i) + \underline{\alpha}^i v^i(\hat{h}) \geq u^i(x^i) + \underline{\alpha}^i v^i(h).$$

If this inequality is satisfied then, since $\hat{h} > h$, the comparable inequality that replaces $\underline{\alpha}^i$ with $\bar{\alpha}^i$ must be satisfied as well: the move to $\hat{h}$ is therefore a $\succsim^i$-improvement. Our earlier analysis of the complete-preferences model therefore implies that if $\sum_i \frac{\underline{\alpha}^i Dv^i(h)}{Du^i(x^i)} > Dc(h)$ then an increase in the public good relative to h will make a Pareto improvement possible. The cases where the new quantity of the public good $\hat{h}$ is smaller than h are similar. Now the worst-case evaluation for individual i is given by the candidate utility with the weighting $\bar{\alpha}^i$ and an allocation will deliver a $\succsim^i$-improvement if it passes a utility test that uses the $\bar{\alpha}^i$ weighting. Hence if $\sum_i \frac{\bar{\alpha}^i Dv^i(h)}{Du^i(x^i)} < Dc(h)$ then there will be a decrease in the public good relative to h that permits a Pareto improvement. In the remaining cases, where $Dc(h)$ lies between $\sum_i \frac{\underline{\alpha}^i Dv^i(h)}{Du^i(x^i)}$ and $\sum_i \frac{\bar{\alpha}^i Dv^i(h)}{Du^i(x^i)}$, no Pareto improvements are possible and the allocation (h, x) is Pareto efficient.

---

[15] Cummings et al. (1986), Hausman (1993).

This efficiency test is sufficiently easy to pass that the set of Pareto-efficient allocations will end up having the maximum possible dimension I, the same dimension as the entire set of allocations, when preferences are incomplete. The range assumption implies that there is a feasible (h, x) such that $Dc(h)$ lies strictly between $\sum_i \frac{\underline{\alpha}^i Dv^i(h)}{Du^i(x^i)}$ and $\sum_i \frac{\bar{\alpha}^i Dv^i(h)}{Du^i(x^i)}$.[16] Moreover, since c and the v^i and u^i are all continuously differentiable, $Dc(h)$ will continue to lie between $\sum_i \frac{\underline{\alpha}^i Dv^i(h)}{Du^i(x^i)}$ and $\sum_i \frac{\bar{\alpha}^i Dv^i(h)}{Du^i(x^i)}$ following any sufficiently small adjustment of the allocation: the adjusted allocation will then also be efficient.

The large dimensionality of the Pareto optima stems from the local incomparability of preferences. When individuals at every point of consumption have a range of margins, a marginal cost for the public good that lies initially amid the interval formed by the sums of the slopes of the agents' supporting price lines will continue to lie in that interval after we change the quantity of the public good by a small amount.

Since utilitarianism takes a stand on how to distribute private consumption in the continuous public goods model, the set of utilitarian optima is not nearly as large as the set of Pareto optima – just as in the complete preferences model the set of utilitarian optima (a singleton) is small relative to the set of Pareto optima. For a utilitarian planner, the two relevant objective functions are $\sum_i (u^i(x^i) + \underline{\alpha}^i v^i(h))$ and $\sum_i (u^i(x^i) + \bar{\alpha}^i v^i(h))$ and hence a feasible allocation is utilitarian optimal in the continuous public goods model with incomplete preferences if there is no feasible allocation that increases both of these objective functions with at least one strict increase. Policy paralysis now appears as a 1-dimensional set of utilitarian optima: the policy goal h is not pinned down but the optimal distribution of income given h is.

Proposition 8.2 *In the continuous public goods model with incomplete preferences, the set of Pareto-efficient allocations forms a nonempty I-dimensional set and the set of utilitarian optima forms a 1-dimensional set.*

The upshot of Proposition 8.2 is a policy indecisiveness akin but not identical to the cost-benefit setting. When h is a continuous rather than a

---

[16] Since each v^i and u^i is concave and differentiable, each is continuously differentiable, as is c. For each h and i, let $x^i(h) = \frac{e - c(h)}{I}$. Since $\lim_{h \to 0} \frac{D\underline{\alpha}^i v^i(h)}{Du^i(x^i(h))} = \infty$ and $\frac{D\underline{\alpha}^i v^i(e)}{Du^i(x^i(e))} = 0$, the continuous differentiability of the v^i, u^i, and c imply that there is a $\bar{h} \in (0, e)$ such that $\sum_i \frac{D\underline{\alpha}^i v^i(\bar{h})}{Du^i(x^i(h))} = Dc(\bar{h})$. For some $h > \bar{h}$ sufficiently near $\bar{h}$, $(h, \frac{e - c(h)}{I}, \ldots, \frac{e - c(h)}{I})$ can serve as the (h, x) above.

0–1 variable, one might have hoped that a policymaker would normally be able to reject arbitrary initial values of h and decree that at least some adjustment should be made. Proposition 8.2 says no: if (h', x') lies in the interior of the I-dimensional set of Pareto-efficient allocations then no value of h near h' can be rejected as inefficient. Small adjustments in the model's parameters therefore no longer call for a policy response: an efficient allocation in the I-dimensional set will normally remain efficient following any small shift in the marginal cost of the public good or in agents' marginal utilities, a marked contrast to the complete-preferences version of the model. Policymakers if they so desire can even carry out an arbitrary direction of change in h or the allocation in response to a parameter change. Economic expertise therefore lose its pivotal role in the machinery of optimization. A utilitarian policymaker, or the maximizers of other social welfare functions, may well respond to a change in the model with adjustments of the distribution of welfare; but even they will not be able to pin down an optimal quantity of the public good. I will explore further the room for interpersonal comparisons of utility when preferences are incomplete in Chapter 10.

The analysis has focused on the dimension of the set of optima: dimension draws a clear mathematical line. But the size of the set of matters as well. A single individual with incomplete preferences – an individual i with $\bar{\alpha}^i > \underline{\alpha}^i$ – is all that is needed to pass a dimensional test of policy paralysis, analogously to our paralysis conclusion for the cost-benefit model. The scale of indecisiveness however will be small if $\sum_i (\bar{\alpha}^i - \underline{\alpha}^i)$ is small.

Instead of trying to assess agents' marginal dollar valuations of public goods directly, economists sometimes measure them indirectly by the amount agents must pay to gain access to the goods, for example, by the increase in the value of land near to a public amenity or by the travel costs agents incur.[17] Applied work can thereby arrive at a single number for a public good's aggregate marginal value. This revealed preference approach to valuation presumes however that agents have well-defined marginal rates of substitution. If instead agents have locally incomparable preferences then, even when agents face a bona fide market price of p per unit of h, we can conclude only that p must fall into each agent's interval of valuations. A marginal increase in h is preferred by an agent only if it costs less than the agent's minimum valuation and a marginal

---

[17] See, for example, Palmquist (1991) and Parsons (2003).

decrease is preferred only if it returns to the agent more than the his or her maximum valuation, and p can sit anywhere between this minimum and maximum. Proposition 8.2 therefore applies and the set of optimal allocations will be vast.

The various schemes for eliciting agents' values for public goods are legion for their wide disparities, even several-hundred-fold for the difference between the valuations agents report and revealed-preference measures.[18] From the vantage of preference incompleteness, such gulfs are to be expected. When agents do not have the valuations that economists demand of them, each elicitation scheme will be slanted by how it frames the valuation problem and gathers information.[19] And if the absence of preference judgments is profound, as is often the case with public goods, the estimated valuations will range widely.

The indecisiveness that arises with incomplete preferences inevitably percolates into the policy arena. When individuals cannot judge a trade-off, it would be remarkable if the government by the wave of an optimization wand could conjure up a neutral resolution for society as a whole.

8.3 POLICY INDECISIVENESS ECONOMY-WIDE

The policy indecisiveness that accompanies incomplete preferences is not tied specifically to the provision of public goods; it applies with equal force to private consumption and to the entire economy. The welfare theorems have classically ruled this terrain but, as we saw at the outset, these results only link Pareto efficiency to competitive equilibria, they do not tell us how effectively the Pareto criterion distinguishes between efficient and inefficient allocations. In a general equilibrium setting, policy indecisiveness occurs when the dimension of the Pareto-efficient allocations is large: a significant set of allocations is then optimal and even policies that seem to call for correction can qualify as efficient. The clearest cases of indecisiveness occur when the dimension of the efficient allocations matches the dimension of the entire set of allocations. Beginning from an efficient status quo, small changes in the parameters of the model will then place few constraints on how policymakers respond: they can leave the allocation unchanged or move the allocation in an arbitrary direction. The volume of the efficient allocations will also form a strictly

[18] Frey et al. (2004).
[19] Kahneman and Knetsch (1992).

positive fraction of the volume of all allocations. As in the case of public goods, the positive volume of the efficient allocations does not tell us if the volume is large or small; moreover size, while it matters, is difficult to judge.

The best-case scenario for the decisiveness of the Pareto criterion occurs when preferences are complete and strictly convex as we saw in Section 8.1. In an exchange economy, efficiency then winnows down the entire set of allocations, which has dimension $(I-1)L$, to a manageable set of dimension $I-1$, where I is the number of individuals and L is the number of goods. To compare this conclusion with the policy indecisiveness that comes with incomplete preferences, I again consider an exchange economy without preexisting distortions except that now each agent i's preference relation $\succsim^i$ will be maximally locally incomparable. Recall from Section 3.3 that a locally incomparable preference $\succsim^i$ is maximal if at each consumption x^i the agent's better-than set $B_{\succ^i}(x^i)$ is supported at x^i by a set of normalized prices that has the maximum dimension $L-1$. Theorem 3.3 shows that this property will usually be satisfied when $\succsim^i$ is the unanimity aggregation of L or more candidate preferences.

If an allocation of goods $x = (x^1, \ldots, x^I)$ is Pareto efficient then a variant of the second welfare theorem implies there must be a common supporting price vector. Formally, if $N^i(x^i)$ is the set of price vectors p that support $B_{\succ^i}(x^i)$ at x^i, then the intersection $\bigcap_i N^i(x^i)$ must be nonempty.[20] Suppose in addition that x satisfies the following two technicalities. Let a Pareto-efficient x be *robust* if (1) there is a common supporting price vector that does not lie on the boundary of any of the $N^i(x^i)$ and (2) each $N^i(x^i)$ varies continuously as a function of x^i in the sense that if p lies in the interior of $N^i(x^i)$ then p also lies in $N^i(\hat{x}^i)$ when $\hat{x}^i$ is sufficiently near to x^i. If a Pareto-efficient x is robust and $\hat{x}$ is a nearby allocation then, since each $B_{\succ^i}(\hat{x}^i)$ will also be supported by a common price vector, a variant of the first welfare theorem will imply that $\hat{x}$ must be Pareto efficient too. And the first welfare theorem is available: its proof does not require preference completeness, only transitivity

---

[20] This conclusion requires neither the continuity nor transitivity of preferences. See Mandler (2014a). The increasingness that comes with local incomparability allows the convexity assumption in Mandler (2014a) to be weakened. Briefly, if x is Pareto efficient then $\sum_i x^i$ must lie on the boundary of $\sum_i B_{\succ^i}(x^i)$: if $\sum_i x^i$ were in the interior then a small disposal of output would harm no agent, in violation of increasingness. We may therefore separate $\sum_i x^i$ from the convex set $\sum_i B_{\succ^i}(x^i)$, which implies the existence of the supporting price vector.

and local nonsatiation, which are implied by local incomparability. We have come to the following conclusion.[21]

Theorem 8.3 *In an exchange economy of agents with maximally locally incomparable preferences, any robust Pareto-efficient allocation is contained in a set of efficient allocations with the same dimension, $(I - 1)L$, as the entire set of allocations.*

If the allocation x is on the boundary of the robust Pareto-efficient allocations, then every p in $\bigcap_i N^i(x^i)$ will also be on the boundary of at least one $N^i(x^i)$. These boundary cases are unavoidable and will arise as x moves from a Pareto-efficient to a Pareto-inefficient region.

In a world of locally incomparable preferences, multiple price vectors will typically support an efficient allocation. There consequently need not be any efficiency drawback to letting different agents confront different prices – as occurs for example when trades are taxed. Violations of the law of one price, although they appear to be paradigmatic distortions that call for correction, do not require a policy response. This conclusion does not contradict any classical welfare theorem; the first welfare theorem asserts the efficiency of competition, not that an absence of competition leads to inefficiency. The argument that a Pareto improvement can always be found when agents face different prices in contrast requires agents to have well-defined marginal rates of substitution. But that assumption, an article of faith of early neoclassical economics, is vacated by local incomparability.

The conclusion of Theorem 8.3 applies to private-good economies with imperfections as well as those that are distortion-free. Suppose that we add consumption externalities to the general equilibrium model above: let the welfare of some individuals now be a function of the consumption of other agents as well as their own consumption. If we begin with no externalities and then increase the magnitude of the externalities continuously, the set of Pareto-efficient allocations will move continuously in response. Consequently any robust efficient allocation will remain efficient when the externalities remain modest. The introduction of a distortion therefore does not call for a remedy; the sweep of economic policymaking accordingly falls short of its original technocratic ambitions.

---

[21] Bernheim and Rangel (2007, 2009), in a similar setting where each individual is a set of behavioral agents, argue in response to Theorem 8.3 that the indecisiveness it demonstrates leaves room for nontrivial policy guidance. See Mandler (2014a) for commentary.

To avoid distractions from the main principles at work, Theorem 8.3 considered the maximally locally incomparable preferences $\succsim^i$ which have a dimension of supporting prices equal to $L - 1$. The bundles that an individual i regards as superior to some x^i will then display a kink at x^i along *any* plane that (nontangently) intersects the set of bundles $B_{\succ i}(x^i)$ preferred to x^i. There are less extreme possibilities. The individual may be able to judge the trade-offs between some pair of goods – say between goods 1 and 2 – but not between other pairs. The lower boundary of $B_{\succ i}(x^i)$ then will not display a kink along a direction from x^i where only x_1^i and x_2^i vary: in this direction the agent will have a well-defined marginal rate of substitution. The dimension of the set of prices that support $B_{\succ i}(x^i)$ then falls from $L - 1$, the maximum possible,[22] and the dimension of the Pareto-efficient allocations consequently falls from the $(I - 1)L$ of Theorem 8.3. Policy indecisiveness is now less severe and, as the number of goods for which marginal rates of substitution are well-defined increases, we converge to the complete preferences case where the dimension of the efficient allocations is $I - 1$. See Mandler (2014a).

Not all marginal utility failures lead to policy indecisiveness. If preferences are safety-biased, strictly convex, and have utility representations, then the standard argument that the set of Pareto-efficient allocations has dimension $I - 1$ applies. The Pareto-efficient allocations will define a utility possibility frontier of dimension $I - 1$ and each efficient utility vector for the I individuals can, by strict convexity, be delivered by only one allocation of goods. To conclude that the dimension of the set of efficient allocations is large, the incompleteness of preferences is pivotal.

While the indecisiveness of policy advice that comes with incomplete preferences is easy to grasp and arises in the simplest utilitarian exercises, a shift of perspective is needed to see the comparable phenomenon in general equilibrium theory; the mathematical facade of the welfare theorems obscures the view. Although the policy implications of the welfare theorems appear to be stark, the Pareto criterion risks providing only the vacuous advice that every policy or a large set of policies is optimal. The void can stem solely from policymakers' limited information or from local incomparability or both.

The problems that beset both social welfare maximization and the Pareto criterion show that the preference foundations of welfare economics are shaky. In Chapter 9, I will lay out an alternative attack based instead on observable trades and production.

---

[22] We saw an instance of this possibility for safety-biased preferences in Section 5.4.

9

Welfare and Policymaking: Pareto without Preferences

With the abundance of optimal allocations that accompanies incomplete preferences, apparent distortions will often no longer call for a policy response; even the label distortion becomes hard to defend. That this difficulty nearly repeats the policymaking dilemmas that arise when individual preferences are unknown suggests that the very aim of using individual preferences to guide allocative policymaking is an inappropriate ideal for welfare economics. A welfare economics built on the shifting sands of nonexistent or unknowable preferences will not provide workable policy advice.

The treatment of welfare economics with incomplete preferences in Chapter 8 assumed an Olympian perspective where optimal allocations are defined directly by agents' preferences. The practical implementation of policies shaped by individual preferences requires a policymaker to infer those preferences from choice behavior. With complete preferences, these inferences are straightforward when agents do not strategically dissimulate. But with incomplete preferences, chosen options need not be preferred to rejected options; inferring preferences then becomes more problematic.

These difficulties force a reformulation of the Paretian principle that policy changes should not harm any individual. Instead of rooting harm in agents' preferences and justifying these policies by the Pareto criterion's normative appeal, I will turn to the political logic that lies behind the Pareto criterion. Changes in economic policy, to be immune to credible objections, must satisfy an "availability test" that gives agents the option of taking whatever actions they took before the policy change. Due to incompleteness, the actions agents actually take following the change need not be preferred to their ex ante actions.

The policies that pass the availability test will come in two varieties. The first and more cautious mirrors the compensationism of Paretian welfare economics. But now the compensation payments agents receive will stand on firmer ground, what agents have been observed to exchange in the past rather than the mirage of their preferences. When policymakers lack the needed information about agents' past trades, we turn to a second variety: the crafting of increases in production efficiency that shield individuals from harm. Instead of the alignment of marginal rates of substitution that Paretian welfare economics focuses on, which allocate a given stock of consumption goods efficiently, these reforms will expand the productive pie.

Production provides an antidote to this book's skepticism about preferences. Inefficiency can in principle arise when there is no price line that supports every agent's better-than set (when marginal rates of substitution do not align in a smooth orthodox model). But that source of inefficiency will arise less frequently when preferences are incomplete and, whether or not preferences are classically rational, the magnitude of those losses pales in comparison to the gains that reorganizations of production can deliver.

When neither of the roads to the availability test is navigable, we must face the thorny cases where all policy options are sure to harm some individual. In Chapter 10, I will resurrect the early neoclassical strategy of comparing the utility of individuals, though now the job will need to be done without the help of utility functions as classically conceived.

9.1 THE AVAILABILITY TEST

Suppose the government subsidizes some good and preferences are locally incomparable: individuals have better-than sets that display kinks at their consumption bundles. To remove or reduce the subsidy while returning buyers of the good to their ex ante level of welfare, a policymaker would need detailed information about the agents' preferences and specifically how much substitution among goods their preferences will allow. The need for information is not special to local incomparability, and we saw in Section 8.1 that a lack of information can hinder the search for Pareto improvements in a world of complete preferences. But the incompleteness of preferences exacerbates the information problems of policymakers in two respects.

With local incomparability, buyers of a subsidized good might not extensively shift consumption to other goods when the subsidy is withdrawn; the compensation payments that will make them whole must therefore be large enough that bundles near to their ex ante consumption will be affordable. Compensation payments will then come close to exhausting the revenue gained from dropping the subsidy, and the reform will enjoy only a narrow margin of error. In the limiting case of no substitution, buyers will stick to their original consumptions, in which case no change in the allocation or in the government's outlays will occur. And short of the limiting case, the cost of discovering agents' preferences could dominate the revenue gained from a diminished subsidy: policymakers will have little wiggle room.

Another, more formidable hurdle stands in the way of reform. How can a regulator even determine when a reform benefits an agent? With complete preferences, there is a straightforward test: we know that an individual is at least weakly better off if we can observe the agent choosing a new reform consumption bundle over his or her prereform bundle. Incomplete preferences, however, disrupt the link between choice and preference. Individuals may well select bundles that are unranked relative to their prereform consumption even when the latter remains available. An observer with enough time and resources could likely distinguish between a switch to an unranked option and a switch to a preferred option; it is reasonable to infer preference when an agent systematically chooses one option over another (see Chapter 6). But the repeated observations of choice behavior that could nail down this observational difference will rarely if ever be available to a policymaker.

To make progress, I will ease the Pareto-improvement requirement that all agents at least weakly prefer their new to their original consumption bundle. Policy changes must instead give agents the option of maintaining their ex ante consumption.

Definition 9.1 *Let x^i be the ex ante consumption of agent i. A policy change passes the* **availability test** *if ex post each agent i has the option of consuming x^i. The policy change passes the* **strict availability test** *if in addition some agent j has the option of consuming a bundle that j strictly prefers to x^j.*

Since agents might not have preferences that rank their ex ante and ex post consumption bundles, a policy change that satisfies even the strict availability test might not lead to a Pareto improvement.

The primary rationale for the availability test is that policymakers should be able to build a consensus for changes to the status quo that pass the test. If some malcontent objects, a policymaker has an effective retort: how can you complain if you have the right to consume what you did before? This rejoinder more closely resembles the arguments put forward in civil law than in welfare economics. When a policy change satisfies the availability test, policymakers can explain to any plaintiff who claims damages that the change has left the agent whole: the agent can replicate every material feature of his or her ex ante life. As in tort law, a valid proof that an agent has not been harmed must rest on externally verifiable claims, which the availability test provides, not on inferences about private psychological states.

The availability test does not rely on the intelligence or sophistication of agents. According to the logic of the first welfare theorem, markets achieve efficiency only because every agent optimizes; Pareto efficiency will not be achieved if just one consumer fails to maximize utility or one firm fails to maximize profits – a fragility I will explore in Chapter 11. The availability test in contrast considers only the options facing agents, not their decisions.

For preference die-hards, there is an alternative defense of the availability test. Call a policy change a (weak) *tenuous Pareto improvement* if instead of insisting that agents weakly prefer the bundles they achieve with a reform to their ex ante bundles we require merely that they do not strictly prefer their ex ante to their reform bundles. So with a tenuous rather than a conventional Pareto improvement, one or more agents may not be able to rank their ex ante and their reform bundles. Any policy change that passes the availability test will qualify as a tenuous Pareto improvement. Unfortunately tenuous Pareto improvements string together poorly. They subject agents to the dangerous trades of Section 6.2: at the conclusion of a sequence of tenuous Pareto improvements every agent can end up strictly worse off. And the offending sequences can even be strict with at least one of the agents strictly better off at each step.[1] Although tenuous Pareto improvements therefore fall short of ideal, we can at least mitigate their drawbacks by comparing the status quo with a single reform policy and rule out of court sequences of tenuous improvements.

---

[1] For example, let there be two goods, three agents, and let each agent i have the incomplete preference $\succsim^i$ defined by $x^i \succsim^i y^i$ if and only if $x^i \geq y^i$. Consider the sequence of consumption profiles that begins with $(x^1, x^2, x^3) = ((4,4),(4,4),(4,4))$ and continues with $((1,5),(5,1),(5,5))$, $((2,1),(6,2),(1,6))$, $((2,2),(2,3),(2,5))$, $((3,3),(3,3),(3,3))$. Each step is a tenuous Pareto improvement and yet every agent's welfare is lower at the end of the sequence than at the beginning. The sequence also therefore defines a cycle of tenuous Pareto improvements.

9.2 QUANTITY INFORMATION

Whichever rationale you prefer, the availability test lays out a path to policy reforms. The test releases policymakers from having to deduce which bundles agents weakly prefer to their ex ante consumption, as they must to find a classical Pareto improvement. In fact policymakers can ignore preferences entirely. If they know the quantities consumers have traded in the past then they can give consumers the opportunity to repeat their trades and hence their ex ante consumption. A policy reform will then pass the availability test.

To illustrate, consider again the removal of a subsidy. Suppose some consumer i initially purchases and consumes a quantity $\bar{x}^i$ of a subsidized good produced under constant returns to scale. If producers face a price equal to their unit cost c and s is the subsidy, then consumers initially pay the price $c - s$. If the subsidy is removed then the price for both producers and consumers will be c. To shield consumers from harm, a policymaker that knows only agents' ex ante trades can pay each consumer i a lump-sum compensation of $s\bar{x}^i$. The sum of what consumer i spent ex ante on the good, $(c - s)\bar{x}^i$, and the compensation payment $s\bar{x}^i$ then equals what i must pay to buy $\bar{x}^i$ under the reform. A subsidy removal combined with the $s\bar{x}^i$ compensations therefore passes the availability test. The government's budget will also balance: expenditures ex ante and ex post will both equal $\sum_i s\bar{x}^i$.

If instead returns are decreasing rather than constant and aggregate supply is an increasing function of price, then the interplay of demand and supply will determine the price that rules when the subsidy is removed. Although preferences when incomplete cannot by themselves determine demand, it is plausible that consumers when choosing among unranked bundles will demand less of a good when its price rises – for example due to the reasons of Becker (1962). As in standard tax analysis, the price p that occurs in equilibrium when the subsidy is removed will then be less than the price $\bar{p}$ (inclusive of the subsidy) that producers received ex ante.[2] Since consumers originally faced the price $\bar{p} - s$ and since $p\bar{x}^i < (\bar{p} - s)\bar{x}^i + s\bar{x}^i$, each consumer i will be able to afford $\bar{x}^i$ when facing p and receiving the compensation payment $s\bar{x}^i$ without having to curtail his or her consumption of other goods. In fact, as long as preferences are increasing, the policy change will satisfy a strict availability test with respect to the consumers.

---

[2] I assume that compensation payments do not shift the demand curve.

It is a different story for the owners of firms or of the fixed factors that are the source of decreasing returns. If p falls relative to $\bar{p}$ they will be worse off. But notice that the compensation payments of $s\bar{x}^i$ to each consumer i are too generous: each i can repeat $\bar{x}^i$ with funds left over. This overshooting turns out to be enough to fund the compensations that suppliers will require to undo their losses: policies that pass the availability test will therefore remain feasible. A more abstract treatment will clarify this point.

To allow for taxes or subsidies that confront different agents – for example consumers and firms – with different prices, let $\bar{p}^i$ be the price vector for the economy's L goods that agent i faces ex ante and let $\bar{z}^i$ be the net trades that i selects ex ante. The sum of the ex ante net trades must be feasible and agents must be able to afford these trades. So I assume that $\sum_i \bar{z}^i \leq 0$ and $\bar{p}^i \cdot \bar{z}^i = 0$ for each i. When i is a firm, $\bar{p}^i \cdot \bar{z}^i = 0$ means that i's sales receipts equal the sum of the firm's factor payments and its return of profits or dividends to its owners.

Subsidies for a good can be incorporated by distinguishing between the good, say k, that consumers buy and the good k' producers sell and letting the government be the intermediary. Letting s and c be the subsidy and unit cost for this good and g the government's index, the prices the government faces ex ante are $\bar{p}_k^g = c - s$ and $\bar{p}_{k'}^g = c$ and its net trades will satisfy $\bar{z}_k^g = -\bar{z}_{k'}^g$. Since the government suffers a loss due to the subsidy, the government's budget constraint, $\bar{p}^g \cdot \bar{z}^g = 0$, will require it to raise revenue by taxing other goods.

The policymaker observes $\bar{p}^i$ and $\bar{z}^i$ for each agent i and then institutes a reform where agents will face a common price vector $p \geq 0$, which the policymaker also observes. To give agents the opportunity to duplicate their prior trades, the government issues a lump-sum payment or tax equal to the difference between what agent i's previous trade now costs with p and what it used to cost with $\bar{p}^i$.

A brute force way to implement these payments is to grant each i the right to repeat at the prices $\bar{p}^i$ any of the trades that i made ex ante and require that when one party to an ex ante trade asks for a repeat, the other party must comply. Agents may resell any goods they acquire through these repeated trades, but resales occur at the new prices p. When agent i is an ex ante net purchaser of good k and p_k rises relative to $\bar{p}_k^i$, that is, if

$$\bar{z}_k^i > 0 \text{ and } p_k > \bar{p}_k^i,$$

then i will want to repeat the ex ante trades to earn $(p_k - \bar{p}_k^i)\bar{z}_k^i$ in arbitrage profits. Agent i will reap these profits even if i does not consume any of good k since after buying $\bar{z}_k^i$ units of k at $\bar{p}_k^i$, agent i can sell them at p_k. When i is an ex ante net seller of k and the price of k rises relative to its ex ante price,

$$\bar{z}_k^i < 0 \text{ and } p_k > \bar{p}_k^i,$$

the agents who bought from i will invoke their right to repeat their trades. So i experiences a negative change in income of $(p_k - \bar{p}_k^i)\bar{z}_k^i$. The cases where $p_k < \bar{p}_k^i$ are similar. In sum, agent i receives arbitrage profits equal to

$$\sum_k (p_k - \bar{p}_k^i)\bar{z}_k^i = (p - \bar{p}^i) \cdot \bar{z}^i.$$

Since each agent i could initially afford his or her ex ante net trade, $\bar{p}^i \cdot \bar{z}^i = 0$,

$$p \cdot \bar{z}^i = p \cdot \bar{z}^i - \bar{p}^i \cdot \bar{z}^i = (p - \bar{p}^i) \cdot \bar{z}^i.$$

Thus each i will receive arbitrage profits that ensure that the agent's ex ante net trades $\bar{z}^i$ remain affordable.

Instead of agents forcing their trading partners to repeat their ex ante trades, a government could achieve the same end by dispensing to each agent i a compensation payment or tax equal to $(p - \bar{p}^i) \cdot \bar{z}^i$, the difference between the ex post and ex ante cost of i's net trades $\bar{z}^i$.

A *quantity stabilization* is a policy where a common price vector p is instituted and each agent receives the compensation $(p - \bar{p}^i) \cdot \bar{z}^i$ – either through government payments or through repeated trades. The government can always afford the compensations. Since $\bar{p}^i \cdot \bar{z}^i = 0$ for each i,

$$\sum_i (p - \bar{p}^i) \cdot \bar{z}^i = \sum_i p \cdot \bar{z}^i = p \cdot \sum_i \bar{z}^i,$$

and since the ex ante net trades were feasible, $\sum_i \bar{z}^i \leq 0$, we have $p \cdot \sum_i \bar{z}^i \leq 0$. The sum of the compensations, $\sum_i (p - \bar{p}^i) \cdot \bar{z}^i$, are therefore nonpositive. The payments will usually be exactly affordable, however, and quantity stabilizations therefore suffer from the no-wiggle-room problem of compensations designed to achieve classical Pareto improvements.

Theorem 9.1 *Any quantity stabilization passes the availability test and the government can afford the required compensation payments.*

To apply Theorem 9.1 to the removal of a tax or subsidy on a good, let the initial price $\bar{p}_k^i$ facing each buyer i of some good k equal a common value $\bar{p}_k^B$ and let the price $\bar{p}_k^j$ facing each seller j equal a different common value $\bar{p}_k^S$. Once the tax or subsidy is withdrawn and the quantity stabilization compensations are paid, a new price p_k for good k emerges. In the special case considered earlier of a subsidy s and unit cost c, $\bar{p}_k^S = c$ and $\bar{p}_k^B = c - s$ and each buyer i has an ex ante net trade $\bar{z}_k^i$ equal to his or her ex ante consumption $\bar{x}_k^i$. In a quantity stabilization, both buyers and sellers then face the price $p_k = c$. Assuming no other prices are affected, each buyer i receives the compensation $(p_k - \bar{p}_k^B)\bar{z}_k^i = s\bar{x}_k^i$ as in our earlier analysis.[3]

Theorem 9.1 appeals only to the affordability of net trades: quantity stabilizations rely only on information about prices and ex ante net trades and invoke no assumptions on preferences. And since Theorem 9.1 does not depend on what prices rule ex post or how they arise, quantity stabilizations do not need to constrain the ex post price vector p. One notable special case occurs when all subsidies and taxes are eliminated and p is the equilibrium price vector of a classical general equilibrium model with transfer payments. Since the quantity stabilization payments do not disrupt the standard proof of the first welfare theorem, the allocation that results will be Pareto efficient not just relative to allocations that can be reached by some policy but relative to all allocations.[4]

The payments agents receive in a quantity stabilization are instances of the Slutsky (1915) compensations that arise on occasion in preference theory: they equal the changes in income that agents would have to receive following a change in prices that would allow them to exactly afford their ex ante consumptions. Slutsky compensations are the lesser known cousins of the Hicks and Allen (1934) compensations that allow agents to maintain their ex ante utility levels. Slutsky never rose above the status of a historical footnote and his compensations are known today only for the curiosity that the derivatives of Slutsky compensated demands coincide with the derivatives of Hicksian compensated demands and for the gold star awarded for preceding Hicks and Allen by twenty years.[5]

Slutsky compensations are however the more obvious way to make agents whole when prices change. Had it not been for the spell cast by the ideology of preference, they would have long ago vanquished the Hicksian competition. Hicksian compensations need not even be well-defined when preferences are incomplete. Given the paucity of indifferent bundles, discussed in Chapter 6, following a price change

---

[3] If, to include the government as an agent, we assign a separate index k' to the good a producer j sells then $\bar{p}_{k'}^j = p_{k'} = c$.

[4] This conclusion requires minor restrictions on preferences (transitivity and local nonsatiation) but not completeness.

[5] See Allen (1936).

there might not be a cheapest bundle that an agent weakly prefers to his or her ex ante consumption.

The advantage of Slutsky compensations is how easy they are to calculate. Even assuming that agents have well-defined preferences, it is not realistic to imagine that policymakers could crank out Hicksian compensation payments; they rely on inherently private information. And while Hicks and Slutsky compensate agents by different amounts, for the goal of Pareto improvements the error of Slutsky compensations goes the right way. The payments overshoot: again assuming that agents have well-defined preferences, Slutsky compensations will usually strictly improve the welfare of their recipients.

The compensation payments received in a quantity stabilization are even easier to calculate than they at first appear. Since $\bar{p}^i \cdot \bar{z}^i = 0$ for each i, the compensation $(p - \bar{p}^i) \cdot \bar{z}^i$ reduces to the simpler $p \cdot \bar{z}^i$. The government thus does not even need to know the ex ante prices $\bar{p}^i$ that faced agent i to pay i the appropriate amount. But despite this simplicity, the compensations would still require too much information in a general equilibrium setting. Policymakers rarely know the entire list of an agent's net trades and hence cannot calculate appropriate payments or enforce repetitions of ex ante trades; economy-wide compensation schemes will therefore usually be too ambitious.

To consider more modest, partial-equilibrium quantity stabilizations, suppose the government knows only the ex ante prices and net trades for the first K of the economy's L goods, $\bar{p}_k$ and $\bar{z}_k^i$ for each agent i and goods $k = 1, \ldots, K$. In the spirit of partial equilibrium, let any policy change affect only the prices of the first K goods: for each good $j > K$ and agent i, the agent will face the same price $\bar{p}_j^i$ that he or she faced ex ante. Agent i's compensation then reduces to

$$\sum_{k=1}^{K} (p_k - \bar{p}_k^i)\bar{z}_k^i.$$

Agents that receive these transfers can again afford their ex ante net trades and the availability test is therefore still satisfied. In this partial-equilibrium setting, policymakers will work under the handicap that they will not know the trades of the last $L - K$ goods and hence will not know $p \cdot \bar{z}^i$. The government consequently cannot rely on the simpler $p \cdot \bar{z}^i$ compensation payments that ignore the ex ante prices; it has to make the compensations specified above.[6]

---

[6] A transfer of $\sum_{k=1}^{K} p_k \bar{z}_k^i$ need not allow agents to repeat their ex ante trades. For example, if $K = 1$ and an agent i with $\bar{z}_1^i < 0$ receives a (negative) transfer $p_1 \bar{z}_1^i$, then i will not be able to repeat his/her ex ante trades.

The brute-force quantity stabilizations that give decentralized agents the right to repeat their ex ante trades will usually enjoy an informational advantage over government transfers. Even when prices change for only a handful of goods, knowledge of the ex ante trades of these goods is likely to be dispersed rather than centralized in the government's hands. Of course, if the government has no access to the $\bar{z}^i$ whatsoever, then agents will repudiate their obligations to trade. But if agents can establish the validity of claims about their ex ante trades in court or before a regulator, say by suing their trading partners if they refuse to honor their obligations to repeat transactions, then agents may be able to achieve on their own what would be difficult for a government to achieve. The mere threat of court action by itself might be sufficient to enforce the repetition of trades. Rental contracts furnish a clean example: tenants can use the government or the courts to enforce a rental at a specific price even though ex ante no repository holds information about all contracts. This enforcement infrastructure in housing markets suggests that reforms of rent control that pass the availability test will be feasible.

Example 9.1 (rent control) Let the first K goods be apartments subject to rent control. The existing tenant i of one of these apartments k has the right to live in k for a rental price $\bar{p}_k$. Other individuals may be willing to pay a far higher price to live in k, often more than i would be willing to pay. Since a simple repeal of rent control would leave many rent-control tenants worse off, this gulf does not by itself imply that the ex ante status quo is inefficient even from a complete-preferences perspective; for a policy to qualify as Pareto inefficient we must identify a Pareto improvement that some other policy can achieve.

The problem with rent control is Coasean: neither current tenants nor owners can reassign properties freely. A quantity stabilization maneuvers around this roadblock. Let the ex ante tenant of apartment k continue to have the right to rent k at the price $\bar{p}_k$ but, instead of requiring the agent to live in k, allow the agent to sublet k to someone else. If k can be sublet for a rent of $p_k > \bar{p}_k$ then the existing tenant can earn a profit of $p_k - \bar{p}_k$, which the agent might choose over living in k. As long as the prices of the non-apartment goods remain unchanged, any tenant can continue to consume his or her ex ante consumption bundle with no added expense: the policy passes the availability test with respect to the tenants. If the subletting market for each apartment k functions competitively and clears at price p_k then, in a classical model without further distortions, the equilibrium allocation will be Pareto efficient relative to all allocations, not just those achievable by some policy.

Inevitably there is a wrinkle. Some apartment k could end up renting for a price that is lower than its ex ante rent-control price, $p_k < \bar{p}_k$. This possibility is by no means pathological. Under rent control, the limited availability of the most desirable apartments may force richer tenants to live in less desirable areas – in Brooklyn rather than Manhattan. The greater availability of desirable apartments could well drive down the value of less desirable apartments. Moreover if $p_k < \bar{p}_k$ then the owner of k will be worse off unless the tenant can be forced to continue to pay $\bar{p}_k$. Such a requirement may be unenforceable if tenants can exit the jurisdiction or may be politically unthinkable.

The government could in principle compensate any landlords suffering a loss by taxing subletting profits, that is, taxing the original tenant of any k with $p_k > \bar{p}_k$. Although the receipts from a such tax might not cover subsidy payments, it is plausible that they would. If subletting profits are taxed proportionally, the tax would effectively be lump-sum and not interfere with efficiency: the original tenant i of k will continue his or her rent-control lease if $p_k > \bar{p}_k$ and continue to sublet k if another agent values k more highly than i does. Such a tax could be implemented using only information from preexisting leases; the overall reform plan would therefore remain informationally accessible. ∎

Policies that use quantity information to meet the availability test stick closely to the Pareto program. While our rationale for quantity stabilizations has sheared away any reference to preferences and relied instead on the continued availability of ex ante trades, the recommendations I have laid out apply without amendment to agents with classical preferences and could be justified by the standard Pareto criterion. The elimination of distortions, such as taxes and subsidies on particular goods, in combination with Slutsky compensations will deliver both Pareto efficiency and a Pareto improvement. One fair reading of this section is that quantity stabilizations provide a low-information route to the welfare goals that economists have long held to be the ideal.

But the information that quantity stabilizations ask of policymakers remains formidable. Our starting point of questioning whether preferences – if they exist – can be discovered argues for a comparable skepticism regarding net trades. There are cases such as apartment rentals where agents leave behind a trail of information about their net trades but they are the exception not the rule.

9.3 PRICE STABILIZATIONS: A PATH TO PRODUCTION EFFICIENCY

The best known principle of welfare economics is depicted by the tangency of indifference curves in the Edgeworth box: an allocation can be Pareto efficient only when agents' better-than sets are supported by a common price line or, if utilities are differentiable and the allocation is interior, when marginal rates of substitution are equal. But when a policymaker does not know agents' preferences or the agents themselves cannot settle on preference judgments, the existence of a common supporting price line can become an empty requirement. The effective multiplicity of potential agents will lead many or possibly all achievable allocations to qualify as efficient. And any gains to be had from a common supporting price line are likely to be small.

The Edgeworth box picture of efficiency fortunately does not capture the main economic benefits that markets deliver. Economic theory's focus on exchange leaves aside the productivity growth and expansions of wealth that typify capitalist societies and can in principle benefit all individuals. Productivity growth however does not arrive as an unalloyed gain. Innovations enhance productivity but they also undermine the income of factors lost in technological backwardness. Schumpeter called these dual effects "creative destruction" and to this day they present the central challenge of economic policymaking: how can we get creative destruction without the destruction?

The same competitive forces that spur productivity growth reconfigure factor prices. Resources must be reallocated to different industries and the relative usefulness of factors within industries will shift. If these changes are combined with the welfare theorem recommendation that consumers and firms face the same prices then some consumers – those that sell factors whose price has fallen – can be substantially harmed. Policymakers can however pass the availability test if they are willing to flout that advice. The availability test will require the relative prices consumers face ex ante to be preserved, while reaping productivity gains will require firms to face prices that incentivize efficient production. The prices consumers and producers confront must therefore diverge.

I will consider economies that suffer from an ex ante production inefficiency: the state could initially be dictating the organization of production, regulators could be sheltering an industry from competition, thereby discouraging the adoption of new technologies, or the state could be requiring industries to use certain factors of production. Policymakers typically know little or nothing about ex ante trades but they do usually know summary facts about markets including the price vector $\bar{p}$ that rules ex ante. If the laws and regulations that foster inefficiency are removed and the prices consumers face remain equal to $\bar{p}$ then the policy change will pass the availability test: each consumer's opportunities for trade will remain unchanged. If in addition the government can distribute money or material endowments to consumers, then some or all of them will be able to afford bundles that make them strictly better off: the policy change will then also satisfy the strict availability test. Alternatively consumers will be able to afford bundles that make them better off if they are net purchasers of a good whose relative price falls or they are net sellers of a good (perhaps their labor) whose relative price rises. I will call prices *stabilized* when changes in the relative prices of goods satisfy these restrictions.

Laissez-faire deregulations and privatizations generally fail to keep prices stabilized. A regulated industry, such as a public utility, may have been mandated by the government to sell to some or all of its customers at a loss, funded either by higher prices charged to businesses or a government subsidy. The industry may also have been rent-sharing with its employees by paying salaries beyond what the labor market requires. A full-scale turn to laissez-faire is likely to harm some of these parties. Since quantity stabilizations will be impossible to devise in the absence of information about ex ante net trades, policies that pass the availability test must stabilize the prices agents face.

For the prices that consumers face, price stabilizations require both that consumption good prices do not rise and that factor prices, including wages and salaries, do not fall. These restrictions need not lead to Pareto inefficiency. Just as individuals with locally incomparable preferences may not know how to trade-off different consumption goods, they also may not know how to trade-off different types of work or how to weigh the disutility of an existing job against the cost of training for a new line of work. Economists have long argued that unions or legislation that raises the wages of low-skilled workers bring an efficiency loss by discouraging workers from investing in new skills. But if workers fail to have a well-defined trade-off between consumption and the costs of acquiring skills, that reasoning is invalid.

But if producers face the same stabilized prices that consumers face then productive inefficiency will likely result. A high wage floor, for example, could choke off the usage of some types of labor. Stabilized prices might even be the initial cause of the ex ante production inefficiency. A government might ex ante mandate that firms trade at prices of its choosing, as when a government in pursuit of votes manipulates wages in the industries it regulates. Price distortions can also become politically intertwined through time with policies originally geared to other ends. When a government concludes that it no longer makes sense to shield a monopoly from competition, the main resistance can come from the rent-sharing workers who siphon off a portion of the monopoly profits. Even when politicians bent on change can withstand the heat from an industry's owners, they may wilt when confronted by the employees.

Price stabilizations can eliminate distortions in production by letting producers face prices that differ from the prices $\bar{p}$ that consumers face ex ante. With a dual system of prices, production efficiency can be achieved without the distributional and political repercussions of market competition.

I will begin with a simple partial-equilibrium case where the producer-consumer price difference applies only to outputs and not to factors and can be enforced by taxes and subsidies. Consider a regulated public utility – say telecommunications or the water supply – that initially is provided only by state-sanctioned suppliers. Two preexisting features of the industry call for reform: entry of competing firms is prohibited or limited which allows the existing providers to produce inefficiently, and the regulator requires the utility to use the revenue earned from one class of customers to subsidize another class.

The ex ante inefficiency in production could take many forms. The government mandates discussed above or simply the absence of market pressure might cause some factors to be used excessively and the lack of competition can allow firms to stick to obsolete technologies.

The difference in the prices faced by the two classes of customers can lead to a different form of inefficiency. In the extreme case where preferences are locally decisive, the price difference will misalign agents' marginal rates of substitution, leading to classical Edgeworth-box inefficiency.

Which of these failures is likely to be the most significant? With locally incomparable preferences, the diversity of prices that customers face ex ante need not be a source of trouble: a common price vector might still support every agent's better-than set initially in which case the ex ante quantities of output will be allocated efficiently. An alignment of the prices customers face then would not make any Pareto improvements available or pass the strict availability test, even assuming that policymakers know the net trades needed to design the right compensation payments. Cases where the different prices faced by consumers do not cause any inefficiency at all may be extreme, but with local incomparability the allocative benefits to be gained from confronting agents with the same prices are likely to be small and – given the difficulty of identifying when an agent has moved to a preferred option – difficult to detect.

The lion's share of the gains will come from repairing the ex ante inefficiency in production. The windfalls that have been reaped from telecommunications deregulations, for example, have not stemmed from improved allocations of given quantities of output. The gains have come from expansions in productivity and the innovations of product and process that previous monopolies had little incentive to pursue.

The orthodox approach to deregulation has been to prescribe a big bang that opens the market to unrestricted competition by letting firms buy or lease the utility's infrastructure and vie for customers. Since market prices will then conform to marginal costs, a big bang combines the increased competition that induces technological progress with an end to cross subsidization. While the first effect potentially benefits all customers, the second effect can be large enough to make the ex ante trades of the previously subsidized agents unaffordable, a violation of the availability test.

To capture the potential productivity gains while passing the availability test, we must redress the production inefficiency while letting the cross subsidization remain partially intact, at least in the short run. Since a diversity of prices facing consumers need not even be a sign of inefficiency when preferences are incomplete, it would be remarkable if eliminating the diversity were important to the cure.

The two classes of customers will be *residences* and *businesses*. I use the label businesses for brevity: it can designate either the owners of the utility's business customers or a class of traditional consumers. Under regulation, the public utility provides service to these two groups at prices $\bar{p}^r$ and $\bar{p}^b$, where $\bar{p}^r < \bar{p}^b$, and the two groups have demand functions for the utility given by $x^r(p^r)$ and $x^b(p^b)$ that are strictly positive at $\bar{p}^r$ and $\bar{p}^b$ respectively.[7] Due to the possibility of incompleteness, it might not be possible to deduce these demands from preferences; the only necessary feature of demand is that no individual i will choose a bundle strictly dispreferred to an affordable bundle. However this indeterminacy is resolved, I assume that a continuous demand function results and that each individual in each class has increasing preferences.

---

[7] The analysis to come would be nearly identical if residences and business paid the same price but the cost of delivering the utility is higher to residences than to businesses.

Under regulation the public utility is assumed to break even. So, if provision of the utility costs $\bar{c}$ per unit initially,

$$\bar{c}(x^r(\bar{p}^r) + x^b(\bar{p}^b)) = \bar{p}^r x^r(\bar{p}^r) + \bar{p}^b x^b(\bar{p}^b),$$

and consequently $\bar{p}^r < \bar{c} < \bar{p}^b$. The quantity $\bar{c} - \bar{p}^r$ is the unit subsidy to residences while $\bar{p}^b - \bar{c}$ is the unit tax on businesses.

The regulatory regime's entry restrictions lead to production inefficiency: I assume that a unit cost $c < \bar{c}$ can be achieved when the utility is delivered by competitive firms. To make sure there is tension between a big-bang deregulation and the welfare of the residences, I assume that $c > \bar{p}^r$.

A big bang ends cross subsidization and companies that deliver the utility will now charge c per unit to both types of customers. Since $c > \bar{p}^r$ the ex ante purchases of residences will now be more expensive. A price stabilization imposes taxes and subsidies on purchases of the utility to ensure that the new price paid by residences does not rise above $\bar{p}^r$. To guarantee that all parties – including the government – can repeat their ex ante transactions at no greater cost, a regulator should set a per-unit subsidy for residential purchases, $s \geq 0$, and a per-unit tax on business purchases, $\tau \geq 0$, to satisfy

$$\bar{p}^r \geq c - s,$$
$$\bar{p}^b \geq c + \tau, \qquad \text{(PS)}$$
$$sx^r(c - s) \leq \tau x^b(c + \tau).$$

A (s, τ) that satisfies these conditions is a *partial-equilibrium price stabilization*. Since the prices that residences and businesses pay are $c - s$ and $c + \tau$ respectively, such policies pass the availability test and the government's subsidy expenditures will be covered by its tax receipts. Given that $c < \bar{c}$,

$$c(x^r(\bar{p}^r) + x^b(\bar{p}^b)) < \bar{p}^r x^r(\bar{p}^r) + \bar{p}^b x^b(\bar{p}^b)$$

and therefore

$$(c - \bar{p}^r)x^r(\bar{p}^r) < (\bar{p}^b - c)x^b(\bar{p}^b).$$

So if we set $s = c - \bar{p}^r$ and $\tau = \bar{p}^b - c$, the inequalities in PS are satisfied: a price stabilization exists. Since moreover the third inequality in PS holds strictly at these values of s and τ and the demand functions are continuous, we can by raising s and lowering τ slightly satisfy all three inequalities strictly. Both residences and businesses can then repeat their ex ante purchases at reduced cost. As preferences are increasing, the adjusted taxes and subsidies pass the strict availability test.

Proposition 9.2 *There exist partial-equilibrium price stabilizations that pass the strict availability test.*

As with the compensation schemes of Section 9.2, price stabilizations can be defended on more conventional grounds: if agents have complete preferences, a price stabilization will lead to a Pareto improvement.

Price stabilizations can satisfy the strict availability test – or can engineer Pareto improvements – because they harness the private information of agents about their ex ante purchases that policymakers do not have. Policymakers do not know which individuals consume the public utility intensively ex ante and therefore cannot determine the lump-sum compensations that would let these individuals repeat their ex ante consumption under a big-bang deregulation. But with a price stabilization the compensations that agents receive in the form of per-unit subsidies are determined by the magnitude of their purchases: those who consume the utility intensively ex ante can therefore continue to do so ex post.

The allocation that results from a price stabilization need not be Pareto efficient relative to the set of all physically feasible allocations: the unit cost will not equal the price either type of agent faces. As noted already, inefficiency is not a certainty since preferences can be locally incomparable. But in addition the relevance of Pareto efficiency, when defined relative to the set of all physically possible allocations, is dubious. If a policymaker cannot identify which policies will Pareto improve on a price stabilization then the price stabilization will qualify as efficient relative to the allocations the policymaker can achieve with the information it has.

Any failure of Pareto efficiency among the physically possible allocations is also likely to fade through time. The raison d'être of price stabilizations is to unleash the productivity-enhancing power of competition among producers, a dynamic process that can continue indefinitely. Marginal costs are assumed to drop immediately to below $\bar{c}$ but they may well keep falling through time. If c descends to a value below $\bar{p}^r$ the tax τ and subsidy s would be self-extinguishing: both classes of customers can then repeat their ex ante purchases at lesser cost when policymakers set $s = \tau = 0$. If productivity does continue to advance, first-best Pareto efficiency will be achieved in the long run. Deregulations of landline telephone services have in time led those services to be delivered at a unit cost near 0; any subsidies to safeguard agents from harm have long become unnecessary. While price stabilizations aim to block the short-run damage that a big bang can inflict on the beneficiaries of cross subsidization, the technological change they induce may be powerful enough that those beneficiaries will gain in the long run even if their subsidies lapse.

Given the attention I have paid to the informational requirements of the laissez-faire policies recommended by the welfare theorems, price stabilizations should be held to the same standard. Since firms supply output elastically at a price equal to unit cost, the parameter c should be easy to infer and a price stabilization (s, τ) can then be readily calculated. To set the information bar higher, suppose for concreteness that all of the gains of a price stabilization go to the residences and businesses. The government's budget must then balance ex post as well as ex ante: $sx^r(c-s) = \tau x^b(c+\tau)$. Given an equilibrium meeting this requirement, suppose the government knows c, again due to the elastic supply assumption, but does not know the demand functions. To implement the equilibrium, the government could set $s = c - \bar{p}^r$ and adjust the tax rate by raising τ when revenue from taxation falls short of expenditures on subsidies and lowering τ when revenue exceeds expenditures,

$$\dot{\tau} = sx^r(\bar{p}^r) - \tau x^b(c+\tau).$$

This rule will lead τ to a price-stabilized value if $x^b(\cdot)$ is sufficiently inelastic and differentiable. Stability will obtain if $\dot{\tau}$ is decreasing in τ, which will be satisfied if tax revenue $T(\tau) = \tau x^b(c+\tau)$ is increasing in τ. Since $DT(\tau) = x^b(c+\tau) + \tau Dx^b(c+\tau)$, stability indeed obtains when $Dx^b(c+\tau)$ is small. Variations on this stability conclusion are available if supply is not perfectly elastic.[8]

Advocates of deregulation usually fold together the cross-subsidization and the production-inefficiency defects of government regulation. In view of preference incompleteness and local incomparability, the magnitude of the efficiency loss from cross subsidization is likely to be small; production inefficiency is the more serious problem. Price stabilizations, which draw only on publicly available information, untie the two problems: by acquiescing to cross subsidization, the policies can both achieve production efficiency and pass the strict availability test.

---

[8] Suppose supplies of residential and business services are given by the differentiably strictly increasing functions $y^r(p^r)$ and $y^b(p^b)$ and let s, p^b, and τ be governed by the dynamical system $\dot{s} = x^r(\bar{p}^r) - y^r(\bar{p}^r + s)$, $\dot{p}_b = x^b(p^b) - y^b(p^b - \tau)$, $\dot{\tau} = sx^r(\bar{p}^r) - \tau x^b(p^b)$. If $Dx^b(p^b)$ is sufficiently small at an equilibrium point of the system, calculation of the eigenvalues shows that the system is asymptotically stable at that point.

9.4 PRODUCTION EFFICIENCY IN THE ECONOMY AS A WHOLE

Price stabilizations can apply to the economy as a whole; by confronting consumers and producers with different prices, the policies again achieve production efficiency and pass the availability test. The chief benefits of competition can thereby be secured without inflicting harm on existing stakeholders, thus deflecting the opposition to reform. In a general equilibrium price stabilization, consumers will continue to face the prices $\bar{p}$ that ruled ex ante, firms will face distinct producer prices $q > 0$, and agents will receive a distribution from the state that consists either of the privatized assets of state firms or financial wealth. Both the consumers that face $\bar{p}$ and the firms that face q optimize and markets clear. If production is initially inefficient, price stabilizations that achieve production efficiency and pass the strict availability test will be feasible; and if preferences happen to be complete then the allocation that results will also Pareto improve on the initial allocation. A price stabilization can be found by progressively doling out greater wealth to consumers until their demands in the aggregate hit the boundary of the set of feasible consumptions: production efficiency is thereby achieved. The producer prices q are defined by the line (hyperplane) that separates aggregate consumption demand from the set of feasible consumptions. I will lay out this argument in more detail in an example below. If we view $\bar{p} - q$ as a vector of commodity taxes, the production efficiency conclusion dovetails with the Diamond and Mirrlees (1971) theory of optimal taxation.

Price stabilizations place modest informational demands on policymakers, compared either to compensations that allow agents to repeat their ex ante trades or to second-welfare-theorem compensations. To institute a price stabilization in general equilibrium, a policymaker only needs to know how to set the tax rates $\bar{p} - q$ and how much wealth to distribute. The former can be determined by adjusting producer prices according to demand and supply: raise q_k, the producer price for good k, when market demand for k at $\bar{p}$ is greater than market supply at q and lower q_k when demand is less than supply. With strictly convex production sets, which ensure that supply functions are well-defined, tax rates will converge to values that support a price stabilization. Convergent adjustment mechanisms for consumer wealth also exist and can run concurrently with the adjustment of tax rates. The adjustment mechanisms for consumer wealth use information only about how aggregate consumer demand responds at $\bar{p}$ to changes in aggregate consumer income; no information about individual preferences or ex ante trades is needed.[9]

Price stabilizations may or may not lead to Pareto-efficient allocations; that will depend on the extent to which preferences are locally incomparable. Either way, policymakers' information constraints will generally make it impossible to find a policy that Pareto improves on a price stabilization.

To keep the discussion concrete I will consider a specific inefficiency, the failure of an economy under autarky to exploit the potential gains from international trade. This choice of an ex ante distortion underscores that the preexisting production inefficiencies can be interpreted broadly: any inefficiency where agents in the aggregate do not initially trade to the boundary of the feasible set of consumptions would do equally well.

The relative prices of an economy sheltered from international trade often differ markedly from the relative prices that rule internationally. The political stakes behind these divergences can be momentous. In Egypt, for example, multibillion dollar subsidies reduce the consumer prices of bread and some other essentials below their international prices, and the elimination of these subsidies in 1977 led to riots and strikes that threatened the Sadat regime. An unquestioned assumption of all subsequent Egyptian governments has been that social peace requires some form of subsidization of bread.[10] International lending organizations, backed by the advocacy in economic theory of lump-sum compensation payments, oppose these subsidies: redistributions of wealth should not target specific goods or distort relative prices and should be directed solely to the poor.

Who is right, the domestic governments driven by political imperatives or the advisers who draw on Paretian welfare economics? In the Egyptian case, probably neither side. The original system of bread subsidies was not applied directly to purchases of bread and instead lowered the price of flour, and recent changes have helpfully given subsidy recipients greater flexibility on what goods they can buy. But the need for domestic tranquility and broad political support – and the limited tools and information about ex ante purchases – argue for subsidizing some consumption goods and giving subsidies a wide franchise that extends beyond

[9] See Mandler (1999a).
[10] See Abdalla and Al-Shawarby (2018) and Alderman (1986).

the poor. However the debate should be resolved, it is implausible that the misalignment between producer and consumer prices or among the various prices that different consumers face could be major impediments to economic growth. Given the doubt that local incomparability casts on the importance of substitution in consumption, the inefficiency that stems from multiple prices in the Egyptian bread market should be given small weight compared to the politics involved or the goal of efficiency in production.

The abstract model considers a small closed economy that must decide whether to open its markets to international trade. An unconditional opening without redistributions would harm some agents. While autarky is Pareto dominated by some free-trade equilibrium with lump-sum redistributions (Samuelson (1939, 1956)), policymakers will not know how to determine those payments; and the information about ex ante trades needed for the compensations of Section 9.2 would be almost as difficult to come by. Price information on the other hand is widely available. By exploiting that information, price stabilizations can capture the most significant gains from international trade and pass the strict availability test.

As usual, there will be L goods and each consumer i has the (possibly incomplete) preferences $\succsim^i$. The technology of the economy under autarky is given by an aggregate production set Y_A. I assume that each $\succsim^i$ is transitive and increasing and that Y_A is closed and convex, satisfies constant returns to scale, and permits free disposal.

In addition to the L traditional goods, the economy has a money or credit, with a price equal to 1, that the state can print in arbitrary quantities. Consumer i's endowment of standard goods is e^i and of money is m^i. Given the price vector p, i's income is then $p \cdot e^i + m^i$. I assume that each consumer i's excess demands – the difference between i's consumption and endowment – are given by a continuous function $z^i(p, p \cdot e^i + m^i)$. As in the partial equilibrium model of Section 9.3, this function presupposes a resolution of the indeterminacy of choice that accompanies any incompleteness of preferences.

An *autarky equilibrium* is a $\bar{p} \geq 0$ and a $\bar{y} \in Y_A$ such that

- $\sum_i z^i(\bar{p}, \bar{p} \cdot e^i + m^i) = \bar{y}$
- $\bar{p} \cdot \bar{y} \geq \bar{p} \cdot y'$ for all y' in Y_A.

Some of the goods are traded internationally. Letting T be the set of L-vectors that can be non-0 only in the coordinates of the internationally-traded goods, $\pi \in T$ will indicate the nonnegative world prices of these goods. The economy under consideration is small: π will be unaffected by its trades with the rest of the world. The set of feasible international trades is therefore $T_I = \{\gamma \in T : \pi \cdot \gamma = 0\}$. When an economy participates in world trade, it has at its disposal the trade-modified production set $Y_T = Y_A + T_I$ that consists of the commodity vectors that, through production or international trade, can be exchanged with consumers. I assume that Y_T intersects the positive orthant only at 0.

Since Y_A is a subset of Y_T, free trade expands the set of feasible aggregate productions relative to autarky. Aggregate production under autarky $\bar{y}$ is on the boundary of Y_A, due to profit maximization, but not necessarily on the boundary of Y_T.

In a price stabilization, consumers continue to face the prices $\bar{p}$ while producers face a distinct price vector q that is comparable to the prices that include taxes and subsidies in Section 9.3. A *general-equilibrium price stabilization* is therefore a $q > 0$, a distribution of money $m_d^i \geq 0$ to each consumer i, and a $y \in Y_T$ such that

$$\sum_i z^i(\bar{p}, \bar{p} \cdot e^i + m^i + m_d^i) = y,$$
$$q \cdot y \geq q \cdot y' \text{ for all } y' \text{ in } Y_T.$$

Production efficiency obtains at a general-equilibrium price stabilization $(q, \{m_d^i\}, y)$ if there does not exist a $y' \in Y_T$ such that $y' \gg y$. An equilibrium is *conditionally efficient* if, defining $z^i = z^i(\bar{p}, \bar{p} \cdot e^i + m^i + m_d^i)$, there does not exist a reallocation of $\sum_i z^i$ that benefits at least one of the consumers and harms none of them, that is, a $(\hat{z}^1, \ldots, \hat{z}^I)$ such that $\sum_i \hat{z}^i = \sum_i z^i$, $\hat{z}^i + e^i \succsim^i z^i + e^i$ for all i, and $\hat{z}^i + e^i \succ^i z^i + e^i$ for some i. Conditional efficiency does not imply full Pareto efficiency since changes in $\sum_i z^i$ might make a Pareto improvement possible.

If production under autarky is in the interior of Y_T, then a nontrivial price stabilization is feasible.

Theorem 9.3 *If $\bar{y}$ is in the interior of Y_T then there exists a general-equilibrium price stabilization that passes the strict availability test and is both production efficient and conditionally efficient.*

The proof proceeds by keeping prices fixed at $\bar{p}$ while expanding the m_d^i distributions of money to agents until the point where aggregate consumption hits a boundary point $\hat{\chi}$ of the set of feasible aggregate consumptions $F = \{\chi \in \mathbb{R}_+^L : \chi \leq \sum_i e^i + y \text{ for some } y \in Y_T\}$. Let $\hat{y} \in Y_T$ be a production that makes $\hat{\chi}$ possible: $\hat{\chi} \leq \sum_i e^i + \hat{y}$. Since Y_T is convex and contains the negative orthant, a separation theorem provides the producer prices $q > 0$ such that $q \cdot \hat{y} \geq q \cdot y'$ for any $y' \in Y_T$. This q, the distributions of money that lead to the aggregate consumption $\hat{\chi}$, and $\hat{y}$ define the price stabilization. The strict availability test is satisfied: since consumer prices remain equal to $\bar{p}$ all consumers can afford their ex ante consumption and those i with $m_d^i > 0$, who enjoy strictly greater wealth, can afford bundles strictly preferred to their ex ante consumptions. Production efficiency obtains: since $\hat{\chi}$ lies on the boundary of F, $\hat{y}$ must lie on the boundary of Y_T. Conditional efficiency follows from a first-welfare-theorem argument (which does not require preferences to be complete).

When there are goods that consumers only buy or only sell, the expansion of demand needed in a production-efficient price stabilization does not have to achieved by disbursements of money. A price stabilization will still pass the availability test if instead the prices for the first class of goods are reduced or the prices for the second class are raised.

Because of the wedge between consumer prices $\bar{p}$ and producer prices q, some goods in a general-equilibrium price stabilization will be subsidized or taxed. As in the partial-equilibrium case, the magnitude of the implicit compensation that an agent receives from subsidies draws on the agent's own information about which goods he or she consumes intensively rather than on policymakers' information.

Due to the taxes and subsidies, the domestic relative price of some consumer goods may fall below their relative price in international trade. Many nations employ such subsidies; the bread subsidies mentioned earlier and the subsidized domestic gasoline prices of oil-producing countries provide two examples. Despite the pleas of these countries that their subsidies are politically indispensable, international lending agencies criticize these subsidies and aid can be contingent on their elimination or reduction. Price stabilization provides an economic theory rebuttal: subsidies can be an efficient device for shielding agents from the losses that accompany unfettered participation in world trade.

Price stabilizations can replace existing, more haphazard policy efforts to protect individuals from harm. When comparative advantage in international trade moves against a previously prosperous industry, the workers in the industry can suffer calamitous harm. The layoffs that result are exacerbated by the wage increases that workers won when they rent-shared in the boom but that did not expire when there were no more rents to share. In a price stabilization, the wages of workers would instead be subsidized, shielding the workers from unemployment and income losses. Since the subsidies are applied to all potential employments of the labor involved rather than only to employment in the threatened industry, some of the labor will be reallocated to other sectors, though the extent of reallocation will normally diminish relative to a laissez-faire policy. It may offend a utilitarian's sense of justice to let the accidental beneficiaries of an industry's earlier boom continue to enjoy privileges. But that charge can be levied against any efficiency standard that seeks to stop agents from experiencing economic losses, the Pareto criterion as much as the availability test.

The scope of taxes and subsidies in a price stabilization is more limited than might initially appear. Since a price stabilization treats international trade as a type of production, the producer prices for the internationally traded goods will be proportional to their prices on the world market. Up to the exchange rate, the producer and world prices of these goods will coincide.[11]

The subsidies enacted under a price stabilization are not directed to domestic producers alone. If they were, the subsidies would shelter domestic producers from lower-cost competitors abroad, which would lead to production inefficiency. The subsidies of a price stabilization simply establish a wedge between consumer and producer prices; and the producer price of a subsidized good will (after accounting for the exchange rate) equal its international price. So when foreign producers are the sole minimum cost producers of a subsidized good, those firms and only those firms will produce the good under a price stabilization. Even if the aim of not harming any agent would justify domestic protectionism, such a sacrifice is unnecessary when price stabilizations are feasible.

9.5 CONCLUSION

The gains reaped by price stabilizations in the previous section stemmed from international trade. Any expansion of production sets or of opportunities for trade would tell the same story. Technological change expands an economy's aggregate production set and those expansions can in principle be exploited to improve the lives of all agents. But when markets are unfettered, technological change will depress the prices of outmoded factors of production and thus endanger their owners. Bitter social conflict can ensue. Rapid productivity growth and the expansion of trade

---

[11] Let q_T be the projection of q onto T. For any $y \in T_I$, $q_T \cdot y = 0$ since $-y \in T_I$ and therefore both $q_T \cdot y \leq 0$ and $q_T \cdot (-y) \leq 0$. Since $\pi \geq 0$ and $q_T \geq 0$ are both orthogonal to every $y \in T_I$ and T_I has dimension $L - 1$, $q_T = \alpha\pi$ for some scalar $\alpha \geq 0$. See Dixit and Norman (1980, ch. 6) for a classical treatment, from the optimal taxation point of view.

have devastated workers and localities tied to heavy industry in developed economies. A price stabilization would have subsidized workers in these industries to allow their reemployment in other sectors while receiving wages that remain unchanged. Although some lapse from efficiency might have resulted, productivity growth and industrial change could then have proceeded without obstruction. Policymakers could alternatively have responded to the deindustrialization of the world's rustbelts with compensation payments that would have allowed displaced workers to replicate approximately their ex ante standard of living. Under either reform strategy, a price or a quantity stabilization, the subsequent political history of the developed economies might have followed a more humane path.

10

Utilitarianism without Utility

10.1 DECOUPLING WELFARE AND UTILITY

Any practical implementation of an economic policy in a large society harms someone. The compensation payments designed to pass the availability test or achieve a Pareto improvement require detailed information about the trades agents would have made without the policy: some of that information is inevitably missing. A price stabilization that exposes firms to competition, though designed to make do with limited information, will never be fine-grained enough to compensate the factors that were expressly built or trained to serve sheltered firms. And reforms of any stripe will never make whole the lucky beneficiaries of the status quo and its general equilibrium consequences. The toll collector's $100,000 a year sinecure will not survive privatization of the toll roads; the tavern next to the shuttered factory will fire its staff.

Policy overhauls require accommodations and shortcuts, and a sense of judgment of when a reform is close enough to its goals. These judgments amount to interpersonal comparisons of well-being, appraisals that the harm done is outweighed by benefits.

Interpersonal comparisons are out in the open when policymakers, instead of trying to compensate agents in harm's way, actively seek to redistribute wealth. In the economic tradition, redistributions of resources are rarely judged by absolute standards, for example, a Rawlsian commitment to the least well off. Economists weigh the gains against the costs imposed. A version of utilitarianism – sometimes veiled as cost-benefit-analysis – usually underlies these schemes.

But when preferences are incomplete, the weighing of gains against losses cannot be accomplished by conventional interpersonal comparisons of utility. The reason is simple: incomplete preferences cannot be represented by utility functions, let alone interpersonally comparable utilities. If preferences display incompleteness with respect to even a minor niche of alternatives then policymakers cannot weigh the utility gains of some agents against the losses of others. Utilitarianism, notwithstanding its 150 year history in economics, thus stands in a precarious position, a vulnerability hidden by economists' allegiance to completeness.

Yet this negative conclusion goes too far. It must be possible to decide that the harm to the featherbedders who lose their protected status are outweighed by sufficiently large gains to the rest of society even when all parties concerned have incomplete preferences. The comparisons of satisfaction implicit in such judgments ought to be detachable from the globally defined utility functions brandished in economics.

In the great solidification of economic theory in the mid 20th century, a new consensus took hold and has reigned ever since: individuals can make preference comparisons among any set of alternatives but society cannot compare the well-being of different individuals. We are free to express normative views about the distribution of wealth and welfare but these opinions lie outside the domain of science. This book has argued so far that individual preferences may be missing; agents may not be able to supply the trade-offs and judgments that provide economics with its raw material.

This chapter rejects the other half of the settlement by assuming that interpersonal comparisons of welfare, unlike individual preferences, are well-defined. In this reversal, individuals cannot judge all the trade-offs among different consumption goods but a planner can compare the welfare of different individuals for specific groups of goods. By splitting apart the allocation of society's resources into small-scale problems, one for each groups of goods, a planner can deliver on classical utilitarianism's ambitions. Planners can in fact display the same level of precision in these interpersonal comparisons that standard utilitarian planners display in their comparisons of the overall welfare of individuals.

This slicing up of social decision-making into separate spheres parallels the way that governments, advocates, and citizens look at policymaking. Few argue for a more equitable distribution of health care or educational opportunities on the grounds that the underserved have a greater marginal utility for consumption as a whole: they reason that resources should be channeled to the individuals and families that have the most pressing need in the sphere at hand. Schools for poor children should be improved not because the poor should consume more in general but because the benefits these children would garner from the particular goods of learning and education outweigh the benefits that other children would receive. Activists rail against fuel-poverty or food-poverty, not poverty in the abstract. Economists under the spell of the second welfare theorem inevitably counter that the most effective way to help the poor is to provide lump-sum transfers and let the poor decide what to spend the money on. The present chapter will come to a more open-minded conclusion.

The reworking of utilitarianism in this chapter will not be presumptuous. Although planners will pin down an optimal distribution of goods, they will not impose upon agents resolutions of the trade-offs that the agents themselves do not know how to judge. So, when a policy question turns on such judgments – as with the scale of public goods in Chapter 8 – a utilitarian policymaker will not be able to eliminate the indeterminacy. It is only the purely distributional decisions that succumb to utilitarian precision. Conversely, distributional equity cannot be addressed by the production cures of Chapter 9 that expand output. After enlarging the pie, both rulers and the ruled need to reckon with how to divide it up.

10.2 UTILITARIANISM GROUP BY GROUP

Preferences will be incomplete when agents do not know how to trade off the benefits of different groups of goods. But individuals may nevertheless be able to identify the benefits of each of these groups and those benefits can be represented by group-specific utility functions. This picture more closely approximates the views of the early neoclassical economists than one might have thought. When an individual confronts a specific optimization problem in Jevons or Edgeworth, the agent's marginal utilities provide a determinate solution. But these specific problems need not knit together: the agent might not maximize a grand intertemporal utility function that weighs every stream of consumption and uncertain contingency. When the early neoclassical economists analyzed questions of distribution, they instead compared the marginal utilities of different individuals for goods that arise in particular arenas of economic life.

I will follow the same path by endowing individuals with utilities that apply to groups of goods. Since the individuals do not know how to compare with precision the utilities delivered by different groups, their preferences will be incomplete. For concreteness a group will consist of the goods delivered at a specific state of the world and the inability of agents to compare utilities across states will appear as a multiplicity of the probabilities that agents use to weight those utilities. The preference judgments agents can make will be given by unanimity aggregations.

As in the Bewley model from Section 3.4, each individual i will have a set of distributions Π^i over a finite state space Ω and the utility that i derives from a ℓ-vector of goods x_ω^i consumed at state ω is given by $u^i(x_\omega^i)$. In addition to our earlier assumptions, let each u^i be strictly concave and let each Π^i be closed. Each π in Π^i defines for individual i a candidate expected utility $\sum_{\omega \in \Omega} \pi_\omega u^i(x_\omega^i)$ for each consumption bundle $x^i = \left(x_\omega^i\right)_{\omega \in \Omega}$ which defines one of i's candidate preferences. A multiplicity of distributions in Π^i indicates that i does not know how to trade off goods delivered at different states: agent i therefore unanimity aggregates the candidate preferences that rule with the various distributions in Π^i. The preference $\succsim^i$ that results is defined by $x^i \succsim^i y^i$ if and only if $\sum_\omega \pi_\omega u^i(x_\omega^i) \geq \sum_\omega \pi_\omega u^i(y_\omega^i)$ for all $\pi \in \Pi^i$. Local incomparability consequently obtains (Theorem 3.4) and, as we saw in Section 8.3, the set of Pareto-efficient allocations can then be a sea of large dimension. The model therefore suffers from a paradigmatic case of policy indecisiveness.

Suppose, for tractability only, there are two states. Letting $\underline{\pi}_1$ and $\bar{\pi}_1$ be the smallest and largest probabilities of state 1 for the distributions in Π^i, $x^i \succsim^i y^i$ holds if and only if

$$\underline{\pi}_1 u^i(x_1^i) + (1 - \underline{\pi}_1)u^i(x_2^i) \geq \underline{\pi}_1 u^i(y_1^i) + (1 - \underline{\pi}_1)u^i(y_2^i)$$
$$\bar{\pi}_1 u^i(x_1^i) + (1 - \bar{\pi}_1)u^i(x_2^i) \geq \bar{\pi}_1 u^i(y_1^i) + (1 - \bar{\pi}_1)u^i(y_2^i).$$

Though this agent may have other candidate expected utility functions defined by values of π_1 between $\underline{\pi}_1$ and $\bar{\pi}_1$, the candidate expected utilities defined by $\underline{\pi}_1$ and $\bar{\pi}_1$ will pin down $\succsim^i$: the above two inequalities are necessary and sufficient for $x^i \succsim^i y^i$ to obtain since they imply, for any $\underline{\pi}_1 \leq \pi_1 \leq \bar{\pi}_1$, that

$$\pi_1 u^i(x_1^i) + (1 - \pi_1)u^i(x_2^i) \geq \pi_1 u^i(y_1^i) + (1 - \pi_1)u^i(y_2^i).$$

There are many equally legitimate utility representations of each of i's candidate preferences. For example, replacing u^i by the increasing affine transformation $\alpha u^i + \beta$ where $\alpha > 0$ would not disrupt any of the above inequalities. Since multiplication of u^i by a probability is also an affine transformation, we can indicate any of the representations by the sum of two functions v_1^i and v_2^i, where each v_ω^i is an increasing affine transformation of u^i.

Formally, define two vectors of functions to be *cardinally equivalent* if one vector can be derived from the other by increasing affine transformations that share a common rescaling of utility units: if $(f_1, \ldots, f_n)$ and $(\hat{f}_1, \ldots, \hat{f}_n)$ are the vectors then there must exist $\alpha > 0$, $\beta_1, \ldots, \beta_n$ such that $f_j = \alpha \hat{f}_j + \beta_j$ for $j = 1, \ldots, n$.

Given some $\pi \in \Pi^i$ and the candidate preference $\succsim_\pi^i$ for i that results, if (v_1^i, v_2^i) is cardinally equivalent to $(\pi_1 u^i, (1 - \pi_1) u^i)$ then the functions defined by $v_1^i(x_1^i) + v_2^i(x_2^i)$ and $\pi_1 u^i(x_1^i) + (1 - \pi_1) u^i(x_2^i)$ are both expected utility functions for $\succsim_\pi^i$. Below I will let $v_1^i + v_2^i$ denote the function that, at $x^i = (x_1^i, x_2^i)$, equals $v_1^i(x_1^i) + v_2^i(x_2^i)$.

Since each candidate preference for i can be identified by a pair (v_1^i, v_2^i), the agent's unanimity aggregation $\succsim^i$ can be represented by a set of such pairs. Let $\mathcal{V}^i$ be a set of pairs of increasing affine transformations of u^i. Define $\mathcal{V}^i$ to *represent* $\succsim^i$ if, for each x^i and y^i,

$$x^i \succsim^i y^i \text{ if and only if } v_1^i(x_1^i) + v_2^i(x_2^i) \geq v_1^i(y_1^i) + v_2^i(y_2^i) \text{ for all } (v_1^i, v_2^i) \in \mathcal{V}^i.$$

The simplest $\mathcal{V}^i$ that represents $\succsim^i$ is

$$\{(\underline{\pi}_1 u^i, (1 - \underline{\pi}_1) u^i), (\overline{\pi}_1 u^i, (1 - \overline{\pi}_1) u^i)\}.$$

But since cardinally equivalent pairs of functions express the same candidate preferences, I will assume that if $(\hat{v}_1^i, \hat{v}_2^i)$ is cardinally equivalent to some $(v_1^i, v_2^i) \in \mathcal{V}^i$ then $(\hat{v}_1^i, \hat{v}_2^i)$ is also in $\mathcal{V}^i$.

Now suppose a utilitarian planner arrives on the scene of an exchange economy with I agents each modeled by a $\mathcal{V}^i$ that represents $\succsim^i$. To undertake the customary utilitarian task of evaluating distributions of goods, the planner examines $\mathcal{V}^1, \ldots, \mathcal{V}^I$ and picks a set $\mathcal{W}$ of utility vectors $((v_1^1, v_2^1), \ldots, (v_1^I, v_2^I))$ that the planner deems to be interpersonally comparable, where each v_ω^i must be an increasing affine transformation of u^i.[1] Each $((v_1^1, v_2^1), \ldots, (v_1^I, v_2^I))$ in $\mathcal{W}$ defines a utilitarian social welfare function $\sum_{i=1}^I (v_1^i + v_2^i)$ that evaluates each allocation of goods $x = (x^1, \ldots, x^I)$. For the early neoclassical economists it was an axiom of faith that a social welfare function should be a sum of individual utilities. But the Harsanyi (1955) aggregation theorem and Hammond (1981) provide foundations for the summing of utilities when state-contingent goods are the objects of preference. A $\mathcal{W}$ encapsulates all that is important about a planner; I therefore use the concepts interchangeably.

---

[1] On the use of sets of utilities in social choice, see Sen (1970), d'Aspremont and Gevers (1977), Roberts (1980), and Bossert and Weymark (2004).

Just as any two pairs of functions in some $\mathcal{V}^i$ that are cardinally equivalent will represent the same candidate preference for i, different $((v_1^1, v_2^1), \ldots, (v_1^I, v_2^I))$ vectors in $\mathcal{W}$ that are cardinally equivalent lead to social welfare functions that represent the same ordering of allocations. I will therefore assume that if two utility vectors are cardinally equivalent and one is in $\mathcal{W}$ then so is the other.

A classical utilitarian planner faces agents with complete preferences and selects a $\mathcal{W}$ with utility vectors that consist of one (v_1^i, v_2^i) from each $\mathcal{V}^i$ such that *any* two utility vectors in $\mathcal{W}$ are cardinally equivalent: if $((v_1^1, v_2^1), \ldots, (v_1^I, v_2^I))$ and $((\hat{v}_1^1, \hat{v}_2^1), \ldots, (\hat{v}_1^I, \hat{v}_2^I))$ are both in $\mathcal{W}$ then the rescaling of utility units that relates (v_1^j, v_2^j) and $(\hat{v}_1^j, \hat{v}_2^j)$ must also govern (v_1^i, v_2^i) and $(\hat{v}_1^i, \hat{v}_2^i)$ for each $i \neq j$. All of the social welfare functions generated by vectors in $\mathcal{W}$ then represent the same ordering of allocations. So, defining the planner's social preferences $\succsim$ over allocations by

$$x \succsim y \text{ if and only if } \left(\sum_i (v_1^i(x_1^i) + v_2^i(x_2^i)) \geq \sum_i (v_1^i(y_1^i) + v_2^i(y_2^i)) \right.$$

$$\left. \text{for all } ((v_1^1, v_2^1), \ldots, (v_1^I, v_2^I)) \in \mathcal{W} \right),$$

$\succsim$ will be complete. If in addition the v_ω^i are strictly concave then maximization of any of these social welfare functions subject to society's resource constraints will determine a unique optimal allocation of goods.

This decisiveness is entirely compatible with a liberal agnosticism about which utilities should represent individuals in $\mathcal{W}$. If $\mathcal{W}$ is chosen by a classical utilitarian then, given any individual i and any (v_1^i, v_2^i) in $\mathcal{V}^i$, there will be a corresponding vector in $\mathcal{W}$ that has (v_1^i, v_2^i) as its ith entry. All of the utility vectors in all of the $\mathcal{V}^i$'s thus appear in $\mathcal{W}$. However $\mathcal{W}$ is constructed from the $\mathcal{V}^i$ sets and whether or not individual preferences are complete, I will call $\mathcal{W}$ *liberal* if for each agent i and $(\hat{v}_1^i, \hat{v}_2^i)$ in $\mathcal{V}^i$ there is a vector $((v_1^1, v_2^1), \ldots, (v_1^I, v_2^I))$ in $\mathcal{W}$ such that $(v_1^i, v_2^i) = (\hat{v}_1^i, \hat{v}_2^i)$.

Now suppose one or more individuals have incomplete preferences: at least one Π^i contains multiple distributions. The planner, who again takes as data a $\mathcal{V}^i$ that represents $\succsim^i$ for each i, will now be unable to select a $\mathcal{W}$ that both pins down a complete ordering $\succsim$ of allocations and remains liberal. If $\mathcal{W}$ is liberal and, say, Π^j contains multiple distributions then, as $(v_1^j, v_2^j) \in \mathcal{V}^j$ varies, the corresponding utility vectors in $\mathcal{W}$ will fail to be cardinally equivalent and $\succsim$ will be incomplete. For example, let $x = (x^1, \ldots, x^I)$ and $y = (y^1, \ldots, y^I)$ vary only in j's consumption and suppose j's candidate expected utilities judge x^j and y^j in opposite ways. So, when $\mathcal{W}$ is liberal, there are $((v_1^1, v_2^1), \ldots, (v_1^I, v_2^I))$ and $((\hat{v}_1^1, \hat{v}_2^1), \ldots, (\hat{v}_1^I, \hat{v}_2^I))$ in $\mathcal{W}$ where, say, $v_1^j + v_2^j$ assigns a greater expected utility to x^j than to y^j and $\hat{v}_1^j + \hat{v}_2^j$ does the reverse, while for $i \neq j$ both

(v_1^i, v_2^i) and $(\hat{v}_1^i, \hat{v}_2^i)$ assign the same expected utilities to x^i and y^i. Neither $x \succsim y$ nor $y \succsim x$ then holds.

Planners in the liberal tradition therefore appear to face a dilemma. Their liberalism requires them not to impose their own views of what an individual should prefer: when agent i cannot decide how likely state 1 is relative to state 2, a planner that wants to respect the diversity of i's candidate preferences should not decide the matter for i. So, just as agent i admits conflicting utility vectors into V^i and unanimity aggregates, a liberal planner must admit conflicting utility vectors into W and should endorse only those changes in allocations that meet the approval of all of the social welfare functions that W generates. Liberalism thus comes at the cost of an incomplete social preference $\succsim$.

But the dilemma is not as acute as first appears. The incompleteness of a planner's ordering need not stop the planner from hammering out a unique optimal policy. While the planner will replicate each agent's inability to judge trade-offs *across* the goods that appear at different states, those gaps do not bear on the *distribution* of goods at any given state. A utilitarian comparison of one agent's marginal utility for a good with another agent's marginal utility for the same good can proceed as usual, with the result that all of a planner's social welfare functions can agree on the distributive judgment calls. In early neoclassical economics, those comparisons were limited to tightly circumscribed allocation problems; in the present setting, the planner's interpersonal comparisons will be restricted to each group of goods – the goods delivered at a particular state.

A planner *makes precise interpersonal comparisons for each group* if, for each $\left((v_1^1, v_2^1), \ldots, (v_1^I, v_2^I)\right)$ and $\left((\hat{v}_1^1, \hat{v}_2^1), \ldots, (\hat{v}_1^I, \hat{v}_2^I)\right)$ in W and each state ω, $\left(v_\omega^1, \ldots, v_\omega^I\right)$ is cardinally equivalent to $\left(\hat{v}_\omega^1, \ldots, \hat{v}_\omega^I\right)$. The planner can then rank any pair of allocations that differs only with respect to goods delivered at one of the states. For example, if x and y have $x_2^i = y_2^i$ for all i then, for any $\left((v_1^1, v_2^1), \ldots, (v_1^I, v_2^I)\right)$ in W,

$$\sum_i (v_1^i(x_1^i) + v_2^i(x_2^i)) \geq \sum_i (v_1^i(y_1^i) + v_2^i(y_2^i)) \text{ if and only if}$$

$$\sum_i v_1^i(x_1^i) \geq \sum_i v_1^i(y_1^i).$$

So, when a planner can make precise comparisons for each group, all of the social welfare functions generated by the $\left((v_1^1, v_2^1), \ldots, (v_1^I, v_2^I)\right)$ in W will order x and y in the same way. Hence either $x \succsim y$ or $y \succsim x$ (or both).[2]

---

[2] Section 8.2 adopted a more informal description of utilitarianism with incomplete preferences. But with regard to distributional decisions (the allocation of private

Planners who make precise interpersonal comparisons for each group partition social decision-making into separate areas, as discussed in the previous section. They weigh the pros and cons of allocations of goods in each group in isolation just as political debate wrestles with the distribution of, say, housing separately from the distribution of health care.

Whether or not individual preferences are complete, a planner that makes precise interpersonal comparisons for each group can always be liberal. Since with incomplete individual preferences a liberal W must lead to incomplete social preferences, a planner can therefore have complete preferences with regard to allocations that differ at only one state even though $\succsim$ seen as a whole is incomplete.

The upshot of this curious combination is that, although the planner like the individuals has incomplete preferences, there will be a unique optimal allocation of goods when standard concavity conditions are in place. Utilitarian planners can judge the optimal allocations of goods for delivery at each state separately, even when they, like the individuals, are stumped about how to trade off goods across states.

Given a planner's social welfare judgments W and the $\succsim$ that results, an allocation x is a *utilitarian optimum* if it is feasible and no other feasible allocation is a strict $\succsim$-improvement. As usual, an allocation x is feasible in an exchange economy if $\sum_i x^i \leq e$, where e is the available stock of goods.

Theorem 10.1 *If a planner can make precise comparisons for each group and each u^i is continuous and strictly concave, then there is a unique utilitarian optimum.*

I argued above that liberal planners will refrain from comparisons of allocations that differ by state that the agents themselves cannot judge. But even if a planner does make those comparisons via W, Theorem 10.1 still holds. The planner could be agnostic or dictatorial about such comparisons: what matters for the uniqueness conclusion is that planners can make interpersonal comparisons of individual utilities group by group.

The proof of Theorem 10.1 is simple. If there were distinct utilitarian optima x and y they would have to assign different consumptions for at least one state ω. But then the feasible allocation z that assigns $z^i_\omega =$

consumption), all of the policymakers' utilitarian objective functions in Section 8.2 made precise interpersonal comparisons – Chapter 8 and the present treatment are therefore compatible.

$\frac{1}{2}x_\omega^i + \frac{1}{2}y_\omega^i$ to each i at state ω and $z_{-\omega}^i = x_{-\omega}^i$ to each i at the other state must, by strict concavity, satisfy

$$\sum_i v_\omega^i(z_\omega^i) > \sum_i v_\omega^i(x_\omega^i) \text{ and } \sum_i v_{-\omega}^i(z_{-\omega}^i) = \sum_i v_{-\omega}^i(x_{-\omega}^i),$$

regardless of which $((v_1^1, v_2^1), \ldots, (v_1^I, v_2^I))$ in $\mathcal{W}$ we select. Hence each candidate social welfare function $\sum_i (v_1^i + v_2^i)$ for the planner is greater when evaluated at z than at x, which contradicts the assumption that x is optimal. Continuity ensures that an optimum exists. Neither the Theorem nor its proof would be affected if we let there be an arbitrary number of states rather than two.

The stark conclusion of Theorem 10.1 rests on two pillars of individual decision-making. The first is the separability of utility functions across groups of goods: for each group there is a group utility that is a function only of goods in that group and each candidate utility is a function only of the group utilities. Separability comes automatically with expected utility theory. The second is the completeness of individual preferences over bundles that vary only with respect to one group. The combination of separability and within-group completeness allows a planner to divide and conquer: each group of goods in effect defines a separate optimization problem. Any setting that enjoys these two features will enjoy a similar uniqueness result. For example, when agents have time-separable utility functions but are undecided about which discount rate should weight the utilities of goods consumed at different dates, a planner could again treat the allocation problems that arise at different dates one-by-one. At each date, the planner can choose a distribution of goods that maximizes the sum of the agents' utilities for goods at that date.

Separability has a long utilitarian pedigree: for Jevons, Marshall, and frequently even for Edgeworth, each good had its own utility function that varies only with that good's consumption level. Early neoclassical economics therefore fits into the setting of Theorem 10.1: each good forms a singleton group and a utilitarian planner can compare the utilities that different individuals derive from that good. In our era, on the other hand, separability assumptions have lost their appeal when applied to consumption goods delivered with certainty at a specific date.

In the absence of separability, we can still define an individual utility function for a group of goods, but we must allow that utility to also be a function of consumption goods outside the group in question. Under uncertainty, the utility of goods at state 1 could then be a function of consumption at state 2; more generally a group utility could resemble a standard utility function that takes all goods as arguments. If planners remain capable of making precise interpersonal comparisons across individuals of these modified group utility functions, they will have a well-defined objective function for each group. But now, since a group utility is a function of outside-the-group consumption, the solution of the planner's problem for one group of goods will affect the planner's solution for other groups. A planner must therefore search for allocations that are efficient across group objective functions: there must be no alternative allocation that is a strict improvement for one of the planner's group objective functions and a weak improvement for the remainder. Letting G be the number of groups and therefore group objective functions, the set of utilitarian optima will generally be contained in a set of dimension $G - 1$. In our example of state-contingent goods, G equals 2 and thus the optima in the absence of separability would be contained in a 1 dimensional set, analogously to the fact that in a two-agent general equilibrium model with complete preferences (a model with two objective functions) the utility possibility frontier has dimension 1.[3] So, when separability cannot be invoked, the decisiveness of utilitarianism will fall short of the uniqueness that classical complete-preference utilitarianism achieves. But we have made progress relative to the profligacy of the Pareto optima under incomplete preferences: the dimension of the set of optima has fallen from $L(I - 1)$ to $G - 1$ – which is a fall since each group must contain a good and hence $G - 1 < L$.

Group-by-group utilitarianism has a further advantage. Amartya Sen has assailed welfarist theories of social choice that determine social decisions based solely on individual utility levels.[4] In Sen's indictment, welfarism sidelines the social and psychological particularities of the decisions facing policymakers: issues as far-flung as the provision of public education and global warming are put through a meat-grinder that reduces all policy changes to their impact on utilities. Classical utilitarianism, not surprisingly, is Exhibit A for the prosecution. The utilitarianism with incomplete preferences in this chapter eliminates this reductionism. When preferences are incomplete, the raw material that feeds the welfarist machine no longer exists: there is no utility function that represents the entirety of an individual's well-being. Space then opens up for separate

---

[3] This problem as well as the simpler separable case are analyzed in detail in Mandler (2020).
[4] See Sen (1979, 1986).

comparisons of individual welfare in various spheres of social decision-making: the weighing of the individual benefits that stem from childhood education can be conducted separately from the weighing of the benefits of a green climate. Group-by-group utilitarianism gives policymakers permission to judge each sphere on its own merits.

The drawback of group-by-group evaluations is that they may clash with agents' judgments of the trade-offs of different goods. A group-by-group planner could determine that agent i's satisfaction from group 1 is stronger than agent j's and that j's satisfaction from group 2 is stronger than i's. The agents themselves might not share these views. Beginning at a utilitarian optimum, there may be transfers of group 1 goods from i to j and of group 2 goods from j to i that make both agents better off (as judged by $\succsim^i$ and $\succsim^j$). Although local incomparability will mean that agents lack well-defined marginal rates of substitution – since better-than sets display kinks – the transfers under consideration might offer exchanges of goods that the agents do judge to be unambiguous improvements. Utilitarian optima, as I have defined them, therefore need not be Pareto efficient.

A strict (but not so liberal) utilitarian would not be disturbed by a conflict between Pareto efficiency and utilitarian optimality: the planner in this view can judge the true value of goods to individuals better than the individuals themselves. Some early neoclassical economists were forthright that planners should trump agents. The assumption that agents discount future consumption has provoked several waves of controversy in economics. The early neoclassical critics of impatience charged that the assumption should not be admitted into the inner sanctum of the theory of rationality. Agents that trade away future consumption for a smaller quantity of current consumption have fallen into error: they are failing to amass as much utility as they could. Thus, according to Schumpeter, discounting is an offense "against the rules of economic reason" (1912, p. 35). A classical utilitarian planner could therefore achieve an improvement by forbidding agents from sacrificing consumption tomorrow for a lesser gain today, even though agents on their own would do so.

Utilitarians that fall short of Schumpeter's doctrinal purity can at least counter that Pareto-utilitarian clashes are unlikely and will become less frequent as the extent of preference incompleteness increases. If preferences are locally incomparable, we can gauge the incompleteness of agent i's preferences when i consumes x^i by the set of prices (or normal vectors) $N^i(x^i)$ that support the bundles i prefers to x^i: a change in i's preferences from $\succsim^i$ to $\succsim^i$ that leads to a $\bar{N}^i(x^i)$ that contains $N^i(x^i)$ indicates greater incompleteness. If given some group-by-group utilitarian optimal allocation x each $N^i(x^i)$ is sufficiently large then there will be a common supporting price vector, a price vector in $\bigcap_i N^i(x^i)$. Since the first welfare theorem applies to the preferences of this chapter even when they are locally incomparable, x must be Pareto efficient. So, in the cases of concern – significant preference incomplete-ness – the conflict between Paretian and utilitarian optimality should be minimal.[5]

---

[5] Other paths to Paretian-utilitarian reconciliation are explored in Mandler (2020).

11

Production and the Enforcement of Rationality

Production has hovered at the outskirts of this book. It was production in Chapter 7 that explained why an economy's endowments, rather than assuming arbitrary values, will land at the points where agents do not have well-defined marginal rates of substitution. Prices can be volatile as a result. It was also production that showed that the intertemporal transfer of resources can mitigate volatility. It was production in Chapter 9 that allowed for policies that both expand output and pass the availability test. By bracketing the relative price changes that harm consumers and letting firms face a different array of prices, an economy can attain the productivity growth that stems from competition among firms without out the downsides of creative destruction. These examples suggest that order and growth and the predictability of economic activity derive from production rather than preferences.

Two interrelated factors underlie the pivotal role of production. First, firms direct production according to an ordering principle: they judge different courses of actions by the profits the actions deliver. Profit maximization is an idealization of course and no firm fits the description exactly. But unlike the diversity of goals that govern consumers, profit maximization applies potentially to all firms.[1] An entrepreneur weighing the most profitable course of action stands out as one of the

---

[1] A grey area appears when markets are incomplete: shareholders then need not agree on how a firm should decide between production decisions that change the distribution of its profits across states. See Drèze (1974) and Grossman and Hart (1979). The problem can be accentuated by disagreement among shareholders about the probabilities assigned to states.

characteristic scenes of a market economy. The claim in modern economics that all agents can rationally order their alternatives takes this case as the prototype. Although that claim is mistaken, its original application in production remains valid.

Profitability as a common ordering principle points to the second reason. When a firm deviates from profit maximization – the family-owned firm that will not fire its longstanding employees or the mismanaged behemoth that rests on its laurels – market competition serves as a regulating mechanism that weeds out these breaches over time. Firms that diverge systematically from profit maximization are shut out of production or pushed into bankruptcy. Profit maximization and productive efficiency therefore do not rely on the contingency that each firm happens to stick to the goal of maximizing profits. The threat of competition and the punishments delivered by the stock market can knock firms into line if they stray from efficient production – or push them into extinction if they do not return. The contrast with individuals is stark. There is no comparable economic mechanism that ensures that individual consumers follow an ordering principle, let alone a common one, and nothing prevents consumers from veering from the ordering principles that may have governed their past actions; a decision that violates your preferences qualifies only as a subjective failure.

Profit maximization as an ordering principle and competition as a regulating mechanism govern other spheres of economic life that do not formally qualify as production. The arbitrage conditions that have laid out the foundations of finance hold due to just this combination of forces. When asset prices deviate from arbitrage restrictions, profit opportunities open up and the traders that ignore these restrictions are driven out of business. It is no coincidence that arbitrage-based finance has given economics one of the rare cases of precise prediction in the social sciences.

One intention of this book has been to discard those putative rules of rationality that individuals do not need to satisfy to pursue their interests effectively: preferences can be incomplete or exhibit safety bias, the tell-tale sign that agents are patching up their incompleteness. I have however supposed that preferences satisfy transitivity, the part of classical rationality that does serve agents' interests. One reason, of course, is that choice behavior will often obey bona fide axioms of rationality. It would also sow confusion to assume otherwise. Any intertwining of incompleteness with genuinely damaging decisions would undermine the case that incompleteness does agents no harm.

But since firms are subject to the regulatory discipline of the market while consumers are not, we can hold the rationality of firms to a more demanding standard. Profit maximization not only serves the interests of the owners of firms, it will dominate in the end even when the market is populated initially by firms that take arbitrary and irrational actions. Profit maximization and the productivity growth that it sets in motion therefore form essential parts of the economic terrain.

11.1 IRRATIONALITY-PROOFNESS

The primary results of the modern theory of competitive equilibria are driven by the simultaneous optimization of agents. Equilibria are Pareto efficient, for example, only if every agent chooses the available action that best serves his or her objective, for a consumer the affordable bundle that delivers the greatest utility, for a firm the feasible production that delivers the greatest profits. If just one agent errs by making a nonmaximizing decision then Pareto efficiency will normally disappear. The first-welfare-theorem conclusion that competition leads to efficiency is thus vulnerable in the extreme. The second welfare theorem is equally fragile.

Production efficiency, on the other hand, does not require each and every firm to maximize profits; the market imposes a discipline on firms that can substitute for rationality. While consumers who fail to maximize utility can persist endlessly in their errors without exiting the economy, markets do not permit firms the same luxury.[2] Due to this asymmetry, the producer side of the economy furnishes stability and efficiency more reliably than the consumer side.

Consider a finite population of firms that consists of two disjoint types, the *rational firms* $\mathcal{F}^R$ and the *irrational firms* $\mathcal{F}^{IR}$ that together form $\mathcal{F} = \mathcal{F}^R \cup \mathcal{F}^{IR}$.[3] A firm j of either type is described by a production set $Y^j \subset \mathbb{R}^L$ that contains the 0 vector where L is the number of goods. Each firm j can choose only a y^j in Y^j. The rational and the irrational firms are therefore capable of aggregate productions drawn from $Y^R = \sum_{j \in \mathcal{F}^R} Y^j$ and $Y^{IR} = \sum_{j \in \mathcal{F}^{IR}} Y^j$ respectively and all firms can together produce from $Y = Y^R + Y^{IR} = \sum_{j \in \mathcal{F}} Y^j$.

---

[2] Lapses of rationality might lead consumers to accumulate less wealth, thus leading to a form of exit, but this mechanism does not enforce utility maximization. See Blume and Easley (1992).

[3] Mandler (2014b) undertakes a broader treatment of economies that mix rational and irrational agents.

Fix the price vector at some $p \geq 0$. A rational firm $j \in \mathcal{F}^R$ maximizes profits: it chooses a bundle from the set of profit-maximizing bundles

$$y^j(p) = \{y^j \in Y^j : p \cdot y^j \geq p \cdot \hat{y}^j \text{ for all } \hat{y}^j \in Y^j\}.$$

An irrational firm $j \in \mathcal{F}^{IR}$ need not maximize profits but it cannot run losses that it cannot cover: a money-losing firm must exit the market. An irrational firm j therefore chooses a bundle from

$$y^j(p) = \{y^j \in Y^j : p \cdot y^j \geq 0\}.$$

The *supplies offered at* p will denote the bundles in $\sum_{j \in \mathcal{F}} y^j(p)$ and these supplies are *well-defined* if $y^j(p)$ is nonempty for each firm j.

For the market to keep the irrational firms on a tight leash, the rational firms must be at least as productive as the irrational firms. Otherwise irrational firms could produce inefficiently and use the earnings from their greater productivity to ward off bankruptcy. Some version of constant returns to scale is also necessary. In a world of decreasing returns, irrational firms could earn strictly positive profits even when facing only rational competitors; and this profit buffer could again shield inefficiency. The model will therefore apply to a long enough run where there are no unpurchasable inputs that can lead to decreasing returns to scale; nondecreasing returns then borders on tautology since production can be scaled up by replication.

The simplest path to efficiency would assume that $Y^R \supset Y^{IR}$ and that Y^R exhibits constant returns. Since these assumptions are needlessly strong, however, I will impose the weaker condition that Y^R *constant returns dominates* Y^{IR}: there is a constant returns set Y^{CR} such that

$$Y^R \supset Y^{CR} \supset Y^{IR}.$$

The rational firms can then have fixed inputs and experience decreasing returns. And when a good is not produced by any irrational firm, constant returns domination imposes no restrictions on the technology that governs that good.

The supplies offered at p are *production efficient* if for each $y \in \sum_{j \in \mathcal{F}} y^j(p)$ there does not exist a $y' \in \sum_{j \in \mathcal{F}} Y^j$ such that $y' > y$ (that is, $y'_k \geq y_k$ for every good k and with strict inequality for at least one k).

Theorem 11.1 *If Y^R constant returns dominates Y^{IR} and the supplies offered at $p \gg 0$ are well-defined then those supplies are production efficient.*

The efficiency of capitalist production thus does not rely on the improbable feat that each and every firm turns out to be a rational profit maximizer. Since Theorem 11.1 does not rely on universal rationality, the result shares ground with evolutionary explanations of the efficiency of firms. But since the market rather the greater rate of growth of more profitable firms drives the efficiency conclusion, the logic underlying Theorem 11.1 is closer to Alchian (1950) or Friedman (1953) than to Nelson and Winter (1982).

A broader principle, that the market is a firm enough taskmaster to deny irrational firms the room to act capriciously, lies behind Theorem 11.1. With constant returns domination, the irrational firms must offer the same supplies to the market that they would make if they were rational. Beginning with a model where the rational and irrational firms are $\mathcal{F}^R$ and $\mathcal{F}^{IR}$, define the irrational firms to *become rational* if we move to a model with the same production sets but where all of the firms are rational.

Theorem 11.2 *If Y^R constant returns dominates Y^{IR} and the supplies offered at prices p are well-defined, then those supplies will remain unchanged if the irrational firms become rational.*

The motives that guide firms thus need not affect the set of actions they can take when they are subject to the discipline of competition. In the long run when constant returns prevails, observers will not even be able to deduce the goals of firms from their market supply decisions.

Theorem 11.1 does not mean that an economy with irrational firms will achieve production efficiency instantaneously. If in the short run firms cannot purchase all inputs and are subject to diminishing returns, then they can produce inefficiently, frittering away the profits their owners could have earned on the capital they previously invested. Efficiency will then emerge gradually as the capital goods of inefficient firms wear out and the set of goods produced under decreasing returns contracts. As the long run approaches and constant returns applies to the production of a good, the irrational firms that produce that good must return to the rationality fold or be driven out of business.

Production inefficiency can also arise when inflows of pioneering firms introduce more advanced technologies or produce new types of goods not yet subject to competition. Their informational advantage allows innovators to earn profits in the short run and thus relaxes the bankruptcy constraints on their actions. Inefficiency can therefore prevail in progressive sectors while being driven out of an economy's stagnant sectors. The presence of irrational firms can thus lead to Schumpeterian entry-exit dynamics. Static efficiency does not reign at every date. Innovators at first have the leeway to indulge their idiosyncratic views about the organization of production; the rationalizing shake-out will occur later once the pioneers have lost their technological edge. Curiously, therefore, a cross section of the sectors of an economy should show a positive correlation between production efficiency and technological stagnation.

As in Theorem 11.1, these dynamics are only quasi-evolutionary: irrational firms are driven from the market due to the price system, not because more profitable firms invest more and hence grow more quickly. The disappearance of irrational firms will therefore be similar to the exit of technologically backward but profit-maximizing firms in Marshallian models of competition.

This sketch illustrates the subtleties that appear when rationality is understood as a regulating consequence of markets rather than an inherent feature of human nature. Efficiency will appear only gradually and when the right market preconditions are in place. As we will see in the next section, policy advice also becomes more challenging. Once we acknowledge the presence of irrationality, the simple recipes of the welfare theorems will no longer deliver unambiguous benefits and policymakers can face difficult choices.

11.2 POLICYMAKING IN THE FACE OF IRRATIONALITY

When economics takes the rationality of economic agents to be axiomatic, policy advice gravitates to the laissez-faire. Governments, it is said, should unleash profit-seeking firms and preference-maximizing consumers onto unimpeded markets. Eliminate the barriers to entry, the distorting taxes, and the tariffs, expose the sheltered industries and the monopolies to competition: efficiency will follow. To buy off those who will be harmed under laissez-faire and who may have the political muscle to block reforms, policymakers in this orthodox vision can simply combine laissez-faire rules with lump-sum compensations. The economy according to this parable can have it all: the gains of economic efficiency and the neutralization of the opposition to change.

In Chapter 8, we saw that governments will not have the information needed to execute this program. I will bracket this objection in this section to focus on a different problem.

When the force that drives efficiency is the competition that pushes backward firms out of business rather than the rationality of individuals, compensations can shelter irrational behavior. If the profits of some firms decline in response to a trade liberalization or deregulation, then compensations can make those firms and their owners whole. But the recipients of these payments may then be able to persist in their ex ante actions and thereby undo the very purpose of a laissez-faire policy reform. Compensations in effect introduce a profit buffer that can sustain the inefficient decisions of irrational firms.

Opening an economy to international trade illustrates this dilemma. Suppose that some sectors of an economy are dominated by irrational firms and that international trade offers the only potential source of disciplining competition – and hence the only path to production efficiency. Free trade may then be able to redress the inefficiency but if the irrational firms are shielded by compensation payments the remedy can be undone.

The irrational and the rational firms in the aggregate will again have production sets Y^{IR} and Y^R that contain 0 and permit free disposal. Some of the economy's L goods are traded internationally. Using the notation of Section 9.4, let $T \subset \mathbb{R}^L$ be the set of L-vectors that can be non-0 only in the coordinates of the internationally traded goods and let $\pi \in T$ indicate the world prices of the traded goods. Some of the goods that can in principle be traded on the world market are protected initially: trades of these goods with foreign firms are prohibited ex ante. Under free trade, the set of achievable net foreign trades is $T_I = \{\gamma \in T : \pi \cdot \gamma = 0\}$, while under protection the set of achievable net trades is

$$T_P = \{\gamma \in T : \pi \cdot \gamma = 0 \text{ and } \gamma_i = 0 \text{ if } i \text{ is protected}\}.$$

The net production of a firm will equal the sum of its own production and the international trades it conducts. Prices are given by a L-vector $p \gg 0$ that satisfies the normalization $\sum_{i=1}^{L} p_i = 1$.

An *equilibrium under protection* is a $(p, y^R \in Y^R + T_P, y^{IR} \in Y^{IR} + T_P)$ such that

- $p \cdot y^R \geq p \cdot \hat{y}^R$ for all $\hat{y}^R \in Y^R + T_P$,
- $p \cdot y^{IR} \geq 0$.

Since the organization of production will be the sole focus of our attention, there is no need to specify a consumer side to the model.

In the absence of the constant returns domination assumption that drives Theorem 11.1, the irrational firms need not produce efficiently in an equilibrium under protection. The irrational firms might for example be the only producers of one or more of the protected goods – the model allows irrational firms to be monopolists that set the prices of their own outputs. Constant returns domination then cannot hold: there will be net productions in Y^{IR} that are not in Y^R. The irrational firms will therefore not be held in check by either domestic or international competition and can use backward technologies without going bankrupt. Even when rational firms also produce the protected goods, those goods could be subject to decreasing returns; agricultural products for example are frequently protected and use untraded scarce resources as inputs. Constant returns domination would again fail to hold and inefficiency can result.

An equilibrium under protection therefore calls out for reform. Instead of waiting for enlightenment to descend onto the irrational firms, supply from abroad can provide a disciplining force that can compel production efficiency. Foreign trade functions in effect like a constant-returns production sector and can thus stand in for part of the dominating set required by constant returns domination.

The sets Y^R and T_I *jointly constant returns dominate* Y^{IR} if there exists a constant-returns set Y^{CR} such that $Y^R \supset Y^{CR}$ and $Y^{CR} + T_I \supset Y^{IR}$.

With this reformulation of constant returns domination, the combination of foreign trade and a constant-returns component of the rational firms' production set dominates the irrational firms' production set. If say a domestic agricultural good is produced only by irrational firms or is subject to decreasing returns, then constant returns domination need not hold domestically. But if the economy can import the good then joint constant returns domination can hold. Foreign production can then potentially confront the irrational firms with enough competitive pressure to force them into efficiency or to shut down – assuming they do not receive compensation payments that cushion the decline in their profits.

If protection is eliminated in its entirety, both the rational and irrational producers can make international trades in T_I rather than T_P. A *free-trade equilibrium with no compensation* is therefore a $(p \gg 0, y^R \in Y^R + T_I, y^{IR} \in Y^{IR} + T_I)$ such that

- $p \cdot y^R \geq p \cdot \hat{y}^R$ for all $\hat{y}^R \in Y^R + T_I$,
- $p \cdot y^{IR} \geq 0$.

If (p, y^R, y^{IR}) is a free-trade equilibrium then $y^R + y^{IR}$ are the *supplies offered* at that equilibrium. Those supplies are *production efficient* if there does not exist a $\hat{y}^R \in Y^R + T_I$ and $\hat{y}^{IR} \in Y^{IR} + T_I$ such that $\hat{y}^R + \hat{y}^{IR} > y^R + y^{IR}$.

Theorem 11.3 *If* Y^R *and* T_I *jointly constant returns dominate* Y^{IR} *then the supplies offered at a free-trade equilibrium with no compensation are production efficient.*

A big bang transition to free trade can thus reap the benefits of production efficiency. If under protection irrational firms previously had the freedom to produce inefficiently – squandering the profits they could in principle have earned – their room for maneuver will disappear under a free-trade equilibrium with no compensation. The downside is that the profits of some firms can fall relative to the equilibrium under protection that ruled initially. The owners of these firms will then usually be harmed; indeed the irremediably inefficient firms will be forced to liquidate, wiping out their owners' equity.

A compensationist regime could use lump-sum payments to protect firms from declines in profits. Let $(\bar{p}, \bar{y}^R \in Y^R + T_P, \bar{y}^{IR} \in Y^{IR} + T_P)$ be the ex ante equilibrium under protection and let p be the prices that rule under the compensations. The rational firms will receive in the aggregate a payment c^R that returns them to their ex ante level of profitability:

$$c^R = \bar{p} \cdot \bar{y}^R - \max_{y^R} p \cdot y^R \text{ s.t. } y^R \in Y^R + T_I.$$

The irrational firms, in contrast, will receive in the aggregate a payment equal to their ex ante profitability $c^{IR} = \bar{p} \cdot \bar{y}^{IR}$. Since the firms in $\mathcal{F}^{IR}$ are irrational, it would not make sense to define their compensation via a maximization problem. But under joint constant returns domination, the maximum of $p \cdot y^{IR}$ s.t. $y^{IR} \in Y^{IR} + T_I$ will equal 0 in equilibrium and c^{IR} will therefore coincide with the value that would arise from a maximization definition akin to the one used for c^R. Behind the aggregate payments, the government may have to set negative compensation payments for some of the profitable firms to cross subsidize the unprofitable firms. All of the payments are lump-sum: they do not vary with firms' production decisions.

Given the equilibrium under protection $(\bar{p}, \bar{y}^R, \bar{y}^{IR})$, a *free-trade equilibrium with compensation* is a $(p, y^R \in Y^R + T_I, y^{IR} \in Y^{IR} + T_I)$ such that

- $p \cdot y^R \geq p \cdot \hat{y}^R$ for all $\hat{y}^R \in Y^R + T_I$,
- $p \cdot y^{IR} + c^{IR} \geq 0$.

The compensation c^R paid to the rational firms does not appear in this definition since it has no impact on y^R: any lump-sum payment adds the same constant to the left- and right-hand sides of the rational firms' profit maximization inequalities.

Since the irrational firms can use c^{IR} to subsidize inefficient production, an equilibrium with compensation need not be production efficient.

Theorem 11.4 *If $c^{IR} > 0$, there is a free-trade equilibrium with compensation such that the supplies offered are not production efficient.*

The proof is trivial: if $c^{IR} > 0$ then the irrational firms could throw away a positive quantity of each good – choose a $y^{IR} \ll 0$ – without violating the constraint $p \cdot y^{IR} + c^{IR} \geq 0$.

Policymakers therefore face a dilemma: to achieve production efficiency, irrational firms cannot be compensated but without compensation payments some agents will be harmed, which can undercut the consensus behind economic reform.

The tough-love advice that firms will produce efficiently only when the threat of bankruptcy hangs over them shares ground with the view that economic downturns cleanse an economy of its technically backward firms. Though championed by Austrians as eminent as Schumpeter and Hayek and by the business press, this position has languished at the fringes of respectable Anglo-Saxon economics.[4] But once the door is open to irrational firms, the institutional role played by an unforgiving market becomes easy to model and defend formally.

11.3 CONCLUSION

Compensationism lays out a conflict-free path to efficiency that converts the losers who suffer under economic change into winners. But in addition to the informational presuppositions discussed in Chapter 8, the path depends upon agents who rationally pursue their self-interest: compensationism will no longer deliver efficiency in the presence of irrationality. The alternative Schumpeterian vision of creative destruction, where the road to production efficiency is littered with bankrupt firms, underscores the difficult facts of economic life: it may be impossible to achieve the full benefits of productivity growth without the social upheaval that can in turn undermine support for economic change.

---

[4] See Schumpeter (1939, 1942) and Hayek (1931) for the Austrian view and Caballero and Hammour (1994) for a contemporary (non-fringe) version of the thesis.

12

Conclusion: Custom and Flexibility

Formal models of the individual and of society, whether in economics, philosophy, or applied mathematics, usually imagine that we can construct an exhaustive list of states of affairs and order them from best to worst. Individual decisions and social rules are then evaluated by this ordering: how high on the list can we get? The alternative is to accept that people are in part creatures of custom: an individual takes an action not because he or she judges the action to be superior to all other options but because the action forms the established status quo and has not yet been successfully challenged. Any different decision that better serves some of the agent's goals will do a worse job of achieving other goals. Individuals can still change their actions – if new possibilities appear or if they can reevaluate their options or goals – but in the absence of innovations they will proceed as they have in the past. We normally judge institutions by the same rubric. A reshuffling of which priorities are served rarely convinces people to overthrow a custom or convention: reformers must find a new arrangement superior to the status quo according to all or most of the priorities or argue that the priorities themselves should be rethought. It may be excessively conservative to give precedence to the weight of tradition. Possibly so, but we should not conclude that deference to the past is irrational.

Economics has long cast a skeptical eye on individual behavior said to be rooted in custom or habit: sooner or later agents will learn how best to pursue their interests. This claim, while worthy of empirical debate, rests upon a presumption that agents always have a best action. That conviction is a fable. It derives from a belief that an agent's interests can be defined objectively, an uneasy fit with the subjectivity and diversity of individual desires so central to the neoclassical tradition.

223

The confidence in economics that agents can always form preferences draws support from the indisputably fierce desires that people do possess; the individuals of a modern market economy strive for material wealth and reliably choose more money over less. These desires do not, however, provide evidence for the preference trade-offs that underlie conventional economic analysis. It has instead been the noneconomic social sciences that have explored how individuals, when they cannot identify their goals, will settle into a pattern of behavior, as for example when Durkheim (1893) argued that contract law does not simply reconcile the clash of individual interests but helps individuals discover what goals to pursue or when Douglas and Isherwood (1979) laid out a symbolic grounding for consumption decisions.

The peculiar tradition of assuming that preferences are exogenous has also obscured the fact that people change and can be changed. When individuals do not know how to trade off the merits of public and private goods, as in Chapter 8, I have portrayed society as stuck; and Chapter 9 accordingly looked to the advancement of productive efficiency as the terrain better suited to government action. It is just as important to investigate how transformation and leadership in culture and politics can overhaul individual preferences. The seemingly intractable problems can then sometimes get unstuck.

Taking individual desires as given has hobbled even our understanding of which desires and attitudes toward trade-offs are best suited to economic growth and prosperity. A resistance to substituting one consumer good for another may not qualify as irrational from the classical point of view, but it can impede economic change. Consider Baumol's cost disease, the slowdown in productivity growth that occurs as resources concentrate in service sectors with little potential for technical change; after 70 years "Waiting for Godot" still requires five actors and two hours.[1] Individuals when they reconceive their desires – accepting videos and perhaps holograms as replacements for a live performance – can move nearer to the neoclassical ideal of substitutability. Welfare improvements are then easier to achieve and cures for the cost disease become available: when audiences adjust their preferences and take a recording to be a partial equivalent of a concert, national income accounts should in principle register a rise in productivity and total output. Individuals thus can not only rethink their desires and which trade-offs they will accept but that imaginative capacity can drive economic progress.

---

[1] Baumol and Bowen (1965, 1966).

Appendix

Proof of Theorem 3.2. Fix some $x > 0$. Given some L-vector p, define y^ε by $(y_i^\varepsilon, y_j^\varepsilon) = (x_i, x_j) + \varepsilon(1, -\frac{p_i}{p_j})$, where $\varepsilon > 0$, and $y_k^\varepsilon = x_k$ for $k \neq i, j$. If p satisfies $p_i > 0$ and $p_j < 0$ then $y^\varepsilon \succ x$. Since $p \cdot (y^\varepsilon - x) = 0$, we conclude, by setting ε sufficiently small, that p cannot define a normal vector for a line of incomparability through x. A p with $p_i = 0$ also cannot define a line of incomparability through x: setting $y_i^\delta = x_i + \delta$, $y_k^\delta = x_k$ for $k \neq i$ we have $y^\delta \succ x$ for all $\delta > 0$ and $p \cdot (y^\delta - x) = 0$. Consider two distinct lines of incomparability through x with normal vectors p and p' such that $\sum_i p_i = \sum_i p_i' = 1$. We therefore have $p \gg 0$ and $p' \gg 0$. Since $p \neq p'$, the intersection of $L_p = \{w : p \cdot (w - x) = 0\}$ and $L_{p'} = \{w : p' \cdot (w - x) = 0\}$ has dimension $L - 2$ and so $L_p \setminus L_{p'}$ has dimension $L - 1$. Almost every bundle in L_p therefore lies in $L_p \setminus L_{p'}$. Let $y \geq 0$ be one such bundle and, for each $\alpha > 0$, define $y^\alpha = x + \alpha(y - x)$ which lies in L_p. Suppose $p' \cdot (y^\alpha - x) < 0$ for one and hence all $\alpha > 0$. The two-dimensional subspace of $\mathbb{R}^L$ through x, y^α, and 0 thus resembles Figures 3.1 or 3.2. Since $p' \gg 0$, there is a $\bar{y}^\alpha \gg y^\alpha$ such that $p' \cdot (\bar{y}^\alpha - x) = 0$. So $\bar{y}^\alpha \succ y^\alpha$. Now if x and y^α are $\succsim$-related then $x \sim y^\alpha$ for all sufficiently small α and so, by transitivity, $\bar{y}^\alpha \succ x$. Letting α converge to 0, $\bar{y}^\alpha$ will converge to x. Since $\bar{y}^\alpha$ is $\succ$-unranked relative to x when $\bar{y}^\alpha$ is near x, we conclude that if α is sufficiently small then y^α is not $\succsim$-related to x. The case $p' \cdot (y^\alpha - x) > 0$ is similar.

To show that $\lambda p + \mu p'$ for $\lambda, \mu > 0$ also defines a line of incomparability, suppose $(\lambda p + \mu p') \cdot (z - x) = 0$ and therefore $(\lambda p + \mu p') \cdot (\alpha z + (1 - \alpha)x - x) = 0$. It is sufficient to show that, for all $\alpha > 0$ sufficiently small, $\alpha z + (1 - \alpha)x$ and x are $\succ$-unranked. If $p \cdot (z - x) = 0$ or $p' \cdot (z - x) = 0$ then $p \cdot (\alpha z + (1 - \alpha)x - x) = 0$ or $p' \cdot (\alpha z + (1 - \alpha)x - x) = 0$. Since p

and p' define lines of incomparability, $\alpha z + (1-\alpha)x$ and x are then $\succ$-unranked when α is small. If $p \cdot (z-x) \neq 0$ and $p' \cdot (z-x) \neq 0$ then $p \cdot (z-x)$ and $p' \cdot (z-x)$ cannot have the same sign: if they did then $(\lambda p + \mu p') \cdot (z-x) \neq 0$. We can therefore label p and p' so that $p \cdot (z-x) > 0$ and $p' \cdot (z-x) < 0$ and therefore $p \cdot (\alpha z + (1-\alpha)x - x) > 0$ and $p' \cdot (\alpha z + (1-\alpha)x - x) < 0$. Suppose $\alpha z + (1-\alpha)x \succ x$ and let $z' \gg \alpha z + (1-\alpha)x$ satisfy $p' \cdot (z'-x) = 0$. Then $z' \succ \alpha z + (1-\alpha)x \succ x$ and hence $z' \succ x$ which, when α is sufficiently small, contradicts the fact that p' defines a line of incomparability. The case $x \succ \alpha z + (1-\alpha)x$ is similar: let $z' \ll \alpha z + (1-\alpha)x$ satisfy $p \cdot (z'-x) = 0$.

Notice that the convexity of $\succsim$ plays no role in this proof. ∎

Proof of Theorem 3.3. Fix x, let $p^1, \ldots, p^m$ be the linearly independent price vectors, and define $p = \sum_i \alpha^i p^i$, where each $\alpha^i > 0$ and $\sum_i \alpha^i = 1$. For any j, linear independence implies that p and p^j are not collinear. Hence there exists a y such that $p \cdot (y-x) = 0$ and $p^j \cdot (y-x) \neq 0$. Since $p \cdot (y-x) = 0$, there must also be a k where $p^k \cdot (y-x)$ has the opposite sign of $p^j \cdot (y-x)$. Select labels so that $p^k \cdot (y-x) < 0$ and $p^j \cdot (y-x) > 0$. Then, for any $\lambda > 0$, $p^k \cdot (\lambda y + (1-\lambda)x) < p^k \cdot x$ and $p^j \cdot (\lambda y + (1-\lambda)x) > p^j \cdot x$. Select candidate preference labels so that p^k and p^j support $B_{\succ k}(x)$ and $B_{\succ j}(x)$ respectively at x. Since p^k supports $B_{\succ k}(x)$, $x \succ^k x + \lambda(y-x)$ for any $\lambda > 0$ and therefore not $x + \lambda(y-x) \succsim^{UA} x$. Since $\succsim^j$ is smooth, $x + \lambda(y-x) \succsim^j x$ for all $\lambda > 0$ sufficiently small, and thus x and $x + \lambda(y-x)$ are $\succsim^{UA}$-unranked for all λ sufficiently small. So, for the preference $\succsim^{UA}$, p defines a line of incomparability through x as does any price vector generated by a different selection of the α^i. It is readily confirmed that $\succsim^{UA}$ is increasing, convex, transitive, and reflexive, and therefore $\succsim^{UA}$ is locally incomparable. Due to Proposition 3.1, p also supports $B_{\succ UA}(x)$.

Since $\{\sum_i \alpha^i p^i : \alpha^i > 0$ and $\sum_i \alpha^i = 1\}$ contains m linearly independent vectors, the set of price vectors in $\{\sum_i \alpha^i p^i : \alpha^i > 0$ and $\sum_i \alpha^i = 1\}$ that satisfy the normalization $\|p\| = 1$ has dimension $m - 1$. ∎

Proof of Theorem 4.3. For manipulation-freeness, let $\langle c^i \rangle$ be the assumed sequential choice function, let $(A^1, \ldots, A^t)$ be an admissible sequence, and let $\bar{x}, x^i, \ldots, x^t$ be alternatives such that $\bar{x} \in A^i$, $x^t \in c^t(A^1, \ldots, A^t)$, and $x^j \in c^j(A^1, \ldots, A^j) \cap A^{j+1}$ for $j = i, \ldots, t-1$. It is sufficient to show that not $\bar{x}\hat{P}y$ for all $y \in \bigcup_{j=i}^t c^j(A^1, \ldots, A^j)$. Due to the first requirement of status quo maintenance, we have not $\bar{x}Py$ for all $y \in c^i(A^1, \ldots, A^i)$. Proceeding by induction, suppose for $j = i, \ldots, \tau - 1$ that not $\bar{x}\hat{P}y$ for all $y \in c^j(A^1, \ldots, A^j)$. By the second requirement of status quo maintenance, if $z \in c^{\tau}(A^1, \ldots, A^{\tau})$ then there is a $y \in c^{\tau-1}(A^1, \ldots, A^{\tau-1}) \cap A^{\tau}$ such that either $z\hat{P}y$ or $z = y$. So, if $\bar{x}\hat{P}z$ the transitivity of $\hat{P}$ implies $\bar{x}\hat{P}y$, in violation of the induction assumption.

For observational intransitivity, implicit incompleteness implies that there exist a and b that are not R^*-related. Then, possibly switching the labels a and b, either (1) there exists a d such that $d\hat{P}a$ and not $d\hat{P}b$ or (2) there exists a d such that $a\hat{P}d$ and not $b\hat{P}d$. In case (1), if $b\hat{P}d$ then the transitivity of $\hat{P}$ would imply $b\hat{P}a$ which violates the assumption that a and b are not R^*-related. Hence b and d are not ranked by $\hat{P}$. In case (2), if $d\hat{P}b$ the transitivity of $\hat{P}$ would imply $a\hat{P}b$ and we again conclude that b and d are unranked by $\hat{P}$. The assumption that $\hat{P}$ is implicitly incomplete therefore implies that there is a triple (x, y, z) such that $z\hat{P}x$, x and y are unranked by $\hat{P}$, and y and z are unranked by $\hat{P}$. Set $A^1 = \{x, y\}$ and $A^2 = \{y, z\}$ and let $\langle c^i \rangle$ be a sequential choice function that is status-quo-maintaining, leads to $\hat{P}$, and satisfies $c^1(A^1) = \{x, y\}$ and $c^2(A^1, A^2) = \{y\}$. The last three properties imply that $\langle c^i \rangle$ is observationally intransitive. ∎

Proof of Theorem 4.4. If, to the contrary, $\hat{P}$ is intransitive then there is a triple (x, y, z) such that $x\hat{P}y$ and $y\hat{P}z$ but not $x\hat{P}z$ and hence an admissible sequence $(A^1, \ldots, A^i)$ such that $z \in c^i(A^1, \ldots, A^i)$ and $x \in A^i$. Since $y\hat{P}z$, $c^{i+1}(A^1, \ldots, A^i, \{y, z\}) = \{y\}$. Since $x\hat{P}y$, the sequence $(A^1, \ldots, A^i, \{y, z\})$ along with $\bar{x} = x$, $x^i = z$, and $x^{i+1} = y$ furnishes a successful manipulation.[1] ∎

Proof of Theorem 5.1. Since $p \cdot a^j = D_{c^j}v(\bar{c}^1, \ldots, \bar{c}^N)$ for j such that $\bar{c}^j > 0$ form $N' < L$ linear equations in the L unknowns p, the solution $\bar{p} \gg 0$ is contained in a set of solutions of dimension at least $L - N' > 0$. Since $\bar{p} \gg 0$ and $a^j > 0$, this set cannot contain only collinear solutions; there are consequently multiple solutions of the same length. For any solution p sufficiently near $\bar{p}$, the inequalities $D_{c^j}v(\bar{c}^1, \ldots, \bar{c}^N) < p \cdot a^j$ remain satisfied for the j such that $\bar{c}^j = 0$. Since $\bar{c}$ continues to satisfy the constraints and complementary slackness holds trivially given that $\bar{p} \gg 0$ implies $\sum_j a^j c^j = x$, $(\bar{c}, p)$ also solves the v-maximization problem when the solution p is near $\bar{p}$. Thus multiple price vectors of the same length support

---

[1] Fishburn and LaValle (1988) and Fishburn (1991) object to money pump arguments on the grounds that they apply static preferences to dynamic choice problems. A rational agent, in this view, should choose a dynamic choice strategy that cannot be manipulated. The same arguments against intransitivity would recur, however, in preferences over dynamic choice strategies. In any event, Theorem 4.4 is immune to these objections: choice is explicitly dynamic.

$B_{\succsim}(x)$ at x for the $\succsim$ defined by u. Due to homogeneity, this conclusion holds for each point in $\Lambda = \{\lambda x : \lambda \geq 0\}$ and so multiple price vectors of the same length support Λ. Since v is increasing, $\succsim$ is weakly increasing and therefore safety-biased. ∎

Proof of Theorem 5.2. Observe first that since u is increasing, the preference that the maxmin utility $\min_{\pi \in \Pi} E_\pi u$ represents is also increasing.

For a bundle $x = (k, \ldots, k)$ that delivers the same vector of goods $k > 0$ at every state, $E_\pi u(x)$ will equal the same value, $u(k)$, for all $\pi \in \Pi$. Suppose that y which need not be constant across states is preferred to x, $\min_{\pi \in \Pi} E_\pi u(y) \geq \min_{\pi \in \Pi} E_\pi u(x)$. Then, similarly to the proof of the Observation, for any $\pi' \in \Pi$,

$$E_{\pi'} u(y) \geq \min_{\pi \in \Pi} E_\pi u(y) \geq \min_{\pi \in \Pi} E_\pi u(x) = u(k) = E_{\pi'} u(x).$$

For any $\pi' \in \Pi$, $Du(k)\pi'$ is the gradient of $E_{\pi'} u$ at x. Therefore, for any y with $\min_{\pi \in \Pi} E_\pi u(y) \geq \min_{\pi \in \Pi} E_\pi u(x)$, we have $Du(k)\pi' \cdot (y - x) \geq 0$ or equivalently $\pi' \cdot (y - x) \geq 0$. Thus π' supports $B((k, \ldots, k))$ at $(k, \ldots, k)$. The preferences represented by $\min_{\pi \in \Pi} E_\pi u$ are therefore safety biased when Π consists of more than one probability distribution: $\Lambda = \{z \in \mathbb{R}_+^L : z = \lambda(k, \ldots, k) \text{ for some } \lambda \geq 0\}$ qualifies as a ray of safe bundles. ∎

Proof of Theorem 6.1. For the first result suppose that $\succsim = \succ \cup \sim$ is classically rational. Since $\succsim$ is complete, $\sim$ coincides with $\sim^*$ and consequently $a \succsim b$ if and only if either $a \succ b$ or $a \sim^* b$. Now suppose in addition that $\sim^*$ is intransitive. Then there is a triple with $x \sim^* y \sim^* z$ but not $x \sim^* z$. Hence either $x \succ z$ or $z \succ x$. In the former case, $z \succsim y \succsim x$ (since $\sim^*$ is symmetric) and yet neither $z \succ x$ nor $z \sim^* x$. The $z \succ x$ case is similar. Next suppose $\succ$ is intransitive. Then there is a triple with $x \succ y \succ z$ but not $x \succ z$. Since $\succsim$ is complete, $z \succsim x$ and therefore, since $\succsim$ is transitive, $z \succsim y$. But since $y \succ z$ implies not $z \sim^* y$, we have $z \succ y$, a contradiction.

For the converse, since $\succ \cup \sim^*$ is complete and $\succ$ and $\sim^*$ are transitive by assumption, we need only show that if $x \succ y \sim^* z$ or $x \sim^* y \succ z$ then either $x \succ z$ or $x \sim^* z$. In the first case, $z \succ x$ cannot hold since, if it did, the transitivity of $\succ$ would imply the contradiction $z \succ y$. Hence either $x \succ z$ or $x \sim^* z$. Similarly, in the second case $z \succ x$ cannot hold and hence again either $x \succ z$ or $x \sim^* z$. ∎

Proof of Theorem 6.5. I outline a proof for $L = 2$. Each $y \approx x$ must be an element of the boundary of $SB(x)$ which I will label bdy $SB(x)$: if $y \in \text{int } SB(x)$ then for some $z \ll y$ we have $y \succ z \succ x$ by increasingness which contradicts $y \approx x$ and if $y \notin \text{cl } SB(x)$ then for some $z \gg y$ such that $z \notin SB(x)$ we have $z \succ y$ and not $z \succ x$, again contradicting $y \approx x$. Suppose there is an infinite sequence of distinct points $\langle y^t \rangle$ and an accumulation point z (possibly on bdy X) such that $y^t \approx x$ for all t and $y^t \to z$. Going to a subsequence, we may assume that either $y_1^t \geq z_1$ or $y_1^t \leq z_1$ for all t. Suppose that $y_1^t \geq z_1^t$ for all t. Define the function f by setting, for each $w = (w_1, w_2)$ near z such that $w \in \text{bdy } SB(x)$, $f(w_1) = w_2$, which may require a relabeling of coordinates. The convexity of $\succ$ implies f is a convex function. Any sequence of subgradients of f at y_1^t must therefore converge to the right derivative of f at z_1 (see Rockafeller (1970, Theorem 24.1)). Consequently $N(y^t)$ converges in Hausdorff distance to a singleton, in violation of the assumption that $\succ$ is nontrivially kinked. If $y_1^t \leq z_1$ for all t then any sequence of subgradients of f at y_1^t must converge to the left derivative of f at z_1, again violating the assumption that $\succ$ is nontrivially kinked. Each $y \approx x$ is therefore isolated and so, since X is compact, there can be only finitely many $y \approx x$ in X.

For the second claim, let $\langle y^t \rangle$ be an infinite sequence of distinct points such that $y^t \in \text{bdy } SB(x)$ and $y^t \to x$. Define the sequence $\langle z^t \rangle = \langle y^t - (\varepsilon^t, \varepsilon^t) \rangle$ where $\varepsilon^t > 0$ for all t and assume for concreteness that $y_1^t \geq x_1$ for all t. Since $y^t \in \text{bdy } SB(x)$ and $\succ$ is weakly increasing, $z^t \notin SB(x)$. Suppose there is a subsequence $\langle \bar{z}^t \rangle$ of $\langle z^t \rangle$ such that it is not the case that $\bar{z}^t \perp x$ and let $\langle \bar{y}^t \rangle$ be the corresponding subsequence of $\langle y^t \rangle$. Since $\bar{z}^t \approx x$ would by transitivity imply $\bar{z}^t + (\delta_1, \delta_2) \succ x$ for all $(\delta_1, \delta_2) \gg 0$ and hence $\bar{y}^t \notin \text{bdy } SB(x)$, we have $x \succ \bar{z}^t$. Since $\succ$ is transitive, $SB(x) \subset SB(\bar{z}^t)$. Since, as in the previous paragraph, the set of normal vectors of common length that support $SB(x)$ at $\bar{y}^t$ converges to a singleton $\{p\}$, $N(z^t)$ must also converge to $\{p\}$ when the ε^t are sufficiently small, which contradicts the assumption that $\succ$ is nontrivially kinked. ∎

Proof of Theorem 11.1. Suppose to the contrary that there are $y^j \in y^j(p)$ and $\hat{y}^j \in Y^j$ for each firm j such that $\sum_{j \in \mathcal{F}} \hat{y}^j > \sum_{j \in \mathcal{F}} y^j$. Then, since $p \gg 0$, $p \cdot \sum_{j \in \mathcal{F}} \hat{y}^j > p \cdot \sum_{j \in \mathcal{F}} y^j$. Since the rational firms maximize profits, $p \cdot \sum_{j \in \mathcal{F}^R} \hat{y}^j \leq p \cdot \sum_{j \in \mathcal{F}^R} y^j$. Hence $p \cdot \sum_{j \in \mathcal{F}^{IR}} \hat{y}^j > p \cdot \sum_{j \in \mathcal{F}^{IR}} y^j \geq 0$. Since $Y^R \supset Y^{CR} \supset Y^{IR}$, there exist $\tilde{y}^j \in Y^j$ for $j \in \mathcal{F}^R$ such that $\sum_{j \in \mathcal{F}^R} \tilde{y}^j = \sum_{j \in \mathcal{F}^{IR}} \hat{y}^j$ and $\sum_{j \in \mathcal{F}^R} \tilde{y}^j \in Y^{CR}$. Since therefore $p \cdot \sum_{\mathcal{F}^R} \tilde{y}^j > 0$ and since $\sum_{j \in \mathcal{F}^R} \tilde{y}^j \in Y^{CR}$ and $Y^R \supset Y^{CR}$, there is a sequence $\langle y^j[n] \rangle$ for each $j \in \mathcal{F}^R$ such that $p \cdot \sum_{j \in \mathcal{F}^R} y^j[n]$ increases without bound and therefore at least one rational firm can make unbounded profits. Hence supplies cannot be well-defined. ∎

Proof of Theorem 11.2. Suppose to the contrary that there are $y^j \in y^j(p)$ for each $j \in \mathcal{F}^{IR}$ such that, for some $h \in \mathcal{F}^{IR}$ and $\hat{y}^h \in Y^h$, $p \cdot \hat{y}^h > p \cdot y^h$ Then $p \cdot \hat{y}^h > 0$ and hence $p \cdot \left(\hat{y}^h + \sum_{j \in \mathcal{F}^{IR} \setminus \{h\}} y^j \right) > 0$. As in the proof of Theorem 11.1, we conclude that supplies cannot be well-defined at p. ∎

Proof of Theorem 11.3. To apply Theorem 11.1, we show that $Y^R + T_I \supset Y^{CR} + T_I \supset Y^{IR} + T_I$. Since $Y^R \supset Y^{CR}$, $Y^R + T_I \supset Y^{CR} + T_I$. Suppose $y \in Y^{IR} + T_I$. Then $y = y^{IR} + y_{T_I}$ for some $y^{IR} \in Y^{IR}$ and $y_{T_I} \in T_I$. Since $Y^{IR} \subset Y^{CR} + T_I$, $y^{IR} = y^{CR} + \hat{y}_{T_I}$ for some $y^{CR} \in Y^{CR}$ and $\hat{y}_{T_I} \in T_I$. Thus $y = y^{CR} + \hat{y}_{T_I} + y_{T_I}$. It is straightforward to show that T_I is convex and displays constant returns. Consequently $\frac{1}{2}\hat{y}_{T_I} + \frac{1}{2}y_{T_I} \in T_I$ and therefore $\hat{y}_{T_I} + y_{T_I} \in T_I$. Hence $y \in Y^{CR} + T_I$. Since $Y^{CR} + T_I$ displays constant returns, Theorem 11.1 implies that if $(p, \hat{y}^R, \hat{y}^{IR})$ is a free-trade equilibrium with no compensation then the supplies $\hat{y}^R + \hat{y}^{IR}$ are production efficient. ∎

Bibliography

Abdalla, M. and Al-Shawarby, S., 2018. "The Tamween food subsidy system in Egypt: evolution and recent implementation reforms," in *The 1.5 Billion People Question: Food, Vouchers, or Cash Transfers?* eds. H. Alderman, U. Gentilini, and R. Yemtsov. Washington, DC: World Bank.

Ainslie, G., 1992. *Picoeconomics*. Cambridge: Cambridge University Press.

Alchian, A., 1950. "Uncertainty, evolution and economic theory." *Journal of Political Economy* 58: 211–221.

Alderman, H., 1986. "Food subsidies and state policy in Egypt," in *Food, States, and Peasants: Analyses of the Agrarian Question in the Middle East*, ed. A. Richards. Boulder, CO: Westview Press.

Allen, R., 1936. "Professor Slutsky's theory of consumers' choice." *Review of Economic Studies* 3: 120–129.

Anscombe, F. and Aumann, R., 1963. "A definition of subjective probability." *Annals of Mathematical Statistics* 34: 199–205.

Armstrong, W., 1948. "Uncertainty and the utility function." *Economic Journal* 58: 1–10.

Armstrong, W., 1950. "A note on the theory of consumer's behaviour." *Oxford Economic Papers (New Series)* 2: 119–122.

Arrow, K., 1951a. "An extension of the basic theorems of classical welfare economics," in *Proceedings of the Second Berkeley Symposium on Mathematical Statistics and Probability*, ed. J. Neyman. Berkeley, CA: University of California Press.

Arrow, K., 1951b. *Social Choice and Individual Values*, 2nd ed. New York: Wiley, 1963.

Arrow, K., 1952. "Le principe de rationalité dans les décisions collectives." *Économie Appliquée* 5: 469–484, translated as "The principle of rationality in collective decisions" in *Social Choice and Justice*, K. Arrow, Cambridge: Harvard University Press, 1983.

Arrow, K., 1964. "The role of securities in the optimal allocation of risk-bearing." *Review of Economic Studies* 31: 91–96.

Arrow, K., 1977. "Current developments in the theory of social choice." *Social Research* 44: 607–622.

d'Aspremont, C. and Gevers, L., 1977. "Equity and the informational basis of collective choice." *Review of Economic Studies* 44: 199–209.

Aumann, R., 1962. "Utility theory without the completeness axiom." *Econometrica* 30: 445–462.

Aumann, R., 1964. "Utility theory without the completeness axiom: a correction." *Econometrica* 32: 210–212.

Aumann, R. and Peleg, B., 1974. "A note on Gale's example." *Journal of Mathematical Economics* 1: 209–211.

Baumol, W. and Bowen, W., 1965. "On the performing arts: the anatomy of their economic problems." *American Economic Review* 55: 495–502.

Baumol, W. and Bowen, W., 1966. *Performing Arts, The Economic Dilemma: A Study of Problems Common to Theater, Opera, Music, and Dance.* Cambridge: Massachusetts Institute of Technology Press.

Becker, G., 1962. "Irrational behavior and economic theory." *Journal of Political Economy* 70: 1–13.

Becker, G., 1976. *The Economic Approach to Human Behavior.* Chicago: University of Chicago Press.

Becker, G., 1991. "A note on restaurant pricing and other examples of social influences on price." *Journal of Political Economy* 99: 1109–1116.

Bernheim, B. D. and Rangel, A., 2007. "Toward choice-theoretic foundations for behavioral welfare economics." *American Economic Review* 97: 464–470.

Bernheim, B. D. and Rangel, A., 2009. "Beyond revealed preference: choice theoretic foundations for behavioral welfare economics." *Quarterly Journal of Economics* 124: 51–104.

Bernoulli, D., 1738. "Exposition of a new theory on the measurement of risk." Translated in *Econometrica* 22: 23–36, 1954.

Bewley, T., 1986. "Knightian decision theory. Part I." Cowles Foundation Discussion Paper 807, Yale University. Also in *Decisions in Economics and Finance* 25: 79–110, 2002.

Blume, L. and Easley, D., 1992. "Evolution and market behavior." *Journal of Economic Theory* 58: 9–40.

Bossert, W. and Weymark, J., 2004. "Utility in social choice," in *Handbook of Utility Theory, Vol. 2: Extensions*, eds. S. Barberà, P. Hammond, and C. Seidl. Boston: Kluwer.

Caballero, R. and Hammour, M., 1994. "The cleansing effect of recessions." *American Economic Review* 84: 1350–1368.

Carson, R., 1997. "Contingent valuation and tests of insensitivity to scope," in *Determining the Value of Non-marketed Goods: Economic, Psychological and Policy Relevant Aspects of Contingent Valuation Methods*, eds. R. Kopp, W. Pommerhene, and N. Schwartz. Boston: Kluwer.

Carson, R., 2012. "Contingent valuation: a practical alternative when prices aren't available." *Journal of Economic Perspectives* 26: 27–42.

Carson, R. and Hanemann, W., 2005. "Contingent valuation," in *Handbook of Environmental Economics, Volume 2*, eds. K.-G. Mäler and J. Vincent. Amsterdam: Elsevier.

Cerreia-Vioglio, S., Dillenberger, D., and Ortoleva, P., 2015. "Cautious expected utility and the certainty effect." *Econometrica* 83: 693–728.

Cettolin, E., and Riedl, A., 2019. "Revealed preferences under uncertainty: incomplete preferences and preferences for randomization." *Journal of Economic Theory* 181: 547–585.

Chakraborty, A., 2021. "Present bias." *Econometrica* 89: 1921–1961.

Chambers, R., 2014. "Uncertain equilibria and incomplete preferences." *Journal of Mathematical Economics* 55: 48–54.

Chipman, J. and Moore J., 1980. "Compensating variation, consumer's surplus, and welfare." *American Economic Review* 70: 933–949.

Conlisk, J., 1988. "Optimization cost." *Journal of Economic Behavior and Organization* 9: 213–228.

Costa-Gomes, M., Cueva, C., Gerasimou, G., and Tejiščák, M., 2022. "Choice, deferral, and consistency." *Quantitative Economics* 13: 1297–1318.

Cubitt, R. and Sugden R., 2001. "On money pumps." *Games and Economic Behavior* 37: 121–160.

Cummings, R., Brookshire, D., and Schulze, W. (eds.), 1986. *Valuing Environmental Goods*. Totowa, NJ: Rowman and Allanheld.

Cunha, A. and Swinbank, A., 2011. *An Inside View of the CAP Reform Process: Explaining the MacSharry, Agenda 2000, and Fischler Reforms*. Oxford: Oxford University Press.

Davidson, D., McKinsey, J., and Suppes, P., 1955. "Outlines of a formal theory of value, I." *Philosophy of Science* 22: 140–160.

Debreu, G., 1951. "The coefficient of resource utilization." *Econometrica* 19: 273–292.

Debreu, G., 1954. "Representation of a preference ordering by a numerical function," in *Decision Processes*, eds. R. Thrall, C. Coombs, and R. Davis. New York: Wiley.

Debreu, G., 1970. "Economies with a finite set of equilibria." *Econometrica* 38: 387–392.

Debreu, G., 1972. "Smooth preferences." *Econometrica* 40: 603–615.

Diamond, P. and Mirrlees, J., 1971. "Optimal taxation and public production. I. Production efficiency." *American Economic Review* 61: 8–27.

Dierker, E., Dierker, H., and Trockel, W., 1984. "Price-dispersed preferences and C^1 mean demand." *Journal of Mathematical Economics* 13: 11–42.

Dixit, A. and Norman, V., 1980. *Theory of International Trade: A Dual, General Equilibrium Approach*. Cambridge: Cambridge University Press.

Douglas, M. and Isherwood, B., 1979. *The World of Goods: Towards an Anthropology of Consumption*. New York: Basic Books.

Drèze, J., 1974. "Investment under private ownership: optimality, equilibrium and stability," in *Allocation under Uncertainty: Equilibrium and Optimality*, ed. J. Drèze. New York: Macmillan.

Duesenberry, J., 1949. *Income, Saving and the Theory of Consumer Behavior*. Cambridge: Harvard University Press.

Durkheim, E., 1893. *The Division of Labor in Society*. New York: Free Press, 1933.

Dworczak, P., Kominers S., and Akbarpour M., 2021. "Redistribution through markets." *Econometrica* 89: 1665–1698.

Edgeworth, F., 1897. "The pure theory of taxation," in *Papers Relating to Political Economy*, vol. 2. London: Macmillan, 1925.

Eliaz, K. and Ok, E., 2006. "Indifference or indecisiveness? Choice-theoretic foundations of incomplete preferences." *Games and Economic Behavior* 56: 61–86.

Fishburn, P., 1970a. "Intransitive indifference in preference theory: a survey." *Operations Research* 18: 207–228.

Fishburn, P., 1970b. *Utility Theory for Decision Making*. New York: Wiley.

Fishburn, P., 1991. "Nontransitive preferences in decision theory." *Journal of Risk and Uncertainty* 4: 113–134.

Fishburn, P. and LaValle, I., 1988. "Context-dependent choice with nonlinear and nontransitive preferences." *Econometrica* 56: 1221–1239.

Frey, B., Luechinger, S., and Stutzer, A., 2004. "Valuing public goods: the life satisfaction approach," CESifo Working Paper Series 1158, CESifo.

Friedman, M., 1953. "The methodology of positive economics," in *Essays in Positive Economics*, M. Friedman, pp. 3–43. Chicago: University of Chicago Press.

Gerasimou, G., 2013. "On continuity of incomplete preferences." *Social Choice and Welfare* 41: 157–167.

Gilboa, I., Maccheroni, F., Marinacci, M., and Schmeidler, D., 2010. "Objective and subjective rationality in a multiple prior model." *Econometrica* 78: 755–770.

Gilboa, I. and Schmeidler, D., 1989. "Maxmin expected utility with non-unique prior." *Journal of Mathematical Economics* 18: 141–153.

Grether, D. and Plott, C., 1979. "Economic theory of choice and the preference reversal phenomenon." *American Economic Review* 69: 623–638.

Grossman, S. and Hart, O., 1979. "A theory of competitive equilibrium in stock market economies." *Econometrica* 47: 293–329.

Guesnerie, R., 1975. "Pareto optimality in non-convex economies." *Econometrica* 43: 1–29.

Hahn, F., 1961. "Theory of value: an axiomatic analysis of economic equilibrium. Gerard Debreu." *Journal of Political Economy* 69: 204–205.

Hammack, J. and Brown, G., 1974. *Waterfowl and Wetlands: Toward Bioeconomic Analysis*. Baltimore, MD: Johns Hopkins University Press.

Hammond, P., 1981. "Ex-ante and ex-post welfare optimality under uncertainty." *Economica* 48: 235–250.

Harsanyi, J., 1955. "Cardinal welfare, individualistic ethics, and interpersonal comparisons of utility." *Journal of Political Economy* 63: 309–321.

Hausman, J., ed., 1993. *Contingent Valuation: A Critical Assessment*. Amsterdam: Elsevier Science.

Hayek, F., 1931. *Prices and Production*. London: Routledge.

Hicks, J., 1939a. *Value and Capital*. Oxford: Clarendon Press.

Hicks, J., 1939b. "The foundations of welfare economics." *Economic Journal* 49: 696–712.

Hicks, J., 1940. "The valuation of social income." *Economica* 7 (n.s.): 104–124.

Hicks, J., 1956. *A Revision of Demand Theory*. Oxford: Clarendon Press.

Hicks, J. and Allen, R., 1934. "A reconsideration of the theory of value." *Economica* 1 (n.s.): 52–76, 196–219.

Hildenbrand, W., 1980. "On the uniqueness of mean demand for dispersed families of preferences." *Econometrica* 48: 1703–1710.

Hurwicz, L., 1979. "On the interaction between information and incentives in organizations," in *Communication and Control in Society*, ed. K. Krippendorff. New York: Gordon and Breach.

Jevons, W., 1871. *The Theory of Political Economy*. London: Macmillan.

Kahneman, D., 2020. "Prospect theory." Invited address to *Decision: Theory, Experiments, Applications*. Paris.

Kahneman, D. and Knetsch, J., 1992. "Valuing public goods: the purchase of moral satisfaction." *Journal of Environmental Economics and Management* 22: 57–70.

Kahneman, D., Knetsch, J., and Thaler, R., 1986. "Fairness as a constraint on profit seeking: entitlements in the market." *American Economic Review* 76: 728–741.

Kahneman, D., Knetsch, J., and Thaler, R., 1990. "Experimental tests of the endowment effect and the Coase theorem." *Journal of Political Economy* 98: 1325–1348.

Kahneman, D. and Tversky, A., 1979. "Prospect theory: an analysis of decision under risk." *Econometrica* 47: 263–291.

Kahneman, D. and Tversky, A., 1984. "Choices, values and frames." *American Psychologist* 39: 341–350.

Kahneman, D., Wakker P., and Sarin R., 1997. "Back to Bentham? Explorations of experienced utility." *Quarterly Journal of Economics* 112: 375–405.

Kaldor, N., 1939. "Welfare propositions in economics and interpersonal comparisons of utility." *Economic Journal* 49: 549–551.

Karni, E. and Levin, D., 1994. "Social attributes and strategic equilibrium: a restaurant pricing game." *Journal of Political Economy* 102: 822–840.

Khan, M. and Vohra, R., 1987. "An extension of the second welfare theorem to economies with nonconvexities and public goods." *Quarterly Journal of Economics* 102: 223–242.

Knetsch, J., 1989. "The endowment effect and evidence of nonreversible indifference curves." *American Economic Review* 79: 1277–1284.

Knetsch, J. and Sinden, J., 1984. "Willingness to pay and compensation demanded: experimental evidence of an unexpected disparity in measures of values." *Quarterly Journal of Economics* 99: 507–521.

Knetsch, J. and Sinden, J., 1987. "The persistence of evaluation disparities." *Quarterly Journal of Economics* 102: 691–695.

Kreps, D., 1988. *Notes on the Theory of Choice*. Boulder, CO: Westview.

Köbberling, V. and Wakker, P., 2005. "An index of loss aversion." *Journal of Economic Theory* 122: 119–131.

Kőszegi, B. and Rabin, M., 2006. "A model of reference-dependent preferences." *Quarterly Journal of Economics* 121: 1133–1165.

Laibson, D., 1997. "Golden eggs and hyperbolic discounting." *Quarterly Journal of Economics* 112: 443–477.

Lancaster, K., 1966. "A new approach to consumer theory." *Journal of Political Economy* 74: 132–157.

Lehrer, E. and Teper, R., 2014. "Extension rules or what would the sage do?" *American Economic Journal: Microeconomics* 6: 5–22.

Leontief, W., 1951. *The Structure of American Economy, 1919–1939: An Empirical Application of Equilibrium Analysis,* 2nd ed. New York: Oxford University Press.

Levi, I., 1980. *The Enterprise of Knowledge.* Cambridge: Massachusetts Institute of Technology Press.

Levi, I., 1986. *Hard Choices: Decision Making under Unresolved Conflict.* Cambridge: Cambridge University Press.

Lichtenstein, S. and Slovic, P., 1971. "Reversals of preference between bids and choices in gambling decisions." *Journal of Experimental Psychology* 89: 46–55.

Lichtenstein, S. and Slovic, P., 1973. "Response-induced reversals of preference in gambling: an extended replication in Las Vegas." *Journal of Experimental Psychology* 101: 16–20.

Lindman, H., 1971. "Inconsistent preferences among gambles." *Journal of Experimental Psychology* 89: 390–397.

Luce, R. D., 1956. "Semiorders and a theory of utility discrimination." *Econometrica* 24: 178–191.

Luce, R. D. and Raiffa, H., 1957. *Games and Decisions: Introduction and Critical Survey.* New York: Wiley.

Mandler, M., 1995. "Sequential indeterminacy in production economies." *Journal of Economic Theory* 66: 406–436.

Mandler, M., 1998. "The economics of incomplete preferences." Cambridge, MA. Harvard University. Mimeo.

Mandler, M., 1999a. *Dilemmas in Economic Theory: Persisting Foundational Problems of Microeconomics.* New York: Oxford.

Mandler, M., 1999b. "Simple Pareto-improving policies." *Journal of Economic Theory* 84: 120–133.

Mandler, M., 2004. "Status quo maintenance reconsidered: changing or incomplete preferences?" *Economic Journal* 114: 518–535.

Mandler, M., 2005. "Incomplete preferences and rational intransitivity of choice." *Games and Economic Behavior* 50: 255–277.

Mandler, M., 2007. "Policy discrimination with and without interpersonal comparisons of utility." *Economic Theory* 32: 523–549.

Mandler, M., 2009. "Indifference and incompleteness distinguished by rational trade." *Games and Economic Behavior* 67: 300–314.

Mandler, M., 2013. "Endogenous indeterminacy and volatility of asset prices under ambiguity." *Theoretical Economics* 8: 729–750.

Mandler, M., 2014a. "Indecisiveness in behavioral welfare economics." *Journal of Economic Behavior & Organization* 97: 219–235.

Mandler, M., 2014b. "Irrationality-proofness: markets versus games." *International Economic Review* 55: 443–458.

Mandler, M., 2020. "Distributive justice for behavioural welfare economics." *Economic Journal* 130: 1140–1160.

Mandler, M., 2021. "A unified explanation of reference dependence, loss aversion, and the reflection effect." London: Royal Holloway College, University of London. Mimeo.

Mandler, M., 2023. "Decision-making for extreme outcomes." London: Royal Holloway College, University of London. Mimeo.

Marshall, A., 1890. *Principles of Economics*. London: Macmillan.

Mas-Colell, A., 1983. "The Cournotian foundations of Walrasian equilibrium theory: an exposition of recent theory," in *Advances in Economic Theory* (Econometric Society Monograph), ed. W. Hildenbrand. Cambridge: Cambridge University Press.

Mas-Colell, A., 1985. *The Theory of General Economic Equilibrium: A Differentiable Approach*. Cambridge: Cambridge University Press.

Masatlioglu, Y. and Ok, E., 2005. "Rational choice with status quo bias." *Journal of Economic Theory* 121: 1–29.

Maskin, E. and Tirole, J., 1999. "Limited unforeseen contingencies and incomplete contracts." *Review of Economic Studies* 66: 83–114.

McCloskey, D., 1973. *Economic Maturity and Entrepreneurial Decline: British Iron and Steel, 1870–1913*. Cambridge: Harvard University Press.

McKenzie, L., 1957. "Demand theory without a utility index." *Review of Economic Studies* 24: 185–189.

Mill, J. S., 1861. "Utilitarianism," reprinted in *Collected Works of John Stuart Mill, Vol. 10*, ed. J. Robson. Toronto: Toronto University Press, 1969.

Mirowski, P., 1984. "Physics and the 'marginalist revolution.'" *Cambridge Journal of Economics* 8: 361–379.

Mirrlees, J., 1971. "An exploration in the theory of optimum income taxation." *Review of Economic Studies* 38: 175–208.

Neilson, W., 1991. "Smooth indifference sets." *Journal of Mathematical Economics* 20: 181–197.

Nelson, R. and Winter, S., 1982. *An Evolutionary Theory of Economic Change*. Cambridge: Belknap Press.

von Neumann, J. and Morgenstern, O., 1947. *Theory of Games and Economic Behavior*, 2nd ed. Princeton, NJ: Princeton University Press.

O'Donoghue, T. and Rabin, M., 1999. "Doing it now or later." *American Economic Review* 89: 103–124.

Palmquist, R., 1991. "Hedonic methods," in *Measuring the Demand for Environmental Quality*, eds. J. Braden and C. Kolstad. Amsterdam: North-Holland.

Parsons, G., 2003. "The travel cost model," in *A Primer on Nonmarket Valuation*, eds. P. Champ, K. Boyle, and T. Brown. Dordrecht: Kluwer.

Pascoa, M. and Werlang, S., 1999. "Determinacy of equilibrium in nonsmooth economies." *Journal of Mathematical Economics* 32: 289–302.

Pigou, A., 1932. *The Economics of Welfare*, 4th ed. London: Macmillan.

Postlewaite, A., 1979. "Manipulation via endowments." *Review of Economic Studies* 46: 255–262.

Radner, R., 1968. "Competitive equilibrium under uncertainty." *Econometrica* 36: 31–58.

Radner, R., 1972. "Existence of equilibrium of plans, prices, and price expectations in a sequence of markets." *Econometrica* 40: 289–303.

Raz, J., 1986. *The Morality of Freedom*. Oxford: Clarendon.

Richter, M., 1966. "Revealed preference theory." *Econometrica* 34: 635–645.

Rigotti, L. and Shannon, C., 2005. "Uncertainty and risk in financial markets." *Econometrica* 73: 203–243.

Rigotti, L. and Shannon, C., 2012. "Sharing risk and ambiguity." *Journal of Economic Theory* 147: 2028–2039.

Roberts, K., 1980. "Interpersonal comparability and social choice theory." *Review of Economic Studies* 47: 421–439.

Robertson, D. H., 1951. "Utility and all that." *The Manchester School* 19: 111–142.

Rockafellar, R. T., 1970. *Convex Analysis*. Princeton, NJ: Princeton University Press.

Roederer-Rynning, C., 2014. "The Common Agricultural Policy: the fortress challenged," in *Policy-Making in the European Union*, 7th ed., eds. H. Wallace, M. Pollack, and A. Young. Oxford: Oxford University Press.

Samuelson, P., 1938. "A note on the pure theory of consumer's behaviour." *Economica* 5 (n.s.): 61–72.

Samuelson, P., 1939. "The gains from international trade." *Canadian Journal of Economics and Political Science* 5: 195–205.

Samuelson, P., 1950. "Evaluation of real national income." *Oxford Economic Papers* 2: 1–29.

Samuelson, P., 1954. "The pure theory of public expenditure." *Review of Economics and Statistics* 36: 387–389.

Samuelson, P., 1956. "Social indifference curves." *Quarterly Journal of Economics* 70: 1–22.

Samuelson, P., 1974. "Complementarity: an essay on the 40th anniversary of the Hicks-Allen revolution in demand theory." *Journal of Economic Literature* 12: 1255–1289.

Samuelson, W. and Zeckhauser, R., 1988. "Status quo bias in decision making." *Journal of Risk and Uncertainty* 1: 7–59.

Savage, L., 1954. *The Foundations of Statistics*. New York: Wiley.

Schlee, E., 2021. "Inertia implies disorder: kinks, incompleteness, and intransitivity." *Pure and Applied Functional Analysis* 6: 851–855.

Schlee, E. and Khan, M., 2022. "Money metrics in applied welfare analysis: a saddlepoint rehabilitation." *International Economic Review* 63: 189–210.

Schmeidler, D., 1971. "A condition for the completeness of partial preference relations." *Econometrica* 39: 403–404.

Schmeidler, D., 1989. "Subjective probability and expected utility without additivity." *Econometrica* 57: 571–587.

Schumpeter, J., 1912. *The Theory of Economic Development*. New York: Oxford University Press, 1978.

Schumpeter, J., 1939. *Business Cycles: A Theoretical, Historical, and Statistical Analysis of the Capitalist Process*. New York: McGraw-Hill.

Schumpeter, J., 1942. *Capitalism, Socialism, and Democracy*. New York: Harper.

Scitovsky, T., 1941. "A note on welfare propositions in economics." *Review of Economic Studies* 9: 77–88.

Sen, A., 1970. "Interpersonal aggregation and partial comparability." *Econometrica* 38: 393–409.

Sen, A., 1973. "Behaviour and the concept of preference." *Economica* 40 (n.s.): 241–259.

Sen, A., 1979. "Utilitarianism and welfarism." *Journal of Philosophy* 76: 463–489.

Sen, A., 1986. *Welfare Economics and the Real World*. Memphis, TN: Seidman Foundation.

Simon, H., 1978. "Rationality as process and as product of thought." *American Economic Review (Papers and Proceedings)* 68: 1–16.

Simon, H., 1979. "Rational decision making in business organizations." *American Economic Review* 69: 493–513.

Slovic, P. and Lichtenstein, S., 1968. "The relative importance of probabilities and payoffs in risk-taking." *Journal of Experimental Psychology Monograph Supplement* 78: 1–18.

Slovic, P. and Lichtenstein, S., 1983. "Preference reversal: a broader perspective." *American Economic Review* 73: 596–605.

Slutsky, E., 1915. "Sulla teoria del bilancio del consumatore." *Giornale degli Economisti* 51: 1–26.

Sondermann, D., 1975. "Smoothing demand by aggregation." *Journal of Mathematical Economics* 2: 201–223.

Sugden, R., 2003. "Reference-dependent subjective expected utility." *Journal of Economic Theory* 111: 172–191.

Taylor, L., 2003. "The hedonic method," in *A Primer on Nonmarket Valuation*, eds. P. Champ, K. Boyle, and T. Brown. Dordrecht: Kluwer.

Temin, P., 1966. "The relative decline of the British steel industry, 1880–1913," in *Industrialization in Two Systems: Essays in Honor of Alexander Gerschenkron*, ed. H. Rosovsky. New York: Wiley.

Thaler, R., 1980. "Toward a positive theory of consumer choice." *Journal of Economic Behavior and Organization* 1: 39–60.

Thaler, R. and Sunstein, C., 2008. *Nudge: Improving Decisions about Health, Wealth, and Happiness*. New Haven, CT: Yale University Press.

Tversky, A., 1972. "Elimination by aspects: a theory of choice." *Psychological Review* 79: 281–299.

Tversky, A. and Kahneman, D., 1991. "Loss aversion in riskless choice: a reference-dependent model." *Quarterly Journal of Economics* 106: 1039–1061.

Tversky, A. and Kahneman, D., 1992. "Advances in prospect theory: cumulative representation of uncertainty." *Journal of Risk and Uncertainty* 5: 297–323.

Tversky, A., Sattath, S., and Slovic, P., 1988. "Contingent weighting in judgment and choice." *Psychological Review* 95: 371–384.

Tversky, A., Slovic, P., and Kahneman, D., 1990. "The causes of preference reversal." *American Economic Review* 80: 204–217.

Walras, L., 1874. *Elements of Pure Economics*. London: Allen & Unwin, 1954.

Walley, P., 1991. *Statistical Reasoning with Imprecise Probabilities*. London: Chapman & Hall.

Winter, S., 1971. "Satisficing, selection, and the innovating remnant." *Quarterly Journal of Economics* 85: 237–261.

Index

Printed in the United States
by Baker & Taylor Publisher Services